OTHER BOOKS BY KAREN LINDSEY

Friends as Family
Dr. Susan Love's Breast Book, with Susan M. Love, M.D.
Falling Off the Roof (poetry)

DIVORCED, BEHEADED, SURVIVED

TIMELINE

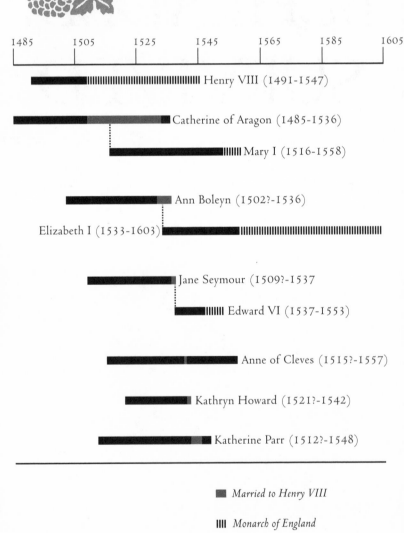

| 1485 | 1505 | 1525 | 1545 | 1565 | 1585 | 1605 |

Henry VIII (1491-1547)

Catherine of Aragon (1485-1536)

Mary I (1516-1558)

Ann Boleyn (1502?-1536)

Elizabeth I (1533-1603)

Jane Seymour (1509?-1537

Edward VI (1537-1553)

Anne of Cleves (1515?-1557)

Kathryn Howard (1521?-1542)

Katherine Parr (1512?-1548)

▆ *Married to Henry VIII*

|||| *Monarch of England*

DIVORCED, BEHEADED, SURVIVED

A Feminist Reinterpretation of the Wives of Henry VIII

KAREN LINDSEY

ADDISON–WESLEY PUBLISHING COMPANY

Reading, Massachusetts   Menlo Park, California   New York
Don Mills, Ontario   Wokingham, England   Amsterdam   Bonn
Sydney   Singapore   Tokyo   Madrid   San Juan
Paris   Seoul   Milan   Mexico City   Taipei

The author gratefully acknowledges the following institutions for permitting her to reproduce portraits from their collections in this book.

Margaret Beaufort (page 2): By permission of the Master and Fellows of St. John's College, Cambridge. *Catherine of Aragon (page 12):* By permission of the Mansell Collection, London. *Henry VIII (page 26):* By permission of the Society of Antiquaries of London. *Ann Boleyn (page 46):* By permission of the Royal Collection © Her Majesty Queen Elizabeth II. *Sir Thomas Wyatt (page 70):* By permission of the Mansell Collection, London. *Thomas Cromwell (page 92):* © The Frick Collection, New York. *Jane Seymour (page 116):* By permission of the Mauritshuis Museum, The Hague. *Anne of Cleves (page 136):* by Hans Holbein, Louvre Museum, Paris, © Photo R.M.N. *Kathryn Howard (page 158):* By permission of the Toledo Museum of Art. *Katherine Parr (page 180):* By permission of the National Portrait Gallery, London. *Mary I (page 204):* By permission of the Isabella Stewart Gardner Museum, Boston. *Elizabeth I (page 216):* By permission of the Mansell Collection, London.

Library of Congress Cataloging-in-Publication Data

Lindsey, Karen, 1944–
Divorced, beheaded, survived : a feminist reinterpretation of the
wives of Henry VIII / Karen Lindsey.
p.   cm.
Includes bibliographical references (p.   ) and index.
ISBN 0-201-60895-2
1. Henry VIII, King of England, 1491–1547—Marriage. 2. Great
Britain—History—Henry VIII, 1509–1547—Biography. 3. Women—
England—History—Renaissance, 1450–1600. 4. Queens—Great
Britain—Biography. 5. Feminism. I. Title.
DA333.A2L56   1995
941.05′2′092—dc20
[B]   94-34505
                                      CIP

Jacket design by Suzanne Heiser
Text design by Janis Owens
Set in 11-point Bembo by Carol Woolverton Studio

1 2 3 4 5 6 7 8 9-MA-98979695
First printing, December 1994

Addison-Wesley books are available at special discounts for bulk purchases. For more information about how to make such purchases in the U.S., please contact the Corporate, Government, and Special Sales Department at Addison-Wesley Publishing Company, 1 Jacob Way, Reading, MA 01867, or call (800) 238-9682.

For Nina and Kim

CONTENTS

CONTENTS

LIST OF ILLUSTRATIONS

ACKNOWLEDGMENTS

My thanks to the friends who have made writing this book possible: Ann Kottel, Marcia Diehl, Til Lamberts, Barbara Berg, Steve Himmelstein, Lynn Leibowitz, and especially Carole Levin; to Sarah Jane Freymann and Kathryn Sand, who have been both excellent agents and supportive friends; to my editors, Amy Gash, who got me started on this book, and John Bell, who, with infinite patience, helped me to shape it; to Rachel Parks, whose painstaking copy editing has added enormously to this book; to my production editor, Beth Burleigh; to Karen Kahn, editor of *Sojourner*; to my father, who has always encouraged my writing, and to my brother Warren, who keeps me going in spite of everything.

WHO WAS WHO IN THE
WORLD OF HENRY VIII

Reading Tudor history is fascinating, but dizzying. There are so many events following closely on one another, and so many people involved in them. Compounding the confusion is the fact that most of these people shared the same small handful of names. There are a dozen Anns and Catherines and Janes, Edwards and Henrys and Charleses. To help alleviate the reader's confusion, here is a list of the most important figures encountered in this book.

Since it was an era indifferent to standardized spelling, people often spelled their own names in a variety of ways. I have taken advantage of this to try to alleviate some of the problem with the overwhelming number of Catherines, giving the names of each of the three Queen Catherines a different spelling. I have done the same with the two Queen Anns.

The symbol Ω indicates that the person was executed during the reign of Henry VIII.

ANNE OF CLEVES (1515?–57) — daughter of the German Duke of Cleves; fourth wife of Henry VIII. Marriage annulled in 1540

ARTHUR, PRINCE OF WALES (1486–1502) — eldest son of Henry VII; heir apparent to the throne of England. Married Catherine of Aragon. His death put his brother Henry in line for the throne

ASKEW, ANNE (1521–46) — the Fair Gospeler; Protestant proselytizer. Ω by burning

BEAUFORT, MARGARET (1441–1509) — mother of Henry VII; grandmother of Henry VIII

BLOUNT, ELIZABETH (1500–40) — Henry VIII's first known mistress; mother of his son Henry Fitzroy, Earl of Richmond. Married Lord Tailboys

BOLEYN, ANN (1507?–36) — second wife of Henry VIII. Ω on charges of adultery and treason

BOLEYN, GEORGE, VISCOUNT ROCHFORD (1503?–36) — brother of Ann Boleyn. Married to Lady Jane Rochford. Ω

BOLEYN, MARY (1500–43) — sister of Ann Boleyn; mistress of Henry VIII. Married to William Carey and later William Stafford

BRANDON, CHARLES, DUKE OF SUFFOLK (1485–1545) — Henry VIII's close friend and courtier. Married Henry's sister Mary. Later married Catherine Willoughby

BRERETON, WILLIAM (d. 1536) — courtier, accused of adultery with Ann Boleyn. Ω

CATHERINE OF ARAGON (1485–1536) — first wife of Henry VIII, after death of her first husband, Henry's brother Arthur. Daughter of Queen Isabella and King Ferdinand of Spain. Mother of Mary I

CHAPUYS, EUSTACHE (1494–1556) — Spanish ambassador to England. Friend of Catherine of Aragon and Princess Mary

CHARLES V (1500–58) — King of Spain (as Charles I) and Holy Roman Emperor. Nephew of Catherine of Aragon

CLEMENT VII (1478–1534) — pope. Refused to grant Henry an annulment of his marriage to Catherine of Aragon

CRANMER, THOMAS (1489–1556) — Archbishop of Canterbury. Proclaimed Henry and Catherine's marriage invalid. Burned at the stake in Mary Tudor's reign

CROMWELL, THOMAS (1485–1540) — Lord Privy Seal under Henry. Ω after debacle over Henry VIII's marriage to Anne of Cleves

CULPEPER, THOMAS (d. 1542) — courtier and lover of Queen Kathryn Howard. Ω

EDWARD IV (1441–83) — grandfather of Henry VIII; King of England between 1461 and 1483. Father of Elizabeth of York and of the princes in the Tower

EDWARD, PRINCE, LATER EDWARD VI (1537–53) — son of Henry VIII and Jane Seymour

ELIZABETH, PRINCESS, LATER ELIZABETH I (1533–1603) — daughter of Henry VIII and Ann Boleyn

FERDINAND OF ARAGON (1452–1516) — King of Spain; father of Catherine of Aragon

FISHER, JOHN (1459–1535) — chaplain of Margaret Beaufort and Bishop of Rochester. Ω for his opposition to Henry's claim to supremacy over the English church

FRANCIS I (1494–1557) — King of France and Henry's political rival

GARDINER, STEPHEN (1483?–1555) — conservative Bishop of Winchester and diplomat under Henry VIII

GREY, JANE (1537–54) — granddaughter of Charles Brandon and Henry VIII's sister Mary. Put on throne in plot to prevent accession of Princess Mary. Executed in Mary's reign

HENRY VII (1457–1509) — King of England and father of Henry VIII

HOWARD, KATHRYN (1520?–42) — fifth wife of Henry VIII. Ω for adultery

HOWARD, THOMAS, DUKE OF NORFOLK (1473–1554) — courtier and statesman. Uncle of Ann Boleyn and Kathryn Howard

LOUISE OF SAVOY (1476–1531) — mother of Francis I of France and, as regent in his absence, a powerful political influence

MARGARET OF AUSTRIA (1480–1530) — regent of the Netherlands. Daughter of Holy Roman Emperor Maximilian I and niece of his successor, Charles V

MARGUERITE OF NAVARRE (1492–1549) — sister of Francis I of France. Duchess of Alençon later queen of Navarre. Humanist author who influenced Ann Boleyn

MARY, PRINCESS, LATER MARY I (1516–58) — daughter of Henry VIII and Catherine of Aragon

MORE, THOMAS (1478–1535) — chancellor under Henry VIII; author of *Utopia*. Ω for his refusal to take the Oath of Succession after Henry's divorce from Catherine of Aragon

NORFOLK, DUKE OF. *See* Howard, Thomas

NORRIS, HENRY (d. 1536) — courtier accused of adultery with Ann Boleyn. Ω

PARR, KATHERINE (1512?–48) — sixth wife of Henry VIII; major Protestant force in his reign. Later married Thomas Seymour and died of puerperal fever

PERCY, LORD HENRY (1502?–37) — Earl of Northumberland; early suitor of Ann Boleyn who later served on jury that convicted her of treason

ROCHFORD, LADY JANE (d. 1542) — wife of Ann Boleyn's brother George. Ω for role in Kathryn Howard's adultery

ROCHFORD, VISCOUNT. *See* Boleyn, George

SALINAS, MARIA DE (d. 1539) — lady-in-waiting and dearest friend of Queen Catherine of Aragon. Married Lord Willoughby de Eresby; mother of Catherine Willoughby

SEYMOUR, EDWARD (1500?–52) — brother of Jane Seymour. Became Duke of Somerset and Protector of the Realm in the reign of the boy king Edward VI after Henry VIII's death. Married Anne Stanhope. Executed in Edward's reign

SEYMOUR, JANE (1509?–37) — Henry VIII's third wife; mother of his only legitimate son, Edward

SEYMOUR, THOMAS (1507?–49) — Jane's younger brother. Gentleman of the privy chamber under Henry; named Lord High Admiral and Baron of Sudelay by Somerset. Later married Katherine Parr. Executed in Edward's reign

SMEATON, MARK (d. 1536) — court musician accused of adultery with Ann Boleyn. Ω

SOMERSET, DUKE OF. See Seymour, Edward

STANHOPE, ANNE (d. 1587) — lady-in-waiting to three of Henry VIII's queens; wife of Edward Seymour

SUFFOLK, DUCHESS OF. See Willoughby, Catherine

SUFFOLK, DUKE OF. See Brandon, Charles

TUDOR, MARGARET (1489–1541) — older sister of Henry VIII. Queen consort of James IV of Scotland and regent after his death

TUDOR, MARY (1496–1533) — younger sister of Henry VIII. Briefly married to King Louis XII of France, hence known thereafter as "the French Queen." Later married Charles Brandon, Duke of Suffolk

WESTON, FRANCIS (1511?–36) — courtier accused of adultery with Ann Boleyn. Ω

WILLOUGHBY, CATHERINE, DUCHESS OF SUFFOLK (1519?–80) — daughter of Maria de Salinas; last wife of Charles Brandon. Influential Protestant and lady-in-waiting to Katherine Parr

WOLSEY, THOMAS CARDINAL (1475?–1530) — Lord Chancellor during first half of reign of Henry VIII

WOODVILLE, ELIZABETH (1437–92) — grandmother of Henry VIII; wife of Edward IV

WRIOTHESLEY, THOMAS (1505–50) — diplomat in Henry VIII's court; made Lord Chancellor in 1540 and Earl of Southampton in 1547, after Henry's death

WYATT, THOMAS (1503–42) — poet and courtier who was a friend of Ann Boleyn

INTRODUCTION

I became interested in the women of Tudor England at around the same time I began my activism in, and writing for, the women's movement—in the early 1970s, when the BBC did its magnificent series *The Six Wives of Henry VIII* and *Elizabeth R*, about Henry's daughter, the splendid monarch who dubbed herself a "prince." Seeing these shows precipitated a rush to the library, where I started reading everything I could find—fiction and nonfiction, scholarly tomes and popular history—about the women and their times. In those early, heady days of feminism, when we were beginning to see ourselves not as natural helpmates to men but as a colonized people, it was easy to fall in love with some set of foremothers, and the discovery of these particular foremothers started a passion that ran a parallel course with my work in the movement itself, both nourishing it and providing an escape from its more grueling and depressing aspects. I wrote about Tudor women in poetry; I read about them in novels.

In the early 1980s, working for a master's degree in women's studies and writing, I wrote my thesis on one of them, the Protestant martyr Anne Askew, whose life was so interwoven with that of Henry's last wife, Katherine Parr. This was a challenging transition. It's one thing to watch television and read historical novels, even to write poetry, which in this context is another form of fiction. It was now necessary to move into the world of serious scholarship.

There was at the time little on which to model the kind of work I wanted to do. Feminist historians tended to write about later women, those of the eighteenth and nineteenth centuries; the women's studies works in my area that were to become classics, such as Joan Kelly-Gadol's "Did Women Have a Renaissance?" came a few years later. Working with Clarissa Atkinson, a historian of religion at the Harvard Divinity School, I was able to use the traditional sources to shape my own theories about Anne Askew.

This work convinced me that I wanted to write more about these women, to see them both in the context of their own times and with the insight feminism provided. I was doing an article for *Ms.* about sexual harassment on the job and reading about Henry's wives in my free time, but it took awhile to put together the fact that Ann Boleyn's position as lady-in-waiting to Henry's wife Catherine of Aragon was her *job*, and that, far from trying to lure Henry away from Catherine, she had spent over a year tactfully trying to repel his sexual advances. I was writing in feminist publications about women's right to their sexual desires, and then reading authors who dismissed Henry's fifth wife, Kathryn Howard, as a "wanton" and a "juvenile delinquent" because she was actively sexual. I was reading about feminist theology and about women who suffered martyrdom for their right to define God according to their own consciences. Slowly, the idea for this book started to grow.

Meanwhile scholarly books began to come out—Retha Warnicke's and E.W. Ives's intriguing interpretations of Ann Boleyn, along with a number of anthologies, all incorporating some of the ideas on the burgeoning scholarly discipline of women's studies. Popular books have followed—Alison Weir's *The Six Wives of Henry VIII* and Antonia Fraser's *The Wives of Henry VIII*. Both have incorporated some of the scholarly women's studies books, and both are informed to some degree by popular feminism. But neither has used the work that seems to me essential in re-exploring any women's histories ("herstories," as some feminist writers prefer to call them)—the writings of activists like Gloria Steinem, Andrea Dworkin, Robin Morgan, Shulamith Firestone, Kate Millett, Germaine Greer, Ingrid Bengis, Adrienne Rich, and hundreds more in the small feminist publications around the country over the past twenty years (*Sojourner, Women: A Journal of Liberation, Off Our Backs, Second Wave,* etc.). It was from this work that much contemporary understanding of women's lives has come—concepts like wife battery, sexual abuse, sexual harassment, and female culture, as well as challenges to male definitions of such diverse areas as work and female sexuality. The understanding of God has been questioned not in terms of Catholicism or Judaism, belief or disbelief, but in terms of women's need to experience spirituality and divinity in light of their own experience. My career as a writer had begun in this tradition, and it seemed to me that through it I could make a contribution to the study of the remarkable women of Tudor times.

The decision to embark on such a project creates a challenge—how to bring this approach to a study of women who lived five hundred years ago without being anachronistic and without projecting wishful thinking onto people whose lives and perceptions were in so many ways different from ours. The first step, obviously, is to thoroughly examine their lives—

to immerse oneself in the world of the sixteenth-century English noble-woman. What was she like? What did she think about? What defined her sense of her morality, of her rights, of her relation to her parents, her husband, her king, her woman friends, her God? What was she *expected* to feel about all these things by the men who controlled and influenced her life?

Second, it's important to look at how these women were perceived by the chroniclers of their own era and those of later periods, and at how these perceptions have been shaped by religious beliefs, political convictions, and assumptions about gender. When the sixteenth-century martyrologist John Foxe writes approvingly of Katherine Parr's relationship with Henry that "she did, with all painful endeavor, apply herself, by all virtuous means, in all things to please his humor," he says something not only about his commitment to Protestantism but about his own (and his society's) sexual politics. Similarly, when the excellent twentieth-century historian Lacey Baldwin Smith says of Kathryn Howard that she "enacted a light-hearted dream in which juvenile delinquency, wanton selfishness and ephemeral hedonism were the abiding themes," he is expressing his own sexual politics. The ways in which successive generations of writers have interpreted these women's lives is almost as interesting, and as revealing, as the stories of the women themselves.

᠅ Any look at women in Tudor England invariably begins with the wives of Henry VIII. There are other equally engaging women—equally brave, equally tragic, equally intelligent, equally victimized, equally triumphant—but because of Henry's glamorously bizarre behavior, those six dominate our perception of the era's women. They hover in our imaginations around the king like faithful satellites orbiting a splendid sun, and the fact that on scrutiny the sun reveals itself as a great, empty mass of hot air does little to lessen the fascination. Henry VIII's monstrous egotism and dynastic misfortune, occurring at a time when Europe was ripe for religious revolution, drew into history six women who were dramatically different from the man who controlled their destinies, and dramatically different from each other. Each became, for varying degrees of time, the most powerful woman in England; each lost that position because she was at the mercy of the most powerful *man* in the land.

Yet the queen, as long as she held the king's affection, or at least his respect, had both personal wealth, with its accompanying economic power, and at least some degree of political power. Henry's first two wives influenced his policy—Catherine of Aragon, because she was shrewder than he and more interested in the nitty-gritty of politics; Ann Boleyn, because by its very existence his marriage to her shaped religious policy at a time when religion and politics were intimately entwined. The later wives had far less influence but were still able to wheedle favors from the king, and his last wife influenced him indirectly by choosing ladies-in-waiting whose ideas mirrored her own. Within the tight, insular court those ladies were able to sway their suitors, Henry's courtiers.

As they had earlier and would do throughout the Tudor and Stuart period, ladies-in-waiting played an important role in the queen's world. The duties of the lady-in-waiting were more restricted than those of the queen's male servants. When Catherine of Aragon came to the throne, she had her own service establishment of nearly one hundred and fifty people—considerably fewer than the king's 500, but certainly substantial. Like the queen consorts who preceded and followed her, she had her own council, whose members, all male, performed such practical tasks as directing and supervising the care of her extensive properties. She had her own chancellor, her master of the horse, her secretary, her chaplains, and a host of other male servants, as well as needlewomen, chamberers, and ladies. The positions that required negotiation with the outside world belonged to men.

That still left plenty for the ladies to do. They were divided, in early Tudor times, into four categories of descending importance—great ladies, ladies of the privy chamber, maids of honor, and chamberers. The great ladies functioned in infrequent, chiefly ceremonial roles, while the ladies of the privy chamber were especially privileged in seeing to the queen's most intimate needs as she readied herself for bed and prepared for the intricate task of getting dressed in the morning. The last category, the chamberers, were the most humble of the queen's personal female servants. Maids of honor were young unmarried women who attended the queen, learning the ways of the court and there attracting the attention of the king's most eligible courtiers. Mothers among the nobility fought long and hard to get their marriageable daughters positions as maids of honor. Minor noblewomen who failed to get their daughters placed in the royal household were often happy to settle for getting them into the households of other great ladies (who were often themselves ladies-in-waiting to the queen). If the king approved of one of his wife's ladies, he might marry her off to an important courtier. In Henry's case, it soon became apparent that he might take her for himself: three of his six wives and both of his known mistresses had begun their court careers as ladies to his current queen.

The ladies had a number of duties. Conspicuous consumption characterized every monarchy of the day; the king and queen must always be seen having their every need attended to. Dinner at court was not simply a meal but a public ceremony illustrating the monarch's wealth, power, and bounty. Most of the service was done by a strictly regulated hierarchy of male attendants, but the queen's most intimate table needs were taken care of by her ladies. At the coronation dinner of Henry's mother, Elizabeth of York, for example, two of her ladies "sat on either side of the Queen's feet all the dinner time" while two others, the countesses of Oxenberg and of Rivers, knelt beside her and "at certain times held a kerchief before her Grace." Years later, when Ann Boleyn was crowned, two noblewomen performed a similar ritual, holding a cloth to Ann's mouth when she wanted to "spit or do otherwise." That such attendance was not confined to coronation banquets is apparent from a letter describing an incident at court during the reign of Ann's successor, Jane Seymour, who, the writer says, was given her water bowl for washing up after dinner by the Marchioness of Exeter.

None of the ladies objected to these menial tasks, which in any case took up relatively little of their time. In a court where leisure was taken very seriously, the ladies and the courtiers accompanied the king and queen in hunting and hawking parties and in elaborate masquerades. The ladies were also expected to attend the frequent jousts, elaborate contests that also served as military training for courtiers, and to applaud the contestants.

Indoors, the queen and her ladies enjoyed playing cards. One account of court life shows the reputedly prim Princess Mary losing money in a card game with the young Duchess of Suffolk, Catherine Willoughby.

Other duties were less colorful. Like any wealthy matron, the queen supervised her household's domestic functioning. Her ladies were at her side, carrying messages to lower servants or, when required, to the king's gentlemen. In the reign of particularly pious queens like Catherine of Aragon, hours were spent each day at chapel—and when the queen prayed, her ladies prayed as well.

They also played music, read, and sewed—sometimes together, with one woman reading or playing the lute as the queen and the rest of her ladies sewed. Medieval and Renaissance queens considered reading religious works and some of the more chaste of the classical writers a wholesome way of keeping young women's minds off the attractions of young men, and sewing seems to have been almost an obsession among the female members of the court. Though the queen's household included numerous sewing women from lower stations, these women did the less creative work. The queen and her ladies spent hours working on the elaborate costumes they wore to masquerades and balls—the green satin costumes with headdresses "made of damask gold with long hairs of white gold" that the French ambassadors admired in their visit to Henry's court in 1518, for example. When Henry went to war with France, his wife's ladies were kept frantically busy making standards, badges, and banners. And they embroidered things like small wall hangings and chair coverings with and for the queen. The rooms of the royal palaces were full of such handiwork.

Sometimes the ladies did less ornate sewing as well. Ann Boleyn had her women make clothing, which she later took on the royal progress and distributed to the poor. Like the reading of good books, such sewing also served to keep them out of trouble. Ann's silkwoman was quoted as praising the queen for keeping her ladies-in-waiting too busy sewing to indulge in "pampered pleasures" or "licentious liberty," as maids were likely to do when given too much free time.

Ann was not unusual in her determination to maintain a chaste court. There was a lot of flirting among these people who worked so hard at their leisure pursuits, and undoubtedly both sexes often went beyond flirtation. But chastity was still expected of the women of the court, even if tempered by worldliness and an attractive air of sophistication. The hallmark of a chaste woman was not, as in the Victorian age, a lack of knowledge about sex. Indeed, the ladies of the court were expected to parry the sexual innuendoes of male courtiers. The woman who didn't at least understand sexual allusions was rare, and not especially admired.

But though she bantered about sex, the "good woman" didn't use her knowledge outside the marriage bed. For the married woman, adultery was dangerous. She could not, early in the Tudor reign, be divorced, but she could be repudiated and left with little money, or she could be kept a virtual prisoner in one of her husband's manors. For maidens, sex was even more dangerous, since pregnancy would lead to instant dismissal from court and the loss of all hope of a prestigious marriage. A woman was expected to come to her first marriage a virgin, though we read occasionally of a lady being sent away from court because of suspected sexual escapades, and during Elizabeth's reign a number of maids—including Bess Throckmorton, the mistress and later wife of Sir Walter Raleigh—were dismissed because of premarital pregnancy.

Nor would it be easy in the medieval or Renaissance court to conceal an affair for any length of time. Royal palaces were busy, public places, and court life was governed at all times by bitter, competitive factions. Every member, no matter how uninterested in political intrigue, had enemies simply by virtue of the fact that relatives and friends took one side or another on a myriad of issues. Enemies loved spying on each other to learn anything that might lead to discredit and disgrace.

Two women did become Henry VIII's mistresses during his marriage to Catherine of Aragon, but adultery with a king was a somewhat different story. The used goods of a nobleman might be forced to marry below her class or enter a convent, but the discarded mistress of a king could be assured of a good match, either at the beginning of the affair, to provide a smoke screen, or at its end, as a payment for services rendered. Bessie Blount was one of Catherine of Aragon's ladies who became the mistress of the king. When she got pregnant, she was quietly sent from court and, after her son's birth, married off to Lord Tailboys. A later mistress, Mary Boleyn, already had a reputation for loose living from her stay in the French court. She was married to William Carey, a gentleman of the king's Privy Chamber, probably during her affair with the king, though it's possible that she was given Carey as a reward when the king had finished with her. It is noteworthy that her reputation for licentiousness stemmed not from her relationship with Henry but from her earlier affairs; there was far less stigma attached to virtue lost to royalty. (Even virtue lost to near-royalty might be overlooked: one of the women Ann Boleyn chose as lady-in-waiting was Bess Holland, the mistress of Ann's uncle the Duke of Norfolk.)

Other stories from the court show that there was a far more complex attitude toward the role of mistress, or potential mistress, to the king. The ideals of female chastity were not always suspended for royalty. There were women who did not want to bed the king, and women whose families did not want them to—either because of the ideal of chastity, or due to the woman's distaste for the particular man. During Catherine of Aragon's reign, two sisters of the Duke of Buckingham were among her ladies. One of them attracted the attention of the king's friend Sir William Compton, who, it was rumored, was merely a go-between for Henry himself. The lady, though married, seemed responsive. Her sister found out about Sir William's overtures and reported the situation to their brother, who, along with her husband, promptly removed her far from court.

During the reign of Henry's last wife, the Duchess of Richmond testified against her brother, the Earl of Surrey, in his trial for treason, declaring that he had urged her to become the king's mistress in order to advance the family's interests. The plan backfired, whether because of the duchess's loyalty to Katherine Parr, her dislike of the king's person, or her own wish to preserve her chastity. She reported the conversation to the king, contributing further to the fury Henry already felt toward the arrogant and doomed young earl, who soon found himself on the block.

Though the daily round of court ladies remained fairly stable throughout the Middle Ages and well into the Renaissance, the environment in which they performed these activities changed dramatically from reign to reign. The monarch created the atmosphere of the court: in the second half of the fifteenth century, Henry VI's court had been spartan; whereas Edward IV's was playful. Richard III was king for too short a period for us to have any sense of what life in his court was like, but his successor, Henry VII, the first of the Tudors, reigned for twenty-four years. Henry's court was stable but austere. He had wrested the throne from Richard in battle, with a very tenuous claim on the monarchy (he was descended, illegitimately, from Edward III), and he was accepted as king by a country beaten down by decades of war and ensuing poverty. There were others with better claim to royal blood than Henry's, most of whom he had put in the Tower or executed on blatantly trumped-up charges of treason. He didn't bother anyone else. Nothing better captures the difference between his character and that of his son than his treatment of the young traitor Lambert Simnel, who tried to pass himself off as the dead Earl of Warwick, grandson of Edward IV. Others involved in the plot were executed, but Simnel, a lower-class youth who was clearly out of his element and posed no threat to the throne after his absurd imposture was exposed, was given a job first in the royal kitchens and later as the king's falconer. The court was a deadly place for anyone who threatened Henry's position, but it was a comfortable, if unexciting, one for everyone else.

In the early days, his son's court seemed to be both comfortable *and* exciting. England was tired of the secure reign of the miserly, colorless old man who had brought its economy back from the shambles of the Wars of the Roses. Henry VIII promised glamour, adventure, youthful pleasures—"pastime and good company," as he wrote in one of the songs that endeared him to his people. The Henry who came to the throne in 1509 was to all appearances a far cry from the roaring tyrant enveloped in layers of decaying flesh that he would become in time. He was startlingly handsome—"handsomer than any sovereign in Christendom," wrote the Venetian ambassador, "very fair, and the whole frame admirably proportioned." The letters of other ambassadors read like the gurglings of infatuated schoolgirls. The young king was charming and charismatic, full of an infectious zest for life that impressed the jaded diplomats. He was the very image of the Renaissance ideal of the monarch. Generous and expansive, he treated his courtiers with an air of equality that paradoxically enhanced his own majesty.

At least one among them saw through the charming facade—the man who had not wanted to be a courtier but was drafted into Henry's service by the king's honeyed insistence. Thomas More gave in gracefully to the king's commands, but he had no illusions. When his son-in-law William Roper waxed enthusiastic over the fact that the king would walk arm-in-arm with Sir Thomas in their gardens, More replied that, though Henry cared as much for him as for anyone, "if my head could win him a castle in France, it should not fail to go."

Few were as discerning as More. They obeyed the king's orders cheerfully because his orders pleased them. He in turn saw their pleasure as the natural, unquestioning deference owed to him, their sovereign. Later, when he came to discover that others didn't always want the same things he wanted, his courtiers would learn that his warmth could quickly turn to fury, and that he would destroy anyone who defied him.

By the second half of his reign, this had become tragically clear. He now got his way through open tyranny, the old charm showing itself only erratically and never wiping out the fear those around him needed to maintain constantly if they were to survive. People still flocked to the court as the center of power and privilege, but it was a different court than it had been in the early days of the reign. Those closest to Henry fell, destroyed by his insatiable ego.

That ego created a new religion. Until Henry wanted to rid himself of a sonless and no longer fertile wife, religion in Tudor England was fairly uncomplicated. The authority of the pope existed on two levels. As a temporal ruler, he could be quarreled with, hated, and even warred against. In his secular capacity, no one expected him to be any better than anyone else. Popes had mistresses and illegitimate children, just as kings did, and like kings they often raised their illegitimate offspring to high positions in government. Whatever the Bible said about fornication, popes were rarely celibate. While many among the English, as among all Europeans, railed against the personal lapses of the pope, it did not affect his position as head of the church. In that capacity, he was revered. Although the doctrine of papal infallibility was not issued until 1870, few Christians challenged the pope's religious pronouncements.

At the same time, the church had always been embattled. There was vicious, internal fighting within the ecclesiastical power structure. Moreover, the lines between the spiritual leadership of the pope and church hierarchy on the one hand and the temporal leadership of secular rulers on the other were far less clear in fact than in theory. Popes and monarchs had always existed in a state of tension and often of out-and-out warfare.

Compounding this situation was the ever-present problem of heresy—a problem that popes and monarchs between them had always managed to keep contained, if not to wholly exterminate. In England, the anticlerical Lollardy heresy, which was influenced by the fourteenth-century scholar John Wycliffe, had for years challenged the power of the church and thus the king, who was seen as God's temporal representative. But Lollardy, though embraced by large numbers of the poor and some of the minor aristocracy, had few proponents among the upper echelons of English society, and most of its open adherents were burned at the stake.

But even the most pious Christians were cynical about the clergy, whose disregard for Christian behavior in their own lives mirrored that of the popes. When, a decade into Henry's reign, Martin Luther defied the pope in Germany and thus opened the rift that would soon grow into the Protestant Reformation, many of the English echoed him. At Cambridge University, the White Horse Inn became known as Little Germany because so many Lutheran sympathizers gathered there.

At first, the boundary between what was considered legitimate questioning and heresy was murky. The New Learning—the greater critical understanding of the Greek and Latin classics that was at the core of Renaissance humanism—eventually led to the rejection of the church's absolute authority, but initially it was in no way antithetical to the religion that had shaped the European worldview for centuries. Catherine of Aragon and Ann Boleyn were both enthusiasts of the New Learning, as were the Catholic martyr Thomas More and the Protestant martyr Anne Askew. Indeed, the word *Protestant* was not used until 1529, and it wasn't common in England until much later. The English tended to lump together all anti-papal believers as "Lutherans"—including followers of John Calvin and even the Anabaptists.

Henry was at first scornful of those who denied church doctrine and rejected ecclesiastical authority, and his courtiers by and large prudently followed suit. The king defended the papacy against Luther, winning from the pope the title Defender of the Faith. With the pope's refusal to annul his marriage to Catherine of Aragon, however, all that changed, and the routinely pious men and women of the nobility found themselves, like the rest of the country, caught in a maelstrom in which religious belief was based not on doctrine but on the king's personal desires, transfigured into theology. It was no longer enough to mutter one's prayers, sit through chapel services, and make pilgrimages to the shrines of royally approved saints.

For a good part of the English people, it was a time of terrifying confusion. Henry would always swear that he was faithful to what was coming to be called the Catholic Church, and that it was the pope who had betrayed it, by betraying him. He did not deny any of the doctrines central to Catholicism—the real presence of Christ in the bread and wine of the Eucharist, for example. Yet he did at times permit the reading of the Bible by the common people, and he had the Archbishop of Canterbury issue a new vernacular version for that purpose. Translating the Bible into the common languages was not heretical—the great Dutch humanist and Catholic apologist Desiderius Erasmus had encouraged lay reading of the Bible—but the centrality of scripture among Protestants, against the authority of the hierarchy and church tradition, made its availability in the vernacular associated with heresy. Henry's dissolution of the monasteries and convents was a greater challenge to the old religion, and the old Catholics protested. Yet Christianity in Henry's England retained much of traditional Catholic dogma. As Henry grew more erratic, people didn't know what they were supposed to believe. Some learned only when they were arrested for heresy.

Each of his queens inevitably played a role in the evolution of Henrician religion. Catherine of Aragon and Ann Boleyn, strong-willed and passionate, became the living symbols of the old and new religions. The others too had their own, often complicated, roles in the early development of English Protestantism. Discovering the political uses of religion, Henry plunged the country into chaos. Doctrines changed as different factions manipulated the king's lust and his ego. Those with deep religious convictions—Catherine of Aragon, Thomas More, Robert Barnes, Anne Askew—were doomed. Those whose beliefs were more pliable had a better chance to remain in the king's good graces—so long as they managed to anticipate his ever-shifting needs and desires. Henry's ultimate God was Henry, and those who failed to worship suffered the fate of all who defy the deity. In one way or another, his wives were all victimized by his unlimited power and his monstrous use of it. But with one exception, each at some point *did* defy this self-invented god, and in the process, defined for herself who she was and what her life meant.

DIVORCED, BEHEADED, SURVIVED

THE KINGMAKER

MARGARET BEAUFORT, COUNTESS OF RICHMOND

She masterminded the plot that brought her son to the throne of England as Henry VII, thus beginning the Tudor dynasty. Margaret was the first in a line of formidable women to influence her grandson Henry VIII.

he word *kingmaker* conjures up the image of the Earl of Warwick, striding magnificently through Shakespeare's plays dealing with the Wars of the Roses. Arrogant, charismatic, ambitious, and brilliant, Richard Neville did indeed turn Edward of York into King Edward IV. But there were other kingmakers besides Warwick, and more successful ones. Not all were warriors; indeed, not all were men. A woman with genius and ambition couldn't dream of ruling in her own name, but she could nonetheless wield great power through the men who, at least in theory, ruled her. Such a woman was Margaret Beaufort—a kingmaker whose work proved far more successful than that of the famous earl, in whose world she moved with deceptive silence.

Born in 1441, Margaret was the only child of John Beaufort, whose grandfather was John of Gaunt, Duke of Lancaster, the fourth son of Edward III. Lancaster had sired four children in respectable wedlock, and four with his mistress of many years, the commoner Katherine Swynford, whom he eventually married. An act of Parliament under Richard II had declared the latter children legitimate, but a later Parliament had, in a legally questionable move, added the stipulation that their descendants be permanently barred from the throne. Margaret Beaufort was one of those descendants.

Margaret's mother appears to have had advanced ideas about the education of girls. True, she made certain her daughter learned the appropriate womanly skills—needlework and the supervision of a large household—but Margaret was also taught to read and write. She was not, however, permitted to study Greek and Latin. She would all her life regret this void in her education, and though she eventually learned "a little percentage of Latin," she was never proficient enough to satisfy herself.

When she was nine, Margaret was given the extraordinary privilege of being allowed to decide which of her two suitors she would marry. One was the eight-year-old son of her guardian, who wanted her wealth to stay in his family. The other was the king's half brother, Edmund Tudor.

Years later, she told her friend Bishop Fisher how she came to decide. She was advised by "an old gentlewoman whom she most loved and trusted" to pray to Saint Nicholas for guidance. She did, and the saint appeared to her in a vision, saying she should marry Edmund. "And by this means," wrote Fisher, "did she incline her mind unto Edmund the King's brother." Soon afterward her guardian was murdered by Yorkists, beheaded with a rusty sword, his body left on the sands of Dover. Edmund Tudor was made Earl of Richmond, and in 1455, at the age of fourteen, Margaret married him.

Within a year, Edmund suddenly fell ill and died. Three months later Margaret's "good and gracious prince, king, and only beloved son" was born. She named him Henry, after his royal uncle, Henry VI. At fifteen, she was a mother and a widow.

The Wars of the Roses had begun the year of Margaret's marriage. Henry VI, docile, kind, and dimwitted, and afflicted with periodic bouts of insanity as well, was incapable of conducting a military campaign, and it was his queen, Margaret of Anjou, who not only organized the battles but at times donned armor and led her army into the field. In the fall of 1460, Richard of York succeeded in seizing the crown, claiming it not for himself but for his descendants after Henry's death. At the end of December, Margaret of Anjou led an army into York itself, where the duke and his men were quartered. After a bloody battle, Richard of York was slain, and the triumphant queen had his corpse decapitated. The head, capped with a paper crown, was impaled on the gate to the city.

Through all this, little Henry Tudor remained in his mother's care— unusual in an era when fatherless children were made wards of a nobleman chosen by the king. In 1459, Margaret Beaufort married Lord Henry Stafford. It was a marriage of convenience, not of passion, one that allowed Margaret to raise her son as she saw fit, teaching him love for learning and, perhaps above all, the value of patience.

In 1461, the tide turned in favor of the Yorkists, and Edward of York, eldest son of the slain Richard, assumed the crown of England as Edward IV. After more battles whose outcomes gave the advantage first to the Lancastrians and then to the Yorkists, the king's only son was killed and the old king himself murdered in the Tower. Henry Tudor was now the sole living male in the Lancastrian line of succession. In the summer of 1471 Margaret sent the fourteen-year-old boy, accompanied by his uncle Jasper

Tudor, to France, which supported the Lancastrians. A storm threw their ship off course, and they landed instead in Brittany, which maintained a cautious neutrality during the Wars of the Roses. The Bretons accepted their guests courteously, and Margaret was assured that her son was, for the time being at least, safe from Edward's soldiers.

Lord Stafford died soon after. Margaret, now thirty, was once again alone. She spent hours at a time in prayer, she fasted frequently, and she occasionally wore hair shirts. She also sought a powerful protector for herself and her son. In 1473, she married Thomas Stanley, later Earl of Derby.

Whether or not her plans were gestating during the reign of Edward IV, circumstances arose in the mid-1480s that dramatically changed Margaret's, and England's, history. On April 9, 1483, Edward died of a sudden illness. He left five daughters and two young sons. In his will, the king had appointed his ambitious brother Richard as protector of the two boys.

Aiming to make his power permanent, Richard claimed that Edward had been betrothed to another woman when he married Elizabeth Woodville. Since a betrothal, or precontract, was considered legally equivalent to an actual marriage, this would have meant that Edward's sons by Elizabeth were illegitimate. He declared himself Richard III, king of England. The young princes, who had been taken to the Tower of London in preparation for the elder boy's coronation, simply vanished from sight.

Whether or not Shakespeare's *Richard III* is an accurate portrayal of this most controversial of kings, he created a murky situation at best. His own claim to the throne was highly questionable; Margaret Beaufort certainly did not accept it. She was sure her own son had a better claim than Richard.

To put young Henry on the throne, she needed help. Her husband had been a loyal Yorkist, which was probably one reason she had married him, believing that she and her son would benefit by their association with one of Edward's firmest supporters. With Edward dead, would Lord Stanley remain loyal to his brother?

Richard's own actions gave Margaret the boost she needed. Stanley was on the new council, as he had been on the old. At one meeting, Richard burst into a sudden fury, raving about a plot against his life. He called in his men-at-arms to arrest several council members, including Lord Stanley. They remained in the Tower for several weeks; then Richard, having a change of heart, sent Stanley home to his wife, gave him back his post of steward of the royal household, and invited him and his lady to attend the coronation.

They could hardly refuse, and duly appeared at the ceremony, Margaret bearing the queen's train and Lord Stanley bearing the mace before the king. All seemed well, but Lord Stanley—who, along with being arrested, had been hit in the head by one of Richard's soldiers—could hardly have felt much affection for his new king. Richard had given Margaret her ally.

Meanwhile, she had been making contact with people she knew would join her cause. One of the most useful, and the most dangerous, of these was her nephew by her second marriage, Henry Stafford, Duke of Buckingham. Buckingham had been Richard's closest ally in his own conspiracy, working cleverly and tirelessly to establish Richard's claim to the throne. Now, with equal fervor, he turned against the king, claiming to be horrified by what he believed to be the murder of the princes. (Some modern historians have suggested that Buckingham himself was the killer.) Whatever the case, Margaret was shrewd enough to spot her nephew's disaffection with Richard and to take full advantage of it.

One day, as Buckingham was riding to Shrewsbury, he happened across Margaret, who was on her way to the cathedral at Worcester. It was too fortuitous a meeting to be a coincidence, but the duke apparently accepted it as such. They discussed many things in that brief encounter, including Buckingham's own royal ambitions. Margaret managed to persuade him that her son's claims were stronger, and that he would do well for himself as a nobleman of high position under Henry Tudor.

There was one other ally Margaret needed to recruit—the one person whose help was crucial if the people of England were to support a virtually unknown claimant. Although Henry would rule in his own name, by right of the Beaufort blood, he would need a queen whose blood was indisputably royal if his children were to inherit and retain the crown. This meant he had to marry one of Edward IV's daughters. Margaret needed the support of their mother.

Elizabeth Woodville had been the beautiful widow of a minor Lancastrian nobleman, Sir John Grey, when the young King Edward met her and became smitten. She refused his advances, saying, "My liege, I know I am not good enough to be your queen, but I am far too good to become your mistress." Edward took the hint and married the ambitious beauty, creating an uproar. No one but Edward liked Elizabeth much, but he liked her enough to sire a quick succession of offspring, which justified their marriage by creating heirs to the throne.

With Edward's death and Richard's ascendancy, everything changed.

Elizabeth fled to sanctuary at Westminster, taking her children with her. She was forced to turn the boys over to Richard. The girls were older—Elizabeth of York was now seventeen—and presumably of less importance to the insecure new monarch. Richard let them remain with their mother.

Soon the princes were gone, possibly murdered. Elizabeth's brother and one of her two sons by her first marriage had been executed. Her marriage to Edward had been declared null and her daughters bastardized. She nearly went mad with grief, screaming and tearing her hair, then falling into silent fits of melancholy. Medical help was clearly called for.

Richard kept a close eye on Elizabeth's visitors, but he could not deny her the services of a physician. Edward Lewis, a prominent Welsh doctor much employed by the English nobility, offered his assistance. After a number of visits he slowly led up to the suggestion that was his mission—for Lewis was also physician to Margaret Beaufort.

Elizabeth's sons were gone, but her daughters were alive, and they carried in them the royal blood of Edward IV. What if the eldest of them, Elizabeth, were to marry Henry Tudor, and Henry were to become king of England? Their children would be Elizabeth and Edward's grandchildren; the usurper and his line would be overthrown.

Elizabeth agreed readily. There was no immediate way of getting the girl out of Westminster without endangering her and arousing suspicion, but with the help of Dr. Lewis, Elizabeth smuggled messages to her relatives and friends. The ousted queen dowager was now the last, and most important, of the conspirators in Margaret Beaufort's plot to make her son king of England.

What did these two strange allies feel toward each other? It's doubtful that the pious Margaret had much respect for the woman who had used her beauty to advance herself socially, and who had abandoned the Lancastrian cause to become the consort of the Yorkist king. And the glamorous, sensual Elizabeth Woodville could hardly have seen the drab, scholarly, ascetic Lady Margaret as a soulmate.

Yet one thing bound them, and bound them deeply. They were both passionately ambitious for their children. Margaret, with all her dreams focused on her one precious son, could understand the pain of the mother who had lost three sons. For her part, Elizabeth could understand Margaret's fierce attachment to the only child she would ever have. Their alliance offered each woman the best possible position for her offspring.

At first all seemed to go smoothly. Margaret sent news of the proposed marriage to Henry, still safely exiled in Brittany, and he agreed.

Next she counseled him to return to England by way of Wales, where the Tudors had numerous supporters. From there he was to lead the army that Dr. Lewis had assembled. Meanwhile, Buckingham was to lead a contingent of rebels in England.

Henry sailed for Wales, but by the time he landed the plan had failed, and Buckingham had been captured and executed. Realizing that the revolt was doomed, Henry returned to Normandy to reorganize the invasion.

Richard had an act of attainder passed against Margaret, declaring her a traitor, but he made no effort to have her executed or imprisoned. Instead he merely turned her over to her husband. Her lands were forfeited, deeded to Stanley for the duration of his life and to the crown after his death. Stanley was ordered to keep Margaret at home, "in some secret place," where she was to have no visitors and receive no messages. Richard trusted Stanley so completely that he didn't bother sending spies to make certain his orders were obeyed.

Margaret was soon at work again, communicating with her old confederates. Richard's leniency seems strange now; apparently it seemed no less strange at the time. "In this troublous season nothing was more marveled at than that the Lord Stanley had not been taken and reputed as an enemy to the King, considering the working of Lady Margaret, his wife, mother to the Earl of Richmond," noted the sixteenth-century chronicler Raphael Holinshed, who attributed Richard's failure to concern himself with Lord Stanley to the fact that "the enterprise of a woman was of him reputed of no regard or estimation."

Richard put his energy into preventing the marriage of Henry Tudor and Elizabeth of York. In March 1484 he was able to cajole or coerce Elizabeth Woodville and her daughters to leave their sanctuary. Elizabeth managed to exact from Richard a solemn vow, taken in the presence of the lord mayor and aldermen of London, that her children would be unharmed. If she believed that Richard had murdered her sons, such a vow could offer little comfort; he had sworn to protect them as well. She may not have been convinced that he was the author of the boys' deaths, or she may simply have grasped at whatever slim thread of hope she saw. Buckingham's death and Henry's retreat had dashed her hopes of any future other than one based on the tenuous mercy of Richard III.

She had entered sanctuary a queen; she left it a private gentlewoman, "Lady Elizabeth Grey, late calling herself Queen of England." Guarded by Richard's squire of the body John Nesfield, she lived a virtual prisoner.

Elizabeth wrote to her son Thomas Grey, Marquis of Dorset,

instructing him to break off the marriage negotiations between Henry of Richmond and young Elizabeth. She also told Dorset to return home. If there is any doubt that she wrote under duress, it should be erased by the second part of her order. It is ludicrous to imagine that the woman who had kept her children in sanctuary for a year to protect them from Richard, who knew that Richard had executed one of her sons and could well have been responsible for the mysterious disappearance of two others, would order a fourth son, safe in Paris, to return and place himself in Richard's power.

Meanwhile, Richard was treating the daughters far better than the mother. When young Elizabeth appeared at court festivities, wearing a dress like the queen's, the growing ranks of Richard's enemies decided that the king was planning to poison his queen and marry "fair Bessie" himself. Although there is no evidence that the rumors were true, they might have spurred Margaret and her son to hasten their planned invasion. Richard's ailing queen died in March 1485, and by summer of that year, Henry, accompanied by his uncle Jasper, landed on England's shores. Learning that the enemy was approaching, Richard quickly seized Lord Stanley's eldest son, Lord Strange, as a hostage. It must have been an excruciating time for Stanley. As Margaret's biographer Linda Simon notes, Stanley's continued support of the coup is eloquent testimony to his respect for his wife's skill and intelligence: "Stanley knew that any apparent defection from the king would cost his son's life. Only Stanley's complete faith in his wife's plan allowed him to gamble for such high stakes."

His faith was not misplaced. On August 22, Richard was killed in the Battle of Bosworth Field. Fourteen years after he had fled England, Margaret Beaufort's son was Henry VII, King of England. Elizabeth of York married him after all, cementing the Tudor dynasty.

Elizabeth Woodville retired to a convent several years after her daughter became queen. But Margaret Beaufort remained a force at court: with the same energy she had used to get her son on the throne, she went about running his various households as well as administering her own considerable lands. Henry gave her a number of lucrative wardships and, perhaps more significant, made her a grant "for life . . . of the right of nomination and appointing the steward, receiver, bailiff, parker and all other officers within the king's lordship of Ware, Co. Hertford" and in other areas around England. Margaret thus enjoyed a degree of autonomy rare for any married woman of the age—her properties were her own, held and controlled by her as "femme sole," not "femme covert."

Margaret took over aspects of domestic supervision that one would have expected the young queen to assume, including the minute details of Elizabeth's confinement as she approached the birth of her first child. Margaret's attitude toward the confinement was creative and surprisingly modern: she insisted on having one window left clear of wall hangings and tapestries, so that the queen "may have light when it pleases her."

In 1495 a young priest came to court, instantly attracting the attention of the king's mother. John Fisher shared her piety, and the two became fast friends, she his patron, he her confessor. Together they worked to recharge religious studies at the two great universities. Both were distressed by abuses in the church—and equally distressed by the heresies that arose in response to those abuses. Lollardy was still strong in small pockets of the country. Aiming to counter it by offering a more accessible orthodoxy to the people of England, Margaret endowed two readerships in divinity at Cambridge, which provided readings of religious works to any who wanted to hear them. She understood that people wanted a greater understanding of the teachings of the Bible than their priests and bishops gave them. The early association with Cambridge led to further involvement, including founding two of its colleges.

Margaret read, sponsored, and wrote a number of devotional works. The love of learning that had been so great a part of her childhood had never left her, though it faded into the background during the years of her great mission. With her son on the throne, she could now indulge this earlier love. She took great delight in translating from the French a treatise called *The Mirroure of Golde for the Sinfull Soule*. She also translated, again from a French version, the fourth book of the *Imitation of Christ*.

Margaret outlived her beloved son, who died in April 1509, by just two months. It is hard to imagine her grief at the loss of the person who had been the focus of her life. She had the comfort, however, of knowing that it was she who had placed him on the throne. As they had both dreamed, his reign succeeded in uniting the houses of York and Lancaster and ending the years of warfare. Her grandson Henry was strong and healthy, and by all indications would make a fine king.

Realizing that she herself was approaching death, she called the new king to her side and urged him to obey John Fisher, now bishop of Rochester, in all things. She died, one hopes, happy in the belief that he would do so. It was not an unreasonable expectation, but in the event it was an inaccurate one. Twenty-five years later, Henry had Bishop Fisher executed as a traitor. And his queen, a pious, proud Spanish princess, was abandoned, repudiated, and replaced for a time by a younger and prettier woman—a sensual and determined woman, a woman perhaps not good enough to be a king's wife, but too good to be his mistress.

Margaret Beaufort and Elizabeth Woodville, different though they had been, had achieved the one thing that, above all others, a woman was valued for: they had both borne living sons. Neither Catherine of Aragon nor Ann Boleyn, equally different and equally remarkable, would be as lucky.

Chapter 1

THE DAUGHTER OF SPAIN

CATHERINE OF ARAGON

Widow of Henry VIII's older brother Arthur, the pretty princess was an appealing bride to young Henry VIII. Her staunch refusal to deny the validity of her second marriage triggered the English Reformation.

Divorced

f Catherine of Aragon had been the eldest instead of the youngest daughter of Ferdinand and Isabella, she might be remembered not as the discarded consort of a marriage-addicted king but as the powerful queen regnant of Spain, following in the footsteps of her formidable mother and altering the course of sixteenth-century European history. Unlike her sister Juana, who was cheated out of the throne, Catherine had much of Isabella's steely purposefulness and intellect.

Catherine, however, was far from the succession. The fifth child and fourth daughter, she had little prospect of inheriting the throne. Her role was to be a matrimonial tool: an alliance with England, flourishing under the firm guidance of Henry VII, could be useful in Spain's frequent battles with France. Catherine was thus betrothed to Henry VII's elder son, Arthur, heir to the crown. Isabella, herself legitimately descended from John of Gaunt, might even have felt, from the heights of her Castilian pride, some condescending affection for the country of her ancestor. England had in the past played an important role in European events—the battle of Agincourt showed its continental neighbors that it was a force to be reckoned with—but the Wars of the Roses weakened both its strength and its prestige, and devastated its economy. Henry VII was impressive, but he was starting a new dynasty in a ravaged country. Marrying his son to the daughter of Ferdinand and Isabella would help validate his claim to the throne and enhance England's battered reputation.

Negotiations for the marriage of the two royal children took some time, however, for Henry was anxious to gain as large a dowry as possible. Great as the honor of marrying his son into Spanish royalty was, the king was not about to accept that honor without appropriate payment. Pulling together an economy destroyed by war determined his priorities throughout his reign.

The dispute over the dowry resolved itself amiably enough. Henry was to receive two hundred thousand crowns, half to be paid on the wedding day and the rest in increments over the next year, as well as cash, jewels and plate that Catherine was to bring to England with her. If the wrangling seemed unpleasant at the time, no one worried much about it, and the awkwardness passed quickly. But it was a harbinger of the first great crisis of Catherine of Aragon's life.

On Whitsunday of 1499, while Catherine waited at home in Spain, Arthur married her by proxy in the prince's residence in Worcester, England. Since bride and groom were both so young—she was fourteen and he thirteen—she remained in Spain for a short while longer, and the two exchanged solemn love letters. Arthur told his "dearest spouse" of his "ardent love" and begged that "your coming to me be hastened."

In May 1501, his wish was granted. Henry had planned lavish ceremonies for the arrival of his new daughter-in-law—a fact that appalled Isabella, who wrote complaining that "it would be more completely in accordance with my feelings and with the wishes of the king my lord if the expenses were as moderate as possible." Some celebration was fine, she added, but the love of Henry and his queen was far more important than gaudy display. It was perhaps the only time in his life that the tightfisted Henry Tudor was rebuked for being spendthrift.

Isabella's own preparations, if not lavish, were thorough. Clothing, jewels, plate, needlework materials, and books were all carefully chosen and packed in leather-covered chests, with Catherine's initials nailed on them.

More important were her companions. Her duenna, Doña Elvira Manuel, was to accompany her, along with Doña Elvira's husband, Don Pedro Manrique, who would be first chamberlain and major domo of Catherine's household. A tutor, a baker, an almoner, gentlemen-in-waiting—all were handpicked by Isabella, as were the ladies-in-waiting who would provide the closest companionship the homesick girl would have in a strange new land. Among these was Maria de Salinas, who became Catherine's dearest friend and remained with her for the rest of her life.

As soon as the ships on which the entourage sailed had left the shores of Spain, a storm hit them. One of the escort vessels sank, and the captain was forced to put into the nearest harbor. Catherine had been ill and terrified by the storm, she told her mother in a letter from Laredo, but now she was impatiently waiting for the journey to begin again. Finally, on October 2, she reached Plymouth.

There she was greeted as she would be by her adopted people for the next thirty-five years—with great rejoicing and great love. Huge bells tolled as her ship anchored, and a grand guard of honor awaited her.

The lavish festivities followed her as she traveled toward London to meet her new husband and his family. Neither Henry nor his subjects heeded Isabella's requests to moderate expenses, for the spare girl who had arrived in England was to ensure the continuance of the new dynasty Henry Tudor hoped to found. Henry had seen to it that his tenuous claim to the throne was bolstered by his wife's blood: Arthur was the grandson of Edward IV. Arthur's sons would be the grandchildren of Ferdinand and Isabella, the sovereigns of mighty Spain. As the girl who would be mother to those sons slowly made her way from Plymouth inland, the local nobility rushed to show their respect. Bonfires were lit everywhere; commoners and nobility alike outdid themselves to pay homage to the princess of Aragon. To a girl far from home, it was all enormously reassuring.

She was to meet her new father-in-law at Richmond Palace, his favorite residence, just outside London. But Henry, acting more like an impetuous bridegroom than an austere father-in-law, gathered together his disgruntled council and, in a chill November rain, galloped toward the palace of the bishop of Bath at Dogmersfield, near London, where Catherine and her company were resting. Informed by the Spanish ambassador that it would be improper for the king to meet the girl in this abrupt fashion, Henry was furious. This was England, he told the ambassador coldly, and as Catherine was to be queen of England, she had best get used to her new country's customs. When a further effort was made to preserve Spanish decorum by the announcement that the princess was indisposed and resting in her bedroom, Henry sternly replied that "the King of England will see the Princess, even if she is in her bed." Her shocked ladies went to relay the news to Catherine, who hastily prepared to meet the king.

Her sense of etiquette was apparently less rigid than that of the members of her retinue—or perhaps she was already adept at smoothing out awkward situations. She greeted Henry shyly but warmly, and when, in the middle of their conversation (conducted in Latin, since she as yet knew no English), her bridegroom also appeared at the door, Catherine embraced him joyfully. She summoned her minstrels and her fool, and an impromptu entertainment for her unexpected guests capped off the meeting. The next day they all headed for London.

The city had outdone itself. Gaily bedecked arches and platforms had sprung up everywhere along the way. Merchants and tradespeople crowded the streets to cheer Catherine. Each guild paid homage to her; pageants and pantomimes were performed. Church bells rang, and choirs stood on the steps of every church singing hymns of joy as she passed by. Great vats of ale stood in the streets, free for the public; as night approached bonfires blazed brightly to remind the weary girl that she was well loved by her new people.

She was also well loved by her new family. Queen Elizabeth's quiet nature was very different from that of the imperious warrior Isabella, but it could be that Catherine found the contrast relaxing. Margaret Beaufort's was probably a more familiar personality—kind and warm, no doubt, but with an unambiguous undercurrent of authority. There was Arthur's boisterous young brother Henry, at ten already given to dominating attention at any public event. And there were his sisters, twelve-year-old Margaret and little Mary.

Unlike their brothers, Margaret and Mary were seeing, in this transplanted princess, their own fates. No princess could reasonably hope to remain in her own country, no matter how much she might love it. A princess was barter, to be sold in marriage to whatever monarch or monarch's son her parents deemed offered the most advantageous alliance. Already Margaret was betrothed to the king of Scotland; soon she would leave her home forever, as Catherine had just done. She must have watched the girl carefully in those early days to see how homesick she was, how well she adjusted to her new country.

What Margaret saw was reassuring. If Catherine's feelings for Arthur were less romantic than their dutiful love letters, written to strangers under the careful supervision of their parents, suggested, she probably found him sympathetic enough. She had never expected to choose her own husband, and the boy she was to spend her life with had a gentle, placid nature. With time, they would doubtless come to love one another as they ruled England together. They would have the children that such a marriage existed for—and suffer together the deaths of some of those children. For even at fifteen, Catherine knew how precarious the lives of children were, and that few women could reasonably expect all their children to live. Isabella of Castile and Elizabeth of York had each lost five children in infancy or in stillbirth.

Whatever sorrows Catherine and Arthur would suffer, however, they would share, and if God willed it, the joys would outweigh the sorrows. Certainly there would be living children to compensate for the lost ones. Catherine would fulfill her role of ensuring the continuation of the Tudor dynasty by giving Arthur several strong sons. Her daughters, for their part, would follow their mother in helping to create political alliances, providing that Tudor blood would run in the veins of royalty all over the Continent.

Catherine could have felt only confidence as, on the morning of

November 14, she was escorted by young Prince Henry from the palace to Saint Paul's, where she was to be married. The wedding was full of the pomp and pageantry that had characterized every step of Catherine's journey through England. Henry VII wanted his people to see, and be impressed by, the joining of the houses of Tudor and Castile. A bridge six feet above the ground had been built from the door of the cathedral to a platform at the altar, over which the bridal party marched in splendor. The Londoners thronging outside cheered wildly, and if their enthusiasm stemmed in part from the simple pleasure of a break from their everyday lives, time would prove that their feelings for their future queen were genuine.

A prominent figure in the wedding festivities was the prince's brother Henry. Flushed with the honor of escorting the bride to the altar, he cheered the mock combatants in the tournament that followed the wedding. After the wedding dinner, young Henry danced wildly with his prim sister Margaret, getting so carried away that he flung off his gown of state and continued dancing in his thin silk shirt, giving his parents "a great and singular pleasure." The king and queen were less pleased that the bridegroom seemed exhausted by the day's events, and danced only once. It was an ominous sign: a prince required vitality if he was to produce heirs to the throne.

Finally, the festivities done, the bride and groom were taken to Baynard's Castle to spend their first night together—not, however, in privacy. First they were publicly bedded down, with Doña Elvira and the Duchess of Norfolk bringing in the bride after Arthur's gentlemen had couched him in the royal bed. Then a priest prayed over them, begging God for a happy and fertile marriage. At last the bed curtains were drawn, and the couple were left more or less alone.

It is hardly surprising, with the grueling festivities and the public nature of their bedding, that the inexperienced girl and the delicate boy failed to consummate their marriage that night. So Catherine would insist in the years ahead, and there is little reason to doubt her. The heady formalities that demonstrated to the world the potency of the new dynasty weren't necessarily conducive to the circumstances for creating heirs to that dynasty.

If Catherine and Arthur were not yet ready to consummate their marriage, they at least appeared, in the weeks following their wedding, to be developing the affection that would make the eventual consummation pleasing to them both. The members of the Spanish court wrote home with delight about the warmth between the two, and Arthur himself wrote his new mother-in-law that he loved Catherine and would be her "true and loving husband all his days."

Henry also wrote to Isabella and Ferdinand, assuring them that he would treat their daughter as "a second father, who will ever watch over her and never allow her to lack for anything he can procure for her." In those early weeks, when all seemed full of promise and it was easy to be a "second father," he was. For Catherine's new life seemed idyllic. There were balls, masques, and tournaments at court and at the homes of various nobles, all anxious to ingratiate themselves with the future king and queen. There was quieter time that she spent with Arthur and his brother and sisters, playing the lute and virginals, regaling them, perhaps, with stories about the court of Isabella and Ferdinand and about Isabella's crusades against the Moors. Probably too the royal children helped Catherine learn English, for it was vital to the girl that she be able to communicate in the language of the people she would reign over.

Soon, however, she was separated from her new family. Arthur was Prince of Wales, the title that belonged exclusively to the heir to the crown, and it was essential that the couple show themselves in the country that had such important symbolic meaning for their future. So on December 2, barely two months after she had landed in England, Catherine was once again traveling to a new land and meeting its people.

She was not the only one to feel ambivalence about the move. That Arthur's health was already fragile is clear from a letter the king sent to Ferdinand and Isabella, justifying the move to Wales. Explaining that the move was "the ancient custom of our realm," he admitted that "the opinions of many were adverse to this course by reason of the tender age of our son." Arthur was fifteen—not a particularly tender age by the standards of the time, either for marriage or for a long journey. Henry himself had been born when his mother was fifteen; Catherine at fifteen had just made a far more difficult journey from Spain to England. The prince's health was delicate enough to merit concern, tactfully masked as solicitude about his age.

The "adverse opinions" of the anonymous dissenters to the move soon proved justified. The weather on the trip was raw and bitter, and it was scarcely better when the entourage reached Ludlow Castle in Wales. Soon Catherine, Arthur, and most of their retinue were ill with the sweating sickness. This bizarre illness was also called "the English disease" because, of all the Europeans it had affected, only the English failed to build an immunity to it. It had first appeared early in Henry VII's reign,

and since then had made several appearances. The others survived this outbreak, but the fragile prince, the hope of England, died on April 2, 1502.
Barely a bride, Catherine of Aragon was now a widow—grieving, confused, and utterly reliant on the kindness of her "second father" until such
time as he sent her home to her own parents, to become once again a
pawn in some other political alliance.

But brides bring dowries, and Henry VII had no intention of losing
any part of the dowry he had haggled so persistently to obtain. On their
side, the rulers of Spain weren't anxious to lose an alliance that would be
valuable in their constant ups and downs with the Holy Roman emperor
Maximilian I and the French king Louis XII. There was an obvious solution. Catherine had been sent to marry the English heir apparent; she
could still do so. Young Henry was next in line for the throne, and as yet
had not been contracted to any future marriage. There was even an
extra—though hardly essential—advantage, in that the children already
knew and liked each other. A slight problem existed, to be sure: marriage
between brother and sister-in-law was prohibited by canon law. But papal
dispensations were easily obtainable for almost any forbidden alliance,
especially if the donations made to the church in gratitude for its leniency were large enough. Indeed, the pope had recently granted just such a
dispensation at the request of Ferdinand and Isabella: their daughter Isabella had died and her husband had married their younger daughter Maria.
There was little reason to doubt that if Henry and the Spanish sovereigns
reached a satisfactory agreement, the pope would find some rationale for
a dispensation.

Neither the prospective bride nor groom was consulted in the negotiations, and at first Catherine appears simply to have assumed that she
would remain in England until the details of her voyage home were
worked out. She was given an establishment at Durham House in London, where her Spanish retinue followed and her English attendants faded
back into the Tudor woodwork. Her days passed pleasantly enough, spent
sometimes in visiting with Henry, Margaret, and little Mary, sometimes in
praying in her private chapel at Durham House or in weaving altar cloths
with her ladies as they all comfortably awaited their return to Spain.

While the larger world that shaped the young widow's destiny was
ruled by Henry and her parents, the small world of her palace was rigid-
ly regulated by Doña Elvira. A long, complicated power struggle began
between Catherine's duenna and the Spanish ambassador, Roderigo de
Puebla. Both wanted to control the princess; neither wanted to consult her
about any of the issues over which they fought. Without her knowledge,

her life was dominated by the machinations of Doña Elvira and de Puebla on the one hand and those of Henry and Ferdinand on the other. As she slowly came to realize the extent to which her views were ignored in all the decisions being made about her life, she grew angry and determined that she would herself direct her own destiny. It was in these early days of confused widowhood that her deceptively quiet, unshakable strength was born.

Then, before the court had finished grieving for Arthur, there was another loss. In February 1503, Queen Elizabeth, the kindly, pallid White Rose of York, died in childbirth at the age of thirty-seven. (Her infant died soon after.)

Henry Tudor, now forty-six, briefly considered marrying his daughter-in-law himself. He was fond of the girl; any children they would have could only further his dynastic schemes; and another bride could easily enough be found for young Henry, which would cement another, perhaps even more useful, alliance.

The king and queen of Spain firmly squelched Henry's proposal, however. Isabella wrote de Puebla that it "would be an evil thing . . . the mere mention of which offends our ears." Henry seems to have dropped the idea with little hesitation. Perhaps he was too grieved by the loss of Elizabeth to wholeheartedly pursue another marriage; or it could be that he had not been serious about the idea in the first place and broached the suggestion only as a means of intimidating Ferdinand and Isabella into agreeing to the best possible terms in negotiating the dowry for his second son's marriage.

It is unclear when Catherine and young Henry were told of the marriage plans. If either had any reservations at the time, history hasn't recorded them. On June 23, 1503, the nuptial treaty was arranged, pending the issuance of a papal dispensation as well as further dowry payments from Spain.

A week later, Catherine lost one of her young companions. Princess Margaret left for Scotland to marry James IV. As always, the feelings of the child played no part in deciding her fate. That a fourteen-year-old girl who had just lost her mother and brother might wish for a little time to grieve with her remaining family occurred to no one—except possibly herself. On the journey, with its inevitable pomp and ceremony along the way, Margaret conducted herself with the dignity of the queen she would soon become, but when she arrived in Scotland, the regal lady gave way to the homesick child. Her letters to her father, dictated to a secretary, are filled with a pathetic petulance. She disliked her husband's beard; she disliked his friends. Her servants were not being treated well. A postscript at the end of one letter, however, scrawled in her own hand, explained all the rest. "For God's sake, Sir, hold me excused that I write not myself to Your Grace, for I have no leisure. . . . I wish I were with your grace, and many times more."

If Catherine knew of her sister-in-law's misery, she could only have commiserated. She herself, awaiting the day of her formal betrothal to young Henry, felt a similar hopeless longing for her homeland. She was frequently ill as a result of the strain.

It soon became apparent to Catherine that, in settling her future, neither her parents nor her father-in-law wanted to spend much money. When Maria de Salinas was approached with a marriage proposal from the grandson of the Earl of Derby, Catherine wrote her parents to remind them that they had promised dowries for her Spanish ladies. They refused to send the money. Catherine was appalled. Once a lady-in-waiting to Isabella herself, Maria had been a good and loyal servant. Catherine pointedly remarked to her father that, since she had forfeited her dower money from her marriage to Arthur, she had no money herself to provide her friend's dowry. Maria's suitor faded away. Perhaps it was as well: Catherine needed Maria with her. There was a deep bond between the women; Catherine, complained the Spanish ambassador, loved Maria "above any other mortal."

Maria was thus still a member of Catherine's household and able to comfort her mistress when in November 1504, less than two years after Arthur's death, Isabella died in Spain. Once more, personal grief was overshadowed by the political implications of a royal death. The Spanish succession was now in question, since Isabella, as ruler of Castile, had been more powerful than Ferdinand of Aragon. The Castilians wanted Princess Juana and her husband, Philip of Burgundy, son of the Holy Roman Emperor Maximilian, to rule Castile. Ferdinand, however, was not about to give up his power, especially to a son-in-law he loathed.

For Henry VII, Isabella's death meant reassessing the value of his son's precontract to the daughter of a king who might soon be ousted. He suddenly felt conscience-stricken—the Tudors had a genius for retroactive attacks of conscience—at having forced his minor son to agree to a betrothal he was too young to understand. Young Henry once more obliged his father, and on June 27, 1505, the day before his 14th birthday, he appeared before the king's council and protested his betrothal to Catherine, asking that, since he had been a minor when he agreed to it, it now be declared null and void.

The remainder of Catherine's marriage portion from her wedding to Arthur had never been sent from Spain. When Henry VII demanded that it be sent and Ferdinand refused, Henry cut off her household allowance. It had been none too generous to begin with, and Catherine already owed her servants back wages. She was also in debt to various tradespeople. Neither monarch would give her money; neither would take responsibility for getting her back to Spain. She constantly wrote letters home, entrusting them to Roderigo de Puebla, in which she reminded her father of her virtually penniless condition. He did not respond. Some of the letters appear never to have reached Ferdinand, for de Puebla withheld some of them and instead reported to Ferdinand that Catherine and her ladies were constantly complaining. Dire distress was dismissed as feminine whining; the princess's uncertain status would continue as long as it suited both monarchs.

The turmoil surrounding her yielded one brief episode of pleasure for Catherine. Henry VII, trying to decide which Spanish faction to support, invited Juana and Philip to visit England. They hesitated, but nature made their decision for them. Sailing in January 1506 from the Low Countries to Spain, they hit a deadly gale, which blew their ship to the Dorset coast. Henry was delighted with the arrival of his unexpected guests, and had them escorted solemnly to Windsor.

For the king of England and the would-be king of Spain it was a politically useful meeting, with a number of possible marriages proposed as bargaining counters, but for Catherine and Juana it was a poignant family reunion. Poignant—but hardly painless. All Europe knew how Juana suffered from Philip's open, callous philandering. Catherine's sister was a deeply unhappy woman who was desperately in love with her husband (known as Philip the Handsome), and who responded to his neglect with moody withdrawal alternating with hysterical outbursts. The princesses' own father had been notoriously unfaithful to Isabella, but the queen had handled his liaisons with finesse, generously finding excellent matches for her husband's mistresses with noblemen far from court. And in turn, if Ferdinand failed to reciprocate his wife's love, he always respected her as his political partner. In the world of sixteenth-century royalty, one didn't expect fidelity from one's husband—only discretion.

Juana had apparently expected both and gotten neither, but her husband's cruelty did nothing to dampen her passion for him. In their brief meeting, Catherine saw in her sister a woman being destroyed by her own emotions. Perhaps she vowed to herself then that, no matter how deeply she might love a man, her love would never overshadow her reason or her pride. If so, her resolution could only have intensified in the months that followed as court gossip brought her further news of her sister's suffering. Philip died of a sudden fever on the journey to Castile and Juana, wild with grief, refused to allow his body to be buried, instead carting the coffin halfway across Spain to the church at Tordesillas. There her father, believing (or choosing to believe) that she was mad, kept her forcibly restrained at a nearby castle for the remainder of his life.

Grief for her mother's death and her sister's misery compounded Catherine's frustration with her ambiguous position at the English court. Abandoned by the young man who had been her betrothed, she was isolated and virtually alone. She did have a few friends, however. Maria de Salinas, of course, was with her, and the friendship of the two women was only strengthened by the ordeal they suffered together and by Maria's unquestioning, uncomplaining loyalty to the mistress she loved as much as she would ever love any husband. There was also an English friend, a powerful nobleman who saw Catherine's plight and visited her often, bringing gifts of fruit and venison from his estates. Edward Stafford, the Duke of Buckingham, was her most important supporter in those early days when she was nearly friendless in Henry VII's court.

But Buckingham's occasional gifts, appreciated as they were, hardly provided enough to feed a large household. Catherine was eventually forced to take the desperate measure of pawning the jewels and the gorgeous Spanish plate that had been part of her dowry. Tableware, after all, was useless without food to put on it.

Nor was there any peace within the household. Doña Elvira's attempts to dominate the now eighteen-year-old Catherine were becoming increasingly annoying. The old duenna was forever making decisions behind Catherine's back, plotting with her brother Don Juan Manuel, a Castilian at the court of Philip of Burgundy who supported the duke's claim to the throne. Things came to a head with the visit of Philip and Juana, and Catherine, fed up with Doña Elvira's duplicity, furiously dismissed her. From now on Catherine of Aragon would control, if not her own fate, at least her own household.

In Spain, Ferdinand had come up with a clever means of restoring his daughter's dignity with a minimum of expense, until such time as the issue of the dispensation was resolved: he appointed Catherine ambassadress to the court of Henry VII, sending a packet of credentials and two thousand crowns—money his daughter badly needed.

It was not enough, as she quickly informed her father; in fact, it allowed her to pay only some of her debts and to redeem the pawned plate.

With Maria de Salinas's abortive plan to marry still smarting, Catherine reminded her father of the sacrifices her loyal servants had made for her, and for Spain. "If it is true that your Highness considers services which I receive as services rendered to yourself, I think there are no persons to whom your Highness is more indebted than to my servants," she wrote sharply.

But the title of ambassadress at least clarified Catherine's position at the English court. Henry could avoid his dead son's widow and his living son's former betrothed, but he could not avoid the representative of the court of Spain. Reluctantly he agreed to meet with her. The audience, however, did her no good. He refused to recognize her betrothal to his son, or to provide her with more money for herself or her household. She again wrote her father, pleading with him for help. Her servants, she said, were ready to go begging for alms. She herself had had to sell a bracelet in order to buy a dress, "for I was all but naked." Indeed, since leaving Spain she had had only two new dresses, and the gowns she had brought with her were now worn out. "I supplicate your Highness to . . . remedy this, for certainly I shall not be able to live in this manner." Ferdinand responded with pious platitudes about conducting herself with the dignity becoming her station, and even reproved her for selling her plate—to which Catherine tartly responded that he knew very well that the remedy for her impoverishment was up to him.

How long this state of affairs would have gone on had the English king's health remained sound is impossible to conjecture. Fortunately for Catherine, on April 22, 1509, Henry VII, worn out with grief for his wife and son, and with the years of rebuilding and holding his country together, died. His son, now nearly eighteen, had, as it turned out, a mind of his own. He announced that his father had expressed a dying wish that he marry Catherine after all, and he intended to honor that wish.

Whether the old king had really voiced such a surprising command to his son, or whether the younger Henry was simply attributing his own wishes to a man no longer alive to refute his story, no one knew. But no argument was possible. The dispensation for the marriage had long since been granted by the pope, the English people adored the Spanish princess, and the new king was firm in his resolve to marry Catherine. On June 11, two weeks before his coronation, Henry took the delighted Catherine to the small chapel of the Observant Franciscans near Greenwich Place, and there they were secretly married.

For Catherine, it was a moment of pure joy. For years, marrying Henry had seemed the only way out of her plight. She had seen little of him in recent years—his father had made certain of that—but she had known him as a child, and the brief glimpses she had of him at court functions only intensified her sense of him as a distant, mysterious prince who could rescue her from her misery. Now he had done so.

Seven years after becoming the widow of the prince of Wales, Catherine of Aragon was queen of England after all. It had been a hard struggle, but it seemed her problems were now behind her.

Chapter 2

MARRIED LIFE

HENRY VIII

This drawing, from a contemporary stained-glass depiction of the youthful king, shows that before his girth and his ego grew to monstrous proportions Henry was considered the most attractive prince in Europe.

he Henry that Catherine of Aragon married on that mellow day in June 1509 was charming, handsome, and full of youthful vigor. He had wanted to marry Catherine, and had done so promptly. Catherine could not have guessed what his single-minded pursuit of his own goals might one day lead to.

If their wedding was quiet and simple, their coronation made up for it. Catherine emerged from the Tower of London in a gown of white satin and gold, the white signifying her virginity. Her thick auburn hair, held by a jeweled coronet, streamed down her back. Her ladies also wore white. She rode in a litter covered with white and gold tissue and drawn by two white palfreys. In dramatic contrast Henry, riding beside her, wore crimson velvet and cloth of gold. He too was much bejeweled. The people in the streets cheered, as they had cheered the Spanish princess when she first arrived in England.

She was twenty-four now, and by all accounts beautiful. Thomas More wrote later that "there were few women who could compete with the queen in her prime." In these early years, Catherine and Henry shared more than physical attractiveness and attraction, though these were an advantage to a king and queen who hoped to produce not only an heir to the throne but numerous other offspring to help them seal political alliances.

Religious devotion was an equally important bond. They heard as many as three masses a day, and spent hours praying together. Henry dreamed of leading a crusade, and he must have been mightily impressed by Catherine's tales of Isabella's successful campaign against the Moors in her own country. At the outset of their marriage the styles of the couple's religious expression were complementary. Catherine's less splashy piety showed womanly modesty, pleasingly highlighting her husband's robust exhibitionism. The young queen's religious faith was deep and internal: she loved her God with a personal passion, and the externals of religion served merely to symbolize that love. She needed neither grand ceremonies nor favors from God, though she was willing to indulge in the former, and always grateful for the latter.

Henry's religion was equally intense, but more external. Fancying himself a theologian, he studied the works of the church fathers. When Martin Luther published his virulently anti-papal *Babylonian Captivity of the Church* in 1520, Henry countered with *The Defense of the Seven Sacraments,* which earned for him the title Defender of the Faith from the grateful Pope Leo X. Henry memorized large chunks of the Bible and other church writings. In the book of Leviticus he must have found the prohibition against marrying one's brother's wife, but at this stage, while Catherine was still young and attractive, and fertile, he apparently conveniently ignored this passage. He loved ritual, the lavish display with which he could show his worship of God, with himself in the foreground. On the whole, however, the differences in the forms of Catherine's and Henry's spiritual lives were barely discernible, though they would become deeply significant as the years passed.

The couple also shared a love of knowledge. Besides theology, Henry studied philosophy, medicine, and science, and he regretted that time forbade his studying more. Without learned men, he told his friend Lord Mountjoy, "we should scarcely exist at all." The Renaissance that had begun in Italy was slowly spreading its way north, and the New Learning was affecting many in England. The king himself corresponded with Erasmus and befriended Thomas More. But again, especially in the early days, Henry's commitment to scholarship was as much to the old learning as the new; his was the conventional approach of the medieval scholastic, glamorized by its atypical association with royalty.

Catherine shared her husband's fascination with learning; she too mingled New Learning with old scholasticism, and she delighted in the king's friendship with men like More. Later she would bring to England her countryman, the humanist Juan Luis Vives, who would help direct the education of the princess Mary and her young friends—two of whom would become leading figures in the political and religious movement that would appall the pious queen.

In the beginning of their marriage, Catherine seemed to share Henry's love of elaborate play. The dancing at court, the jousts, and a continual round of banquets always centered on the king and his new bride. In keeping with the sensibility of the age, these amusements involved much intricate play-acting. One evening a band dressed as Robin Hood and his merry men suddenly appeared in her chambers demanding alms for the poor. "The queen and her ladies were greatly amazed," wrote one witness, "as well for the strange sight as for the sudden appearance." Discovering that the bandit of Sherwood Forest was her own husband, Catherine provided both the alms and further entertainment for her ladies and her husband's retinue. Such "disguisings" took place frequently and in various contexts. Catherine and her attendants always showed suitable surprise or confusion, as the particular disguise demanded, and wonderment when the players turned out to be Henry and his courtiers. Their surprise was certainly as ritualized as the men's disguises. Though a number of writers assume that Henry was taken in by the exclamations of amazement, surely even he was never *that* dense. It was perhaps inevitable that Catherine, six years older and more sober by nature, would weary of such games long before Henry did, but in the early years of their marriage she was a cheerful companion for an exuberant overgrown boy.

She did not love power the way Henry did, but she did show political astuteness that rivaled his, especially in the first years of his reign, when most of the work of administering his realm consisted of allowing policy to be formulated and implemented for him while he hunted, feasted, and planned romantic if anachronistic crusades. Ferdinand kept her in her capacity of ambassadress, a role in which neither Henry nor Catherine seemed to find what a later age would call conflict of interest. Despite Ferdinand's neglect during the years just past, she still had absolute faith in his political judgment. At the beginning, trusting that her father was always right, she was more effective in representing Spain than serving as queen of England, since she thoroughly identified her new country's good with that of her old country. Early in her marriage she wrote to Ferdinand that "in this life I have no other good than in being your daughter. . . . As to the King my lord, among the reasons which oblige me to love him much more than myself, the one most strong, although he is my husband, is his being the true son of your Highness, with desire of greater obedience and love to serve you than ever son had to father." Ingenuously, Catherine took for granted that Henry would always want to follow in Ferdinand's footsteps, but it was inevitable that a time would come when the charming boy would have policies of his own that would clash with those of his Spanish "father"—and when it did, Catherine's roles of wife and diplomatic envoy would also clash.

Her rival in political influence was Henry's royal almoner, a priest from Ipswich named Thomas Wolsey. Wolsey, the son of a butcher, had great intellect and greater ambition. Though he rose to a bishopric and dreamed of becoming pope, there was little piety in Wolsey's makeup; like many clerics, he viewed the religious life solely as a stepping-stone to power. It had served him well. In 1505 he had become Henry VII's chaplain, and he was now a fixture in the new king's court. The grinding details of daily administration were daunting to the exuberant young monarch, but they posed no problem to the power-climbing prelate. He gladly took on the tedious job of running Henry's country for him, while obsequiously pandering to Henry's vision of himself as a brilliant statesman. It was perhaps not a bad division of power. After years of Henry VII's drab court, England needed the glamour Henry VIII brought with his tournaments, masques, and endless hunting parties as much as it needed the political skills of Wolsey. Wolsey's titles eventually caught up with his power: in 1514 he became Archbishop of York and 1515 Chancellor of England.

In the middle of 1509, Catherine became pregnant. Henry moved the court to Richmond for the Christmas holidays, celebrating the birth of the savior and awaiting joyfully the birth of his own son. On January 31, the child was born. It was a daughter, and it was stillborn.

Henry and Catherine grieved at this first tragedy in their married life. But they knew other children would follow. What was crucial was for Catherine to get well after her physical and emotional ordeal. Catherine's grief was compounded by a sense of failure. That she was acutely aware of bearing children as a political task is evident in the poignant letter she wrote her father, in which she said that the stillbirth was "considered in this country a great calamity." Anticipating Ferdinand's anger, she begged, "Pray, your Highness, do not storm against me! It is not my fault; it is the will of God!"

Fortunately, she had other duties besides that of providing heirs, and Henry emphasized these, enlisting her aid with a feast planned at Shrovetide for the ambassadors of all foreign nations. Tactfully, he included both of her functions in his plans: she would attend both as queen and as Spanish ambassadress. Later that year Ferdinand sent a special envoy, Don Luis Caroz, to work with her. Catherine was cordial, but paid him little heed. She was performing her role to her own satisfaction.

New Year's Day 1511 brought the birth of a living child—a son this time—and the country went wild with rejoicing. Bonfires lit the streets of every town in the country. Henry promptly paid a pilgrimage of gratitude to the shrine of Our Lady of the Grey Friars, known as the Shrine of Kings because so many of his royal predecessors had made pilgrimages there. Again there were tourneys and feasts and the masques of which Henry was so fond. Then, in the middle of the festivities, the tiny prince suddenly became ill. On February 22, less than two months after his birth, he died.

Henry, according to one contemporary, "made no great mourning outwardly; but the queen, like a natural woman, made much lamentation."

As she found herself failing in one of her jobs, she began also to have trouble in the other. Perceptive though she was, she was too well trained in filial obedience to question her father's wisdom on political matters. Ferdinand was more than willing to manipulate his daughter's trust in him for his own ends. He enlisted Henry's help in a war against France: when they had crushed the French king, Henry would get as his part of the spoils the former English possession of Guienne. The campaign was a disaster, and it was soon clear that Ferdinand was merely exploiting the English in his rivalry with France. As Henry's ambassador to Spain noted bitterly, he was a man who "attaineth many things to other men's pains." Ferdinand's ambassadress urged her husband to continue the campaign, and Henry followed her advice. Then in April 1513, Ferdinand quietly and unilaterally signed a treaty with France.

Henry took his anger out on Caroz rather than on Catherine, and was somewhat soothed by Ferdinand's promise that he would get Guienne for Henry in the next year, in spite of the new treaty. Henry this time had the sense not to wait for the Spanish king and made his own plans to invade France. In this he was happily supported by Catherine, who had been raised to see the French as devils second only to the Moors. Indeed, since Louis XII had quarreled with Pope Julius II and now with his successor, Leo X, Catherine and Henry were able to persuade themselves, with Ferdinand's help, that this invasion was really a holy war. With great pomp, Henry went off to Calais with his navy, leaving Catherine regent in England—entrusting her with more power than a female regent had ever before been given in England.

Matrimonial politics had given Catherine and Henry a strange enemy in this war. King James IV of Scotland, husband of Henry's sister Margaret, was France's ally. As Ferdinand played on Henry's gullibility, Louis played on James's. He was ably assisted by his shrewd wife, Anne of Brittany. Homely, aging, and vulnerable only to her own ailing body, Anne wrote to James as a damsel in distress, sending him a glove and a ring and begging him to rescue her from the combined villainy of Ferdinand, Henry, and the Emperor Maximilian. (She was canny enough to enclose fourteen thousand crowns in her next letter. Though rings and gloves established the right mood for the chivalric drama, its actors needed to be paid.)

James's commitment to France greatly displeased his own queen, who loathed and distrusted this ally. Margaret's marriage had never been romantic, but it was a good partnership. The fey Scottish king owed much to his

practical-minded wife, who had given him, in addition to political guidance, two sons. But Margaret remained an Englishwoman to the core. She
paid lip service to her new country's sovereignty, but she never really
believed it, preferring to see Scotland as England's vassal. Just as Catherine
was her father's representative in Henry's court, Margaret saw herself as
Henry's representative in James's court. After Anne of Brittany's plea for
rescue, Margaret set up a counterdrama, weeping and accusing James of
being unfaithful to her and in love with Anne—though she had for years
comfortably tolerated his numerous actual mistresses.

For all Margaret's efforts to undermine James's alliance with France,
the Scottish king persisted. When Henry invaded France, James invaded
England. With the able assistance of the aging Thomas Howard, Earl of
Surrey, Catherine, as regent, conducted the war against her brother-in-law.

Margaret too was now regent of Scotland. But she was incapable of
seeing Catherine as her enemy. She begged James to take her with him on
his campaign if he would not abandon it, for she believed the two queens
could between them effect a peace. "If we shall meet," she wrote him,
"who knows what God, by our means, might bring to pass?"

Sadly, neither God nor the queens were given a chance to find out.
James threw himself into the thick of battle. On September 9, on Flodden
Field, he died—along with nine thousand Scottish and fifteen hundred
English soldiers. The credit for this most impressive victory in England's
sorry war with France belonged not to Henry but to his wife, the regent
Catherine of Aragon.

Hers was no nominal regency. She took charge with great gusto.
When Surrey sent her the news of James's death, she relayed it to Henry
with gleeful pride. "You shall see the great victory that the Lord hath sent
your subjects in your absence." With somewhat less tact, she continued:
"To my thinking, this battle hath been more than should you win all the
crown of France." Sending him a piece of the dead king's coat, she added,
rather morbidly, that she would have preferred to send James's body
instead, "but our Englishmen would not suffer it." Catherine followed her
military victory with a diplomatic move that was perhaps motivated as
much by compassion as by diplomacy: she sent a message to Margaret
assuring her that Henry would support her as regent for the new king, her
eighteen-month-old son James. Margaret wrote back thanking Catherine
for her sympathy.

Catherine, pregnant throughout the war, now gave birth—to a stillborn son. She must have wondered, bitterly, if the new king of Scots
would one day be king of England because she, unlike Margaret, seemed

unable to produce a living heir. She and Henry had now been married four years—not time enough to despair, but certainly time enough to worry. When would she provide the son the king so needed?

❧ Catherine's Scottish victory did much to enhance her husband's international reputation. The Venetian ambassador wrote home that, in light of Flodden Field, "hitherto, small mention has been made of King Henry, whereas for the future the whole world will talk of him." Henry's own victories in France were far less impressive, for Louis, embroiled in battles in Italy, had his troops fight only tepidly against the English. The English captured Tournai and Thérouanne, small, insignificant cities on the outskirts of Hapsburg territories in the Low Countries.

As the English rejoiced over their victories in Scotland and France, Henry's allies, Ferdinand and Maximilian, quietly made a separate treaty with France. Maximilian's daughter, the astute Archduchess Margaret of Austria, who ruled the Netherlands as the emperor's regent, denounced this move in a letter to her father: "Monseigneur, unless you give [Henry] cause to the contrary, he will help you both with his person and his money without deceit . . . the promises made should not be broken." Ferdinand's daughter, by contrast, continued to act as her father's uncritical representative.

Henry did not long remain in ignorance. His young sister Mary had been betrothed to Charles, grandson of both Maximilian and Ferdinand. The marriage was to take place in May 1514. Now, suddenly, there were inexplicable delays—delays that must have seemed ominously familiar to the English queen, who had waited years for the confirmation of her own betrothal to Henry. Henry guessed that there were diplomatic reasons for the delay, and it didn't take much ferreting to find out he'd been badly used. As the details of the secret agreement among Spain, the Holy Roman Empire, and France became clear, Henry was furious.

In his rage, the king made a significant comment to the Venetian ambassador, Sebastian Giustinian. "I do not see any faith in this world save in me," he said bitterly, "and therefore God Almighty, who knows this, prospers my affairs." He had every reason to be angry, but the jump in logic from the treachery of his allies to his own purity was a large one, and the consequent alliance between himself and God even larger.

Henry's first move against the monarchs who had betrayed him was to cancel the betrothal of Mary and Charles. Mary agreed with alacrity. But though Henry assumed she was simply displaying feminine modesty and obedience, he learned otherwise when he negotiated a new marriage for her.

Her former intended had been a boy four years her junior. Her new one was thirty-four years older, "a feeble and pocky man," as one enemy described him. But he had one all-important attraction for Henry—he was king of France. Henry realized he had to make his own truce with Louis XII if England was not to be swallowed by the three continental powers now so ominously united. Anne of Brittany had died, leaving the aging king with no son. A new young wife, healthy and strong, could make up for that lack.

Mary Tudor was healthy and strong, and more: she was reputed to be one of the most beautiful women in Europe. Even taking into account the flattery routinely given to women in the royal family, the descriptions are impressive, and they come from varied sources. Margaret of Austria's ambassador wrote that Mary "was one of the most beautiful girls that one would wish to see; it does not seem to me that I have ever seen one so beautiful." According to the Venetian ambassador to France, she was a "paradise." Meeting her while she was still betrothed to Charles, Erasmus rhapsodized, "O thrice and four times happy our illustrious prince who is to have such a bride! Nature never made anyone more beautiful; and she excels in goodness and wisdom."

As changes in the plans for her future were being made, no one bothered to ask Mary how she felt. Why would they? It was a question rarely asked of women. But though Mary's motto was "*La volenté de Dieu me suffit*"—"The will of God is sufficient for me"—she was about to prove that she had a will of her own.

Mary had strong feelings about her future. She had fallen in love with her brother's bluff, handsome friend, Charles Brandon, the Duke of Suffolk, and wanted to marry him. Such a match should have seemed out of the question for her: Brandon was a nobleman only because of his father's services to Henry VII at Bosworth Field and the affection young Henry retained for him. He had no royal blood in his veins, and no pretensions beyond being a good soldier and a good companion to the king.

But the king's sister worshiped him. And when the plans for her marriage to Charles crumbled, she began to hope that she might now be free to marry the man she was in love with. Brandon, she knew, was attracted to her, and at the moment he too was free—having managed to get two marriages annulled and a precontract broken. (Mary was not the only woman to have been overwhelmed by Charles Brandon's charms.)

Then came the staggering news that Mary was to marry abroad after all—not the young Charles but the aging Louis. She had reason, in the abstract, to have a positive regard for her first fiancé, who was the nephew of her beloved sister-in-law Catherine. If she did not feel romantic passion for him, at least she could console herself with the thought that she would have an appealing husband, one she could admire and respect. But Louis had always seemed a monster to her—the fiendish king of an evil land across the sea. Now she was to leave her beloved England, and her beloved Charles Brandon, to become the bride of this decrepit villain.

Mary did the unthinkable: she refused to marry the French king. She wept and sulked and carried on until it became clear that her astonished brother would not give in to the bizarre demand that she be allowed to choose her own husband. When Mary realized her cause was hopeless, she hit on an ingenious device. Suddenly reverting to the submissiveness Henry had always known, she bowed to his will—with a condition. Louis was old and in poor health, she reminded Henry, and she would probably outlive him. She would be a docile wife and work for England's good while Louis lived—if Henry promised that, after Louis's death, Mary could choose her own husband.

Henry must have been furious with his sister, but he agreed. A promise cost him nothing—hadn't he just learned that monarchs don't have to keep their promises? Probably he thought he was clever to convince Mary that she would get her way after her husband died. But Mary Tudor, as Charles's betrothed, had also experienced the betrayal of Ferdinand and Maximilian. She too was learning to be devious.

She was married first by proxy in an elaborate and, to the twentieth-century eye, comical ritual. After she exchanged vows with the Duc de Longueville, substituting for the French king, the marriage was symbolically consummated. Mary changed into a ceremonial nightgown, and Catherine and her ladies led her to a large bed, in which she lay awaiting her "bridegroom." Longueville arrived with equal ceremony, removed his boot, lay in bed beside her, and, with his naked foot, touched her bare leg. Their passions thus quenched, they went back to their respective quarters, again donned their clothes, and rejoined the company for dinner and dancing. The fake wedding night had been pleasant enough, but the princess must have shuddered to imagine what the real one would be like.

A month later she left for Paris. Once again, Catherine relived her own departure from Spain. Did she feel any regrets for the years of sadness and frustration that had followed? Or had it all been worth it, since she was now married to her handsome, loving Henry?

Arriving in Paris, Mary met her husband and learned that he lived up to his reputation: red-faced, bloated, fat, and hunchbacked, looking older than his 52 years. But she made the best of it, appearing gracious and even merry. When Louis sent most of her entourage back to England—permitting only a few inconsequential maids of honor such as the sisters Mary and Ann Boleyn to remain—Mary wrote a furious letter home, but she did not show her anger to her husband. She was pleasant to him and to his noblemen, and she even took the opportunity to ask the Duke of Albany, who was on his way to Scotland to serve as regent, to offer protection to her sister, the Queen Dowager Margaret. (Though a Frenchman, Albany was the nephew of King James's father, James III.)

The newlyweds were expected to celebrate their marriage, and celebrate they did—every day and night. After her coronation, Mary and Louis entered Paris in state, accompanied by six hours' worth of pageants involving gods and goddesses, cardboard castles, and all the usual accouterments. Mary glowed, but her husband was too worn out from the celebrations to attend the banquet afterward. Nevertheless, for weeks he acted like a young man, dancing and hunting, going to bed late and rising early. The Venetian envoy cynically dubbed him a sick old man whose infatuation for his wife would soon kill him.

It did. On New Year's Day 1515, three months after his marriage, Louis of France died. It would be an exaggeration to say that as kindly a woman as Mary deliberately hastened her husband's death, but she certainly did nothing to discourage the wild burst of activity that killed him, and she could not have been sad at his loss. The anticipation of his death had made her marriage bearable, and now she would have time to plot her course.

French custom gave her the breathing space she needed to make her plans. For six weeks, the queen dowager retired to the Palais de Cluny, where she was allowed access to no man except the new king, Francis I, and her confessor. There was a practical as well as a ceremonial reason for this—if the queen happened to be pregnant, it was crucial to be certain that her child's father was the dead king.

In her forced isolation, Mary worked out her course of action. She knew that Charles Brandon, as Henry's favorite, would be among the courtiers sent to bring her back to England at the end of the six weeks. She also knew her brother's promise was not to be trusted. She had heard rumors of Henry's plan to marry her to another Spanish prince.

Mary needed an ally, and she knew where to find him. Francis of Valois, the new king, was like her brother—vain, ambitious, charming. But unlike Henry, he had acquired a reputation as a womanizer; among others, he had had an affair with one of Mary's own ladies, Mary Boleyn. It was, for Mary Tudor's purposes, a useful reputation. She wrote anxious letters to Henry, saying that Francis was making advances toward her.

Perhaps Mary was simply telling the truth, but it seems unlikely. Francis *was* a womanizer, and he was probably attracted to the beautiful widow. But he wasn't stupid, and he very much wanted to remain king. He could ill afford to risk siring a bastard who, as Louis's son, would be king of France. Frances might flirt with the lovely lady, but he would never go beyond that, and Mary knew it.

However, fear of being dishonored by the lecherous Francis might provide Mary an excuse for a hasty marriage—an excuse her brother would have to sympathize with. And she was most certainly planning a hasty marriage. The dowager queen and the new king had many conversations in the privacy of Cluny, and she told him about Charles Brandon. She wanted to marry Charles, she told Francis, but she needed his help.

When Charles arrived in Paris, he didn't stand a chance. Francis came to him and demanded that he admit his feelings for Mary. Charles equivocated at first, but finally confessed he wanted to marry her. With a great display of brotherly affection, Francis insisted on helping the star-crossed lovers, offering to write to Henry and plead their cause. He suggested that the sooner they were married, the better.

Francis had played his part; now it was up to Mary. Since the six-week period of seclusion had ended, Brandon was granted—or perhaps thrust into—a private audience with the queen. Greeting him warmly, she wasted no time in making her demands known. Henry, she said, planned to break his promise to her and force her into a Spanish marriage. But she would *not* marry a Spanish prince. She would marry only a man of her choosing. And that man, she told Brandon firmly, was himself. If he preferred not to marry her, that was his prerogative. She would enter a convent, no longer letting herself be used as a political counter by her brother.

When Charles argued with her, she burst into floods of tears. "She weeped," he wrote piteously to Henry. "I never saw a woman so weep." What could he do, this handsome, brave, but not overly bright courtier, caught in the machinations of the cunning beauty and the wily French king? Miserably certain his own king would never forgive him, he capitulated.

Why did Francis help Mary in her determined, unorthodox wooing of her beloved Charles? Partly, one imagines, because it would be embarrassing to Francis—to France—if the dowager queen became a Spanish princess. There may have been a less political motive as well. Francis had been preparing himself for the throne of France for years, and he had listened enviously to reports of the dazzling king of England. What better way to start his reign than by helping the English king's sister humiliate her brother? Henry would be outwitted by a mere girl, and the world would laugh at him.

There was probably a third motive—and a third conspirator. Francis may well have been directed by his politically shrewd, ambitious mother, Louise of Savoy. She had lived only to put her son on the throne, scheming for him as successfully as Margaret Beaufort had schemed for Henry Tudor, and was undistracted by the charms of voluptuous ladies or the pretty trappings of royalty. Louise was perhaps more keenly aware than her son of the possible implications of an embarrassing marriage of the young dowager queen. She was also aware that Mary's presence in France, once she left the confines of Cluny, could be dangerous. Even when she was back in England, rivals of the Valois might court the young beauty who had once been their queen. It would not hurt to have the romantic young lady marry her less than chivalrous knight.

So they gathered together in the tiny chapel at the palace. Under its exquisite lace-domed ceiling, the Dowager Queen of France became the Duchess of Suffolk. Quickly and efficiently, Mary had turned her own life and Henry's policy around. She had turned herself from a piece of disposable royal property into the chief determiner of her own fate. It was an accomplishment many women, and more than a few men, might envy. All her life she had known strong women who unquestioningly accepted the fates their parents and brothers laid out for them. Francis I's brilliant sister Marguerite, the Duchess of Alençon, had acquiesced to a marriage she found repugnant. Mary's own sister had sulked at her marriage, but never challenged it. Her sister-in-law Catherine, for all her strength of character, never thought of using it to choose her own husband, or her own home. Even Henry himself had not been able to choose his own wife until after his father's death.

Mary and Charles returned to England to an irate but ultimately forgiving Henry. He made his acceptance of their marriage contingent on their "repayment" of the dower moneys he had lost through his sister's short-lived reign as queen of France. With Charles Brandon, Mary went on to live a life of quiet graciousness, its drama seemingly finished in that one masterful achievement. We might almost think she was unaware of what an astounding feat she had pulled off, were it not for one thing. Tactfully, she and Charles named their first son after her brother. There were many women she and Charles might have chosen to honor in naming their second child, a daughter—her mother, Elizabeth; her sister, Margaret, her sis-ter-in-law, Catherine. Instead, the girl was given the name of the conspira-tor in the plot that had won Mary the husband of her choice. The daughter was named Frances. For the rest of her life, Mary was always known in England as the French Queen, never as Duchess of Suffolk—a constant reminder that she had married beneath her, and that she remained royalty.

With Mary's return, Catherine was reunited with a dear friend, and she could only rejoice in her sister-in-law's marriage. Her own marriage remained happy—at least according to contemporary observers. She still played a lively part in Henry's endless round of pageants and disguisings, still dancing, still acting dutifully surprised when Robin Hood or the masked knight turned out to be her own beloved husband.

On January 22, 1516, Ferdinand of Spain died. At first Henry was afraid to let her know of her father's death, for she was pregnant again, and he feared the shock would bring on yet another miscarriage. The baby was born on February 18, a strong, healthy child with only one flaw: it was a girl. Henry was publicly optimistic. "We are both still young," he told the Venetian ambassador. "If it is a daughter this time, by the grace of God sons will follow."

Watching his queen lie in bed, exhausted and ill from this most recent childbirth, Henry had time to contemplate his disappointment. Catherine had not given him a living son. She had been the instrument of some of his military failures because of her zealous support of Ferdinand's policies. She had also been the instrument of Henry's greatest military success, Flodden Field, but that was easy to ignore when God's voice began to whisper softly in his ear—a whisper that would soon grow into a roar.

Now Catherine's father was dead, replaced by Charles I, an untried boy of sixteen. Charles showed no interest in releasing his mother from her ten years' imprisonment in the castle of Tordesillas, and he was unlike-ly to feel strongly protective of the aunt he barely knew. Ferdinand's death had changed the international political scene, and it also changed the polit-ical usefulness of his daughter.

Equally important to Henry, Catherine herself had changed. She was now past thirty, and time had not treated her gently. It was less than seven years since she had married Henry, but they were hard years, physically and emotionally. The many stillbirths and miscarriages had thickened her waist and sallowed her complexion. Henry was hardly the philanderer his father-in-law had been. Indeed, for a king, he had been almost faithful.

But in 1514 he had begun an affair with one of Catherine's ladies-in-waiting, Elizabeth Blount, and the affair was still going on. There were rumors of other affairs: Jane Popyngcort, a friend of Mary's from her days in France and briefly maid of honor to Catherine, was possibly one amour. Catherine, like most royal wives of the time, pretended not to notice.

More ominous than the liaisons common to kings were rumors that Henry planned to repudiate Catherine. In 1514, while Henry romped with Bessie Blount, the Venetian ambassador had written to the pope that "it is said that the king of England means to repudiate his present wife . . . because he is unable to have children by her." It's doubtful that the rumor had any truth to it: Catherine was pregnant at the time and might well have been carrying a son. But it's possible that Henry had become bored with her sexually and angered by her continual failure to give him an heir, and that the idea of repudiating her if this pregnancy failed was in the back of his mind, pushed forward in a moment of pique, and then ignored again. Now at least Catherine had given him a daughter—a daughter who might if need be come to the throne.

They named the girl Mary, probably for the French Queen and, in Catherine's mind at least, for her beloved Maria de Salinas. Mary lived and thrived, and her father made a great display of loving her. But she was not a son, and he could not forget that—especially not in 1519, when Bessie Blount gave birth to a boy, whom the king named Henry Fitzroy.

In the spring of 1516, Henry's sister Margaret made a brief return to England. Margaret, like her sister Mary, had married for love after the death of her royal husband. But the aftermath of their alliances were dramatically different. In part this was because Mary happily embraced a life of unambitious domesticity while Margaret was an ambitious politician, and in part because of the nature of the men they loved. Charles Brandon was a caring, loving husband. Margaret's husband, Archibald, Earl of Angus, was a treacherous self-seeker who quickly earned Margaret's bitter nickname, the Earl of Anguish.

Aside from her marital problems, Margaret was also facing political struggles with the powerful Scottish lords who wanted neither a female nor an English regent to control their country. She planned a visit to England. Her younger son had died; his brother, the boy king, was under the control of the lords and their French leader, the Duke of Albany. She had recently given birth to Angus's child, a pretty little girl named for herself. Margaret took the baby with her to London, where she and her brother showed off their little daughters to one another. For Catherine, the rare opportunity to share maternal gurglings must have been a delight—mitigated, perhaps, by the knowledge that both her sisters-in-law had sons while she had none. Still, she did have this daughter. Little Mary might one day marry Margaret's son and join the crowns of England and Scotland—an idea Henry had put forth and both Margaret and Catherine found appealing.

For a year, Catherine, Margaret, and Mary reveled in one another's company. Different as their lives now were, they had much in common; they had all been princesses sent from their homes as brides to unknown princes. They shared something else as well, which created differing degrees of damage in their lives—a misplaced trust in the man all three loved, King Henry.

They also shared a sense of compassion, which was revealed by a terrifying event. On May 1, 1517—Evil May Day, as it would come to be called—ugly riots erupted in the streets of London, the violence ignited by English workers' and apprentices' growing resentment of the highly skilled Flemish, Spanish, French, and Italian craftsmen who lived in the city, holding jobs that unemployed Londoners coveted. That these foreigners were patronized by the king and his Spanish queen didn't help matters, and there were outbursts of hostility from time to time. Wolsey ordered a city-wide curfew, which only served to further antagonize the apprentices and their supporters. On May Day, a furious mob ran through Whitehall, where most of the foreigners lived, pillaging and setting fire to the houses and shops of Spanish merchants.

Thomas More, then undersheriff of London, tried to calm the riots and might have succeeded, but for the arrival of the arrogant Duke of Norfolk. The people respected More, whose compassion for them was well known, and they hated Norfolk. Norfolk returned their loathing, and his hatred was far more lethal than theirs. His troops rounded up all the rioters they could get their hands on, executing them instantly on gibbets erected over the merchants' own shops. Dozens of rioters were hanged, drawn, and quartered. Hundreds more were imprisoned, awaiting a similar fate.

They might have met that fate without an unexpected upsurge of female solidarity. The mothers, wives, and sweethearts of the prisoners made a slow procession toward the palace, where they stood outside the wall, weeping and wailing. Did they hope to reach the king, safely sheltered behind his palace walls? Possibly. The people adored Henry, and perceived him as a loving father. Or it may be that they instinctively geared their cries to the queen—a mother and wife like themselves.

Catherine heard their cries. So did Mary and Margaret. As the nineteenth-century historian Agnes Strickland tells it, the three women rushed to Henry's chamber, throwing themselves at Henry's feet and begging him to spare the lives of the boys Norfolk had condemned to death.

He might, of course, have heeded their pleas at once, but to do so would be to lose a great theatrical opportunity. Henry and Wolsey waited ten days. Then, on May 11, the prisoners and their supporters were treated to the spectacle of Henry under a handsome canopy, high up on a dais, surrounded by the three queens. The prisoners were sent for—"poor younglings and the old false knaves, bound in ropes, all along one after the other in their shirts, and everyone with a halter about his neck, to the number of 400 men and eleven women."

Wolsey dramatically reviled the youths, cursing Norfolk and the aldermen who had not instantly hanged them all. Henry looked on sternly in his role of impartial arbiter of justice while the women in the back of the hall cried out to him, "Mercy, gracious lord, mercy!" For Henry and Wolsey it was a sadistic farce, performed to show the king's great mercy even to his undeserving subjects, but to the rioters and their families it was deadly serious.

Once again, the three queens threw themselves on their knees in front of Henry, their spontaneous gesture on May Day now repeated as a small piece of the drama being enacted by Good King Hal. Wolsey watched it all with the relish of a superb director; at just the right time he suddenly joined the women, apparently moved by their feminine charity, and knelt before Henry to add his pleas to theirs. Henry then offered his carefully rehearsed forgiveness. The prisoners, weeping, threw off their halters and left with their families, all cheering for the gracious king.

Like the apprentices' victims, Catherine was Spanish, and she might have been expected to use her influence to avenge her countrymen. Instead she sided with her adopted people. A ballad that was heard in the streets of London in the wake of the pardons shows that the people understood what that meant:

> What if [she said] by Spanish blood,
> Have London's stately streets been wet,
> Yet will I seek this country's good
> And pardons for their children get . . .
>
> For which, kind queen, with joyful heart,
> She heard their mothers' thanks and praise,
> And so from them did gently part,
> And lived beloved all her days.

Margaret departed for Scotland again shortly after these events. It was as well for her that she did, for an epidemic of the mysterious disease known as the sweating sickness now broke out in England. It was particularly virulent, hitting the young and healthy as well as the old and infirm. It attacked suddenly, with an intense fever and profuse sweating, followed by nausea and constricted breathing. "It killed some within three hours," wrote the Tudor chronicler Edward Hall, "some within two hours, some merry at dinner and dead at supper." Thomas More wrote to his friend Erasmus, "Many are dying all around us; almost everyone in Oxford, Cambridge, and London has been ill lately and many of our best and most honored friends have perished." Henry and Catherine fled from court to court, desperately trying to avoid London and outrun the epidemic. Wolsey, remaining in London to do the king's work, contracted the disease but, to Henry's relief, survived it.

On November 10, 1518, Catherine gave birth for the last time—to a girl, who died a few hours after her birth. With such personal and social turmoil, the queen began more and more to turn to the religion that had always been a solace to her. The need to resign herself to the fact that she would never bear a son was almost certainly the chief reason for her increase in fasting and other religious observances. It was probably in these years that she began to wear a hair shirt—unconsciously imitating that other pious, determined lady, her husband's grandmother Margaret Beaufort.

Meanwhile, political changes abroad continued, changes that would affect the queen's future. The delicate balance of power between France and Spain veered in France's favor with the death of the Holy Roman Emperor Maximilian in January 1519 and the election of Charles of Spain in his place the following June (the same month Bessie Blount bore Henry's illegitimate son). The Holy Roman Empire was never as grand as its name suggested; in the eighteenth century Voltaire airily dismissed it as neither holy, nor Roman, nor an empire. It did, however, keep many of the German states as well as most of the Low Countries and parts of present-day France and Italy under a single ruler. The union of the empire with Spain thus gave Charles a frightening amount of power, and Henry was unsure of what his course should be. Should he ally himself with Charles against France? Or seek instead to join with Francis I against any encroachments by Charles's empire?

On a more personal level—and Henry's politics were always personal—Charles rounded out the trio of competitors that would vie with each other for European power and prestige for the next twenty years. Henry was now twenty-eight, Francis I twenty-five, and the new emperor only nineteen. Both Henry and Francis put much stock in extravagant clothing and display, whereas Charles utterly lacked charisma. His colorless personality seems to have fooled Henry for a time. Odd-looking, with a jutting jaw that sometimes made his speech slur, the new emperor was in reality the shrewdest statesman of the three. His throne was not an extension of his ego, and he did not leave the real work of statecraft to a Cardinal Wolsey or a Louise of Savoy.

Charles had once negotiated for the hand of Henry's sister Mary. Now he asked for the hand of Henry's daughter Mary, who in 1518 had already been betrothed to the young French dauphin.

Henry met separately with each of his rivals in 1520. In May Charles paid a brief visit to England, chiefly to dissuade Henry from his planned formal meeting with Francis in Calais, the English-held territory on the French seacoast. Arriving with a minimum of fanfare, he treated Henry with deference. Henry greeted his nephew cordially, refusing his request but agreeing to a later meeting with him in Flanders.

The meeting with Francis took place on what came to be called the Field of Cloth of Gold. It was a gorgeous but empty piece of royal theater. On June 7 the two monarchs met in the Vale of Ardres—today, Alison Weir wryly notes, a turnip field—gorgeously dressed for three weeks of pageants, displays, counter-displays, and general showing off.

The make-believe town was splendidly appointed. Three months before the event over two thousand artisans, including master masons, tailors, smiths, joiners, and carpenters, had arrived at Ardres to create a huge artificial castle, timbered and painted, with glazed windows, canvas roof, a private chapel complete with choir, tapestried walls, and, leading to the thrones on which the monarchs would sit, a carpet lined with pearls. Henry, accompanied by an entourage of four thousand, along with Catherine, with twelve hundred attendants of her own, was going to show Francis what kingliness was about.

Francis had the same idea. His section of the field was filled with tents covered by cloth of gold, cloth of silver, and purple velvet, while his pavilion, 120 feet high, glittered with its gold brocade exterior.

The French and English met officially at the border of the English "village." Cannon boomed, trumpets blasted, and Henry and Francis rode toward each other on horseback, bejeweled and gorgeous in cloth of gold and silver. They dismounted and embraced, swearing their great love and eternal loyalty to each other amid the cheers of the French and English nobility and of those commoners who were able, outside the six-mile limits prescribed by Francis, to stare down from the hills above the Picardy plains. Not everyone was fooled. "They hate each other cordially," wrote the Venetian ambassador.

For two weeks the meeting continued, a constant round of feasts, tourneys, masques, and everything but political discussion. A few tense moments occurred when the braggadocio of the kings threatened to expose the hostility behind their expansive displays of brotherly love: a wrestling match proposed by Henry and avidly accepted by Francis ended, as one biographer put it, with "Henry of England . . . flat on his royal rump on the grass." Rising, Henry demanded a rematch. The strain was dissipated by the two queens, who laughingly tugged at their husbands' arms and pulled them away from one another.

Catherine and Francis's queen, Claude, provided the one breath of sincerity in the clotted air of the pompous spectacle. Tricked out as much as their husbands in garish royal finery, they nonetheless managed to inject some simple human reality into the proceedings. Both were, at this stage, temperamentally unattracted to the masques and jousts; in addition, Queen Claude was seven months pregnant. They found each other comfortable companions in the brief weeks of their acquaintance. One incident stands out in its warm common sense. On the morning after their arrival, during the solemn mass presided over by the splendid Cardinal Wolsey, they were offered the cross to ceremonially kiss. But which should kiss the cross first? Each repeatedly tried to defer to the other. Suddenly struck by the unnaturalness of the formality, they solved the problem by turning away from the cross and kissing each other instead.

Among the other women present were Francis's mother and sister, the Queen Dowager Louise of Savoy and Marguerite, Duchess of Alençon. The royal women had their ladies to attend them. Queen Claude almost certainly had brought along one of her ladies-in-waiting, the English Ann Boleyn, who could act as a valuable bridge between the two cultures. Ann was elegant and sophisticated, polished in the French fashion Henry so admired. But if she was there, no one paid much attention to her. Catherine certainly didn't. The queen might have felt a twinge of envy toward her new friend Claude, who had given her husband two healthy and thriving sons, but she had no cause to feel threatened by any other woman there—certainly not by the obscure, dark-haired English girl who charmingly and unobtrusively served Queen Claude in the evanescent fairy-tale town of Henry's creation.

Chapter 3

THE GREAT WHORE

ANN BOLEYN

For years, Ann tried to escape King Henry's sexual advances.
Failing, she strategized, with spectacular success but tragic consequences, to become his wife.

Beheaded

f all of Henry VIII's wives, Ann Boleyn is the one who has attracted the most popular interest, and her character has perhaps been subjected to the most intense distortion. She has been called a whore, a homewrecker, a soulless schemer, a commoner who used religion to advance herself but who had no true religious convictions of her own. She has been described as ugly, hideously deformed by a huge wen hidden by high-necked gowns, and a sixth finger on one hand.

The image is fun, and it makes for great melodrama. All it lacks is accuracy. Ann Boleyn's sexual activity, even by the standards of the age, was not excessive: there is no evidence that she engaged in sex with anyone but her husband, although she was flirtatious in the courtly mode that had existed throughout the Middle Ages. She did catalyze the timing of Henry's scheme to get his marriage annulled, but she was not its cause: Henry had already begun to question why he had no legitimate son. Nor was she a commoner. Her grandfather, the Earl of Surrey, was one of the highest-ranking noblemen in England. As for her religious faith, she was a serious evangelical, one whose views bordered on Protestantism. She bravely gave her patronage to reformers whose beliefs were dangerously close to heresy—a patronage that could only have been based on conviction, since it threatened to alienate her from the more conservative king. She could not have hidden a wen on her neck, since court women of the day wore low-necked gowns.

The extra finger, the wen, and all the other deformities appear only in works written decades after her death, yet there were plenty of contemporary observers who despised her and wrote numerous unflattering accounts of her. One of these was the Spanish ambassador Eustache Chapuys, who gleefully ferreted out all the sordid gossip he heard about Ann and included it, along with his own hostile observations, in his voluminous reports to the emperor. Yet this crafty politician, who could easily have bribed ladies-in-waiting for information, never mentioned wens or moles or extra fingers. One contemporary, writing to the imperial court at Brussels, did describe a goiter on her neck—but he said that her high ruff concealed it, so it's difficult to know how he saw it (or how the other witnesses missed it, for that matter).

George Wyatt, writing more than fifty years after Ann's death, had had conversations with a number of people who had known her. One was her lady-in-waiting Ann Gainsford, who would have had a fairly intimate knowledge of her mistress's body. According to Wyatt, Ann "had upon the side of her nail upon one of her fingers some little show of a nail" and had a few small moles "incident to the clearest complexions." It seems odd that Chapuys never learned of either the extra nail or the moles: if they existed, they must have been tiny indeed.*

Why, then, all the fuss about Ann's looks and behavior? And why her endless fascination? She fascinated Henry five hundred years ago; she fascinates us still. Ann Boleyn, moles or no moles, lovers or no lovers, was a sexy woman. She was never described as a great beauty, but even those who loathed her admitted that she had a dramatic allure. Her dark complexion and black hair gave her an exotic aura in a culture that saw milk-white paleness as essential to beauty. Her eyes were especially striking: "black and beautiful" wrote one contemporary, while another averred they were "always most attractive," and that she "knew well how to use them with effect." Her sexuality resonates through the pages of Henry's cloying love letters and of Chapuys's diatribes. It reverberates through all the stories of the king's seven-year obsession with the woman who refused to become his mistress and yet held absolute sway over his desire.

Perhaps this is the reason Ann holds us in her spell even today. Pursued by a king whose advances she at first resisted, she turned the lust from which she could not escape into a means of achieving power for herself: captured, she became herself the captor. Even in defeat, she was never fully Henry's. Like the falcon she chose as her emblem, she was a wild creature used, curtailed, but never truly tamed; she was a sexual woman whose vitality belonged only to herself. For years Henry tried vainly to control that vitality; finally, unable to mold it to his purposes, he killed her.

---

*For a credible argument that Ann could not have had any such deformities, see Retha M. Warnicke, *The Rise and Fall of Anne Boleyn: Family Politics at the Court of Henry VIII* (Cambridge: Cambridge University Press, 1989), pp. 58–59.

஥ Ann Boleyn had never, in her early life, imagined herself becoming queen. Born somewhere between 1501 and 1507 (scholars debate the year fiercely, but we can't know for certain), as the daughter of one of Henry VIII's prominent courtiers, she expected to make a good marriage with another member of the high nobility, in England or in Europe. Perhaps it was with this in mind that her father, Sir Thomas Boleyn, sent the girl to the court of Margaret of Austria at Malines in the Low Countries in 1513, where he had himself earlier served as Henry's ambassador.

It was excellent training for a budding English noblewoman. Though the cultural flowering in the lands held by the dukes of Burgundy had begun to fade, Margaret presided over the leading court of Europe, to which the elite of other nations sent their children. There the archduchess maintained an ambience of both artistic and intellectual sophistication and political power. Since the death of Isabella of Spain nine years earlier, Margaret had become the most powerful woman in all Europe. She brought to her rule in the Netherlands an enviable knowledge of the courts of Europe that few male rulers could match. Betrothed at the age of three to the French dauphin, she had lived for the next ten years at the French court. When Margaret was eleven, the French regent Ann de Beaujeu decided on a better match for the boy king, and Margaret's betrothal was abruptly repudiated. Six years later she married Catherine of Aragon's brother Juan and lived briefly in the court of Isabella and Ferdinand. Juan's death soon after the marriage left Margaret again alone, although this time without the stigma of rejection. She bore a child who died shortly after birth, leaving her doubly devastated. In 1501 she married Philibert II, Duke of Savoy. He died in 1504, and Margaret decided that she had had enough of wedlock. Though her father, Maximilian I, tried to arrange other marriages for her (including one with the widowed Henry VII), she firmly refused them all.

In 1507, the emperor appointed her regent of the Netherlands for her nephew Charles of Burgundy, making her in effect the ruler of the Low Countries. She had done spectacularly well. Everything she had learned at the courts of France, Spain, and Savoy she brought to the already exquisite court of Burgundy. Most important was the influence of France. She had learned painting, drawing, lute playing, dancing from the greatest French masters. Her own musical abilities were legendary, and her court organist, the famous Henri Bredemers, taught the young Charles and his sisters. Dancing was also a major art form, practiced not only by itself but as part of the intricate pageants and disguisings, of which the English variants so loved by Henry were but a pale derivative. (In one pageant, Margaret appeared as queen of the Amazons, bejeweled, beplumed, and flourishing a real sword.)

To this court, then, the girl Ann Boleyn went in 1513, and she remained there for the next year. She seems to have quickly picked up the skills she had been sent to learn. "I find her so bright and pleasant for her young age," Margaret wrote to the gratified Thomas Boleyn, "that I am more beholden to you for sending her to me than you are to me." A French observer later wrote of Ann that she "listened carefully to honorable ladies, setting herself to bend all her endeavor to imitate them to perfection, and made such good use of her wits that in no time at all she had command of the language."

As she became fluent in French, she probably acquired more substantial duties as well. After Henry's victory over the French at Thérouanne, the English king met Maximilian in the Flemish town of Lille, where Margaret and her court joined them. A month later came the successful siege of Tournai, and again Maximilian sent for his daughter. Grumbling that widows did not go around visiting armies, Margaret nevertheless obeyed the emperor's summons. Though there is no record that Ann was with Margaret on these occasions, it seems likely: Thomas Boleyn was with the English army and, more important, Margaret and Maximilian would both recognize the girl's usefulness as an interpreter.

The following year, when Henry's sister Mary went to Paris to marry Louis XII, Ann was sent to join her entourage, thus moving from the Burgundian court to the equally sophisticated French court. There, in the quaint assessment of the nineteenth-century historian J. A. Froude, she "could not have failed to see, to hear, and to become familiar with occurrences with which no young girl can be brought in contact with impunity." Her sister Mary was also there and, if later reports are to be believed, soon fell into a lifestyle of sexual activity that she would continue as Henry VIII's mistress. Mary, wrote one ambassador, had acquired a reputation "as a very great wanton."

When Louis died and Mary Tudor eloped with her beloved Charles Brandon, Ann stayed on as a lady-in-waiting to the new queen of France. Claude, the daughter of the dead King Louis, was a homely, shy, fifteen-year-old. Perhaps, as E. W. Ives suggests, Ann had endeared herself to the girl earlier when, awkward and knowing no English, the princess needed help in communicating with her stunning eighteen-year-old stepmother. Ann stayed at Claude's court for seven years.

Although her major duties kept her by the queen's side, she was also exposed to two other, more dazzling women. During Francis's early days as king his mother, Louise of Savoy, was as much responsible for French policy as he was, combining the roles that Catherine of Aragon and Cardinal Wolsey held in England. Ann's year in Malines had shown her that a woman could hold and use power directly. Now she was finding that, even in a country that barred women from the throne, a shrewd woman with influence over a king could wield a great deal of power as well.

Whereas Louise of Savoy influenced French policy during Francis's reign, her daughter, Marguerite of Alençon, influenced French culture. Marguerite was a poet of note; more important for Ann, she was just beginning her support of religious reform, which would strengthen throughout her life. Young, elegant, knowledgeable, and intellectually challenging, Marguerite was an obvious role model for a girl who was acquiring those characteristics herself, and it is likely that the duchess's burgeoning interest in ecclesiastical reform paved the way for Ann's own.

Thomas Boleyn recalled his daughter to England in 1521 to arrange a marriage between Ann and the son of a distant relative, Piers Butler, in the hope that it would settle a long-standing land dispute between the families. The intermediary for this marriage was Cardinal Wolsey. The wedding plans were suddenly and mysteriously dropped, and Ann was once again appointed as a lady-in-waiting to a queen—this time, England's Catherine of Aragon. She was probably relieved by the failure of the marriage plans, for the disputed estate where she and her husband were to have lived was in Ireland—a primitive land far removed from the courtly life Ann had so fully adapted to.

What did she feel about England itself? It wasn't Ireland, but it wasn't France either. Yet it had its advantages. In the French court, Ann was one among many, standing out only on the occasions when her linguistic skills were called on. In England she was unique; she emanated the continental elegance of France and Burgundy that the English court tried so hard to emulate. A French courtier wrote that "no one would ever have taken her to be English by her manners, but a native born Frenchwoman." It is appropriate that the first record we have of Ann in her new job is her appearance at a pageant performed for the ambassadors from Charles of Burgundy, now Holy Roman emperor. Charles, whom she had known as an awkward boy in her year at Margaret of Austria's court, was again betrothed to a Tudor princess—not, this time, Henry's sister, but his daughter.

The pageant was nearly as elaborate as one of Margaret of Austria's— a complex depiction of the assault by eight courtiers on the Château Vert, in which Beauty, Honor, and their six attendant ladies dwelled, each representing a different female ideal. Ann was given the role of Perseverance, to which she was as well suited as her one-time mistress, the French Queen, was to her role of Beauty.

Along with the opportunity to dazzle the English court with her continental sophistication, Ann found another means of reconciling herself to her new life at home. The queen's ladies-in-waiting had ample time to meet and mingle with the courtiers who attended the king and his all-powerful chancellor, Cardinal Wolsey. Among Wolsey's retinue was the attractive young Henry Percy, son of the Earl of Northumberland. While the cardinal was at court, Percy amused himself by flirting with the queen's ladies. Sometime before the fall of 1523 his attention focused on one of those ladies—the glamorous new arrival from France, Ann Boleyn.

According to Wolsey's gentleman-usher George Cavendish, Ann returned Percy's interest. "There grew such a secret love between them that at length they were insured together, intending to marry," he wrote. They decided to keep their betrothal secret, however, realizing that neither family was likely to approve of the match. But the court was an all too public environment, and secrets rarely lasted long. When word reached Wolsey of his protégé's indiscretion, he was incensed. The betrothal must be broken instantly.

Wolsey confronted Percy. "I marvel not a little of thy peevish folly that thou wouldest tangle and assure thyself with a foolish girl yonder in the court," he sneered. Reminding him that at his father's death he would inherit "one of the most worthiest earldoms of this realm," Wolsey added that the young man, rather than contracting a secret betrothal, should have asked his father's and the king's consent: the king might have had another marriage in mind for him. In fact, Wolsey added, the king had another match in mind for Ann herself.

The rebuke stung, and Percy, frightened, burst into tears. But he insisted that he had a right to choose his own wife, and asked Wolsey to intercede with both the king and his father—a request Wolsey scornfully refused. The young man protested that he had committed himself to Ann "before so many worthy witnesses that I know not how to avoid myself nor to discharge my conscience," but his words fell on deaf ears. It was true that, according to the letter of the law, an agreement to marry, even if it did not involve sexual consummation, was binding, but it was equally true that in practice such an oral contract was easy to break—especially with the cardinal's influence behind the effort.

Northumberland, who had been sent for, publicly berated his son, calling him a "proud, presumptuous, very unthrifty waster," and threatening to disinherit him. Ann was sent away from court to her father's country house, Hever Castle. She did not, Cavendish tells us, take Wolsey's interference in her life happily. Furiously, she declared that if she ever had the opportunity she would "work the cardinal as much displeasure" as he had done her.

There is some debate as to who really instigated the breakup of Ann and Percy. Cavendish, writing thirty-five years later, insisted that it was the king, who had already cast an eye on the new lady-in-waiting. Later scholars argue that the events took place too early for this to be the case, since Percy was married to Mary Talbot by 1524, when Henry was presumably still having his affair with Ann's sister Mary. But the two ideas aren't mutually exclusive. Cavendish may be our only source for the notion that it was Henry's doing, but he is a reliable one. He was Wolsey's close and trusted servant, and he speaks with authority. After so much time he may well have forgotten many things, but hardly something as fundamental as whether Wolsey was acting under Henry's orders when he confronted Percy about his engagement to Ann Boleyn. And his explanation for Ann's appeal to the king has the ring of truth: "for her excellent gesture and behavior did excel all other." Henry, anxious to match the elegance of his counterparts in Paris and Malines, must have noticed Ann as soon as she set foot in his court. Perhaps his role as chief assailant against the ladies of the Château Vert suggested to him that actual pursuit of Lady Perseverance might have more charm than his palling affair with her compliant sister.

We don't know exactly when Henry's obsession with Ann began. J. J. Scarisbrick suggests that a "light dalliance" had become far more serious by 1525. Though Scarisbrick offers the idea casually, it may be an important insight into the nature of Henry and Ann's early relationship, for the "dalliance" might easily have begun several years earlier, at least in the king's own mind. That he was sleeping with her sister would hardly prevent his being attracted to Ann, and we need not assume that only a passionate infatuation would lead him to stop her from marrying the man she was in love with. If he fancied her as his next mistress, he might well want to choose her husband himself, as he chose her sister's husband, thus assuring himself of a comfortable cuckold, well rewarded for his tractability with royal favors. The future Earl of Northumberland was unlikely to be bought off as easily as plain William Carey, Mary Boleyn's husband, nor would he be flattered that his wife had attracted the king's lust.

It would take a grossly self-absorbed person to destroy two people's happiness because of his own, possibly mild, attraction to a woman. But Henry was such a person. We need not assume that he changed overnight from a compassionate man to a monster. It seems more likely that his essential ruthlessness was masked by charm, and by the fact that nothing had yet occurred to call that ruthlessness forth. He might well have decided that it was worth keeping the elegant maiden from France available for his future use. And it would be wholly in keeping with his character as we know it from later years for him to make Wolsey the instrument of his will, so that any antagonism Ann, or even Percy, felt would be diverted from the king himself.

Percy's father had for many years been negotiating a possible marriage for his son with Mary Talbot, the Earl of Shrewsbury's daughter. Now the betrothal was quickly arranged, and by early 1524, the miserable Henry Percy had married a woman he bitterly resented. The marriage turned out as badly as one might expect under the circumstances, and the rest of Percy's life is a story of wretched unhappiness, ending with his death twelve years later.

With Percy married, Ann returned to court and Queen Catherine. It would be interesting to know what these two made of each other in the early days of Ann's service. Catherine was usually kind to her ladies, and probably fond of most of them. She may well have enjoyed the company of the newcomer, though she would not have been pleased by Ann's French manners. Except for her friend Queen Claude, France represented to Catherine wickedness and self-indulgence. Fiercely Spanish as she was, she never trusted the French, and she despised their king, calling him "the greatest Turk" that had ever lived. (One wonders whether she knew of Francis's cruel observation about her, when he remarked that "my good brother of England has no son because, although young and handsome, he keeps an old and deformed wife.")

For her part, Ann had reason to like the queen. In her piety Catherine resembled Claude, and in her intellect Margaret of Austria. Though glamorous, Ann was not shallow, and she could appreciate the queen's goodness and intellect, while pitying her dowdiness and, of course, the tragedy that had come to define Catherine, her failure to have a son.

Even this Ann might not have perceived as an unmitigated tragedy. In the courts she had come from there were women who managed to triumph without sons. Claude was the daughter of a queen, Anne of Brittany, who had been extremely influential in her husband's reign, notwithstanding her lack of sons; to some extent Claude, as queen consort, was redeeming her mother's chief fault by giving birth to several sons and preserving her father's blood, if not his name, on the throne of France. And the most powerful woman in Europe, childless Margaret of Austria, had done the unthinkable. Though still of childbearing age, she had given up on marriage and thus on that ultimate female goal of producing sons, becoming instead a foster mother to her nephew Charles and ruling the Netherlands for him. In the world Ann Boleyn knew, having sons was the most important thing a woman could do—but if that didn't succeed, there were other options.

Ann is unlikely to have harbored doubts that she herself would have sons, once the right husband was found for her. Heartbroken though she was over the loss of Henry Percy, she would not shroud her heart in a lifetime of mourning. She was ambitious, the daughter of an ambitious courtier, and she wanted such power and influence as shrewdness and sophistication could provide her. A woman's power required a direct relationship with a powerful man, as even the example of Margaret of Austria showed. For most women, that meant having a powerful husband. Such men were found by being at court and shining there, making certain one's beauty and charm were well known and universally admired. Among other things, this entailed playing the game of courtly love, and not only in pageants and disguisings. It had to be played at every possible moment.

It was a game Ann played carefully and well, always managing to be both flirtatious and chaste—and again, her continental training stood her in good stead. She seemed to relish the contest, and she acquired a number of admirers, among them her cousin, the poet Thomas Wyatt.

The nature of their relationship has fascinated scholars because of the hints Wyatt gives in a host of brilliant love poems. Only a handful of the poems are clearly about Ann, and it's hard to be certain how seriously to interpret them: poets of the era were fond of writing laments about the cruel mistress, and the pretense of an affair may have simply made for good sonnets.

Wyatt's grandson George, writing fifty years later of conversations he had had with one of Ann's ladies-in-waiting, believed that there had been a flirtation between the two that was taken seriously by Wyatt but not by Ann herself. According to George, his grandfather, though a cousin of Ann's, first saw her when she came back to England, and, "coming to behold the sudden appearance of this new beauty, came to be holden and surprised somewhat with the sight thereof; after much more with her witty and graceful speech, his ear also had him chained unto her, so as finally his heart seemed to say, *I could gladly yield to be tied forever with the knot of her love.*"

Ann was probably attracted to Wyatt, who seems by all accounts to have been an appealing man (though his notoriously adulterous wife didn't seem to think so). But the cautious and canny lady-in-waiting who had learned the art of chaste flirtation at the court of France, where her sister had chosen a more reckless path, was unlikely to destroy her chance of an advantageous marriage by having an affair with a married suitor. It was far safer—and perhaps even far more pleasurable—to take on the courtly role of the unattainable beloved. As for the poet, whatever passions he had for Ann ended when he realized that Henry was serious about her and that she intended to respond to the king's courtship. Wyatt was no more self-destructive than Ann herself, and when the passion was no more a game but a serious danger to them both, it burned itself out.

For it was not long before the king's mild interest in his wife's exotic new lady-in-waiting grew into something more serious. Mary Boleyn too had been in France, but for a shorter time; she had not been formed in the most refined continental courts. In any case, easily conquered, she had begun to bore him. It was time to move on to a new mistress, and Mary's sister was looking increasingly interesting. She would of course take a little wooing; she would of course express the proper degree of maidenly resistance before giving in to him. That was part of the pleasure, making her inevitable surrender all the more enjoyable.

But the king was in for a rude surprise: Ann Boleyn did not surrender. Impossible though it might seem to the monarch everyone adored, someone was immune to his charms.

And so he succumbed to hers.

Nevertheless, it was not because of Ann Boleyn that Henry VIII decided his marriage to Catherine of Aragon was invalid, though his infatuation with Ann certainly determined the timing. He had long wanted a son, and his sexual life with Catherine was over. The birth of his bastard son, Henry Fitzroy, in 1519 must have confirmed his conviction that it was Catherine, not he, who was unable to produce living sons, and it is possible that that event caused him to consider seriously the idea that had only been a bitter fantasy five years earlier.

In 1521 Edward Stafford, the Duke of Buckingham, was executed, charged with treason for, among other things, suggesting to friends that the death of Henry's son was willed by God and that he, Stafford, being of royal descent, was the obvious candidate to succeed as England's next king. The words were treasonous enough, but Henry's reaction suggests his anxiety about his lack of a son, as well as his disaffection from Catherine, whose dear friend he was willing to kill. In the following year, Henry first consulted his confessor, John Longland, Bishop of Lincoln, about the possibility of extricating himself from his marriage.

By 1525, when Henry was no longer having sex with Catherine, the idea of finding a way out of the marriage must have been with him for a while. Probably the thought of an annulment and the captivation with his wife's intriguing lady grew side by side for several months before they coalesced. And it's likely that his initial visions of a second wife were the same as Wolsey's—she should be another European princess, probably a French one. That was the way kings married. Kings also had mistresses—women honored, in their way, given privileges and even titles. Surely Ann Boleyn would come to understand that, and to accept his advances.

But she didn't; that much is clear from a series of seventeen letters (unfortunately, they're undated) Henry wrote to his would-be mistress. From references within the letters it is certain that there were others that are no longer extant. Henry hated writing letters, making Wolsey compose most of his correspondence, so the fact that he wrote so many bespeaks an intense infatuation. But since we don't know the dates, we can't be sure of the sequence of the letters and the events they mention. Some clearly refer to events after the two had become involved: he assures her in one that "this bearer and his fellow be dispatched with many things to compass our matter and to bring it to pass as our wits could imagine or devise." Others obviously date from some earlier stage, when they were not yet lovers but Henry had reason to believe that she desired him and was willing to grant him some form of sexual favor: he ends one with the wish that he was "in my sweetheart's arms, whose pretty dukkys I trust shortly to kiss."

The dating of the others is less easy to determine. Cavendish's explanation for the breakup with Percy, along with historians' assumption that Ann willingly received Henry's advances, is significant. Most scholars have thought that the letters began in 1524. But they may have started earlier than that. Scarisbrick's offhand observation about the "light dalliance" of the early 1520s is important, as is Ives's more recent interpretation of the sequence of the letters. The first three, Ives says, "belong to the period when the conventions of courtly romance began to change into something more serious." In other words, Ann had been flirting with Henry in the belief that such flirtation was safe—that it didn't imply an actual sexual relationship was expected. But Henry started wanting more. With what is apparently the first letter that survives he sent Ann a gift—a buck he had hunted and killed—and complained that she was not answering his letters.

Why does a woman not answer a suitor's letters—especially a powerful suitor's? Probably to accomplish that most delicate task: to convey that she doesn't return his interest without openly rejecting him. In the second letter, Henry complained again. In the role of courtly love he had decided to play, the suitor is the servant of the lady. Yet Ann had insisted that she was *his* servant, since he was king and she his subject. "Although it does not appertain to a gentleman to take his lady in place of a servant," he grumbled, "nevertheless in compliance with your desires, I willingly grant it to you. . . . " He willingly granted it, but he refused to accept its meaning. She didn't want to be his lady, but simply his subject—she didn't want a sexual relationship.

In spite of his promise to let her stay "in the place by you chosen"— the place of a loyal subject only—Henry kept up the pressure. Today, Henry's approach to Ann would be instantly identifiable as sexual harassment. Ann, however, had no social or legal recourse against the man who ruled the country. She continued, as so many women before and since have done, to dodge her pursuer's advances while sparing his feelings. It didn't work.

Henry's next letter demanded that she explain her position once and for all. He had been "above one whole year struck with the dart of love" and still didn't know how she felt. It was the deliberate ignorance of the absolute narcissist, for surely she had given clear enough signals. He persisted. He wanted her to love him "in a way that is beyond common affection." Still she tried to hold him off.

After more than a year of this, Ann must have been growing pretty desperate. Henry was by now offering to make her his official mistress, mimicking the practice of other European courts, one that had never before existed in England. She did not want this. She wanted, in all likelihood, the kind of marriage she had been raised to want—a good, respectable marriage with a suitable nobleman. Perhaps she still wanted Henry Percy. What is clear is that she did *not* want Henry Tudor.

But Henry Tudor wasn't letting go. She stayed away from court, refusing to return even if chaperoned by her mother. He assured her that if he "knew for certain that you wished it of your own will" he would cease importuning her and "put from me little by little my mad infatuation."

It was a hellish position. Could she really tell the king to his face that she had no interest in him? She could reiterate her desire to keep her chastity and her honor, but clearly he didn't respect that. She could ignore his letters and stay away from court, but he refused to take the hint. To offer him the outright insult he asked for would be to risk not only her own but her father's and brother's careers at court. She undoubtedly kept hoping he would tire of the chase and transfer his attentions to some newer lady-in-waiting.

But he didn't, and she was trapped: there was no chance of her making a good marriage when every eligible nobleman knew the king wanted her. She began to realize she would have to give in. Thomas Wyatt's magnificent poem, looming so largely in the story of Ann Boleyn, takes on chilling significance:

> *Whoso list to hunt: I know where is a hind.*
> *But as for me, alas I may no more:*
> *The vain travail hath wearied me so sore,*
> *I am of them that farthest cometh behind.*
> *Yet may I by no means my wearied mind*
> *Draw from the deer, but as she fleeth afore*
> *Fainting I follow. I leave off therefore,*
> *Sithins in a net I seek to hold the wind.*
> *Who list to hunt, I put him out of doubt,*
> *As well as I may spend his time in vain,*
> *And graven in diamonds in letters plain*
> *There is written in her fair neck round about:*
> *"Noli me tangere, for Caesar's I am,*
> *And wild for to hold, though I seem tame."*

Virtually every account of Ann's story cites the poem, yet its central image is ignored. Ann was a creature being hunted, and hunted by the king—like the buck he had killed and so proudly sent to her. There could be no refuge from the royal assault; no one would risk protecting her from Henry's chase. She could run, hide, dodge for a time, but the royal hunter would eventually track down his prey. And he would destroy her. The hunt was not an archaic metaphor in sixteenth-century court life; it was a vivid, integral part of that life, and everyone knew what happened to the wild creature at the hunt's end.

But perhaps there was, after all, one escape, an ingenious and daring one. If she could not flee her hunter, she could survive by being captured on her own terms. Henry was talking of annulling his marriage; Wolsey was scheming for a French princess to supplant Catherine of Aragon. But why should the new queen not be Ann herself? Historians hostile to Ann assume that she had no feelings for either Henry or Catherine, but only raw ambition; those more sympathetic suggest that she was in love with the king. But it may be that neither is true. She may have been sympathetic to the queen, but she knew that Catherine's marriage was doomed. She could turn Henry's cruelty to her own advantage. She would not have forgotten the story of Henry's grandmother Elizabeth Woodville, the beautiful noblewoman who had chastely resisted the advances of Edward IV and become his queen. Elizabeth had borne Edward two sons. And though the king had been unfaithful to her throughout their marriage, he had never repudiated her as Henry was now planning to repudiate Catherine, because she had given him male heirs. Ann too would have sons. Then her position as Henry's wife would be safe; her position in his heart would have served its purpose.

It must have been at about this point that Ann sent Henry an intriguing gift, described in one of his letters. It was a diamond pendant depicting a solitary woman "tossed about" in a ship. Henry, as well as later historians, interpreted this token as representing her commitment to him—he was the ark that would rescue and protect her. Perhaps: her letter, "so warmly couched," presumably suggested the same thing. But Ann was a woman with a strong sense of irony, capable of subtle and bitter humor. In her own mind the ship might have represented a desire to escape Henry and his courtship, to sail back to the court of Paris or Malines. Henry was not the ship, then, but the stormy sea on which she tossed, helpless unless she could manage to steer her own course.

That course included marriage. She could not have decided on such a path until she knew, or strongly suspected, that Henry planned to repudiate his wife. Again, we simply can't be certain as to when that was. By 1525 the king had ceased to have sexual relations with Catherine, who had apparently gone through menopause, but there are indications that he had not yet decided to discard her. Two interesting, and paradoxical, events support this. In June of that year he created his illegitimate son, Henry Fitzroy, Duke of Richmond, the title Henry VII had held before he became king of England. The six-year-old Richmond was now first peer of England. Catherine resented the insult to herself and was alarmed by the possibilities the boy's elevation to the title suggested, but there was little she could do about it. Piqued that she would dare to express anger, Henry avenged himself by dismissing three of her ladies-in-waiting.

Later that same year, Henry sent the nine-year-old Princess Mary (who had been jilted by her cousin Charles V) to Ludlow Castle, where she would take up her duties as Princess of Wales. This title unambiguously belonged to the heir to the throne, and Henry's move can only be seen as a recognition of his daughter's claim. It may be that in giving little Henry Fitzroy the Richmond title Henry was only providing a back-up heir in case Mary, whom the Venetian ambassador described as "thin, spare and small," died young. Or perhaps Henry, anguishing over the lack of a legitimate male successor, was casting about for other solutions.

The separation from her daughter was painful for the queen, and her letters to the girl show that Henry had withdrawn from her as well: "The long absence of the King and you troubleth me," she wrote sadly, in a letter that went on to address her daughter's studies.

The first official record we have of Henry's doubts about the validity of his marriage dates from May 1527, but by this time the king had researched the question thoroughly. In 1529, at the hearings before the court of the papal legate summoned at Blackfriars, Henry claimed that the doubts had been planted by French ambassadors: when a marriage between the princess Mary and the French king's son was being negotiated, he said, the ambassadors had expressed concern about Mary's legitimacy. Catherine and others believed it was Wolsey who first sowed the seeds of skepticism in Henry's mind. Modern biographers, however, tend to see the idea as Henry's own, not Wolsey's. It may have been a combination of the two. Wolsey, sensing what the king wanted, might have encouraged him to think of ridding himself of Catherine—either subtly insinuating the original idea, or reinforcing it after the king suggested it. Catherine had long been a thorn in the great cardinal's side. Her political influence on Henry had remained strong over the years, interfering with Wolsey's pro-French policies. A French princess would serve his purposes far better.

However the idea of annulment originated, once Henry got it into his head, it stuck. He wanted a son, badly, and ridding himself of Catherine was the only way to get one.

It was true that the absence of a son was a serious problem for a monarch. In a society that held that women were by nature inferior, one in which both women and men routinely sent letters of condolence to a woman who gave birth to a daughter, the thought of a female leader was unsettling. Even the early feminist Christine de Pisan, writing in defense of womankind in 1405, followed her descriptions of successful female rulers with a disclaimer that leadership was a role properly belonging to men, not women. There were several levels to the problem. But each level lent itself to a far less drastic solution than the one Henry came up with.

To begin with, there was the question of whether a woman had the

ability to rule. How could the inferior female mind cope with the responsibilities of leadership? How could men obey a ruler who was, paradoxically, beneath them by virtue of her gender even as she was above them
by virtue of sovereignty? Yet, as Henry knew full well, women had ruled
and continued to do so—some with outstanding effectiveness. Catherine's
mother, Isabella, as queen of mighty Castile, was more powerful than her
husband, Ferdinand; she was also the more able ruler of the two, and with
her husband she ruled Spain brilliantly for thirty-five years. The regent
Margaret of Austria ably governed the Low Countries. Henry, in his many
dealings with Margaret, knew her capability well. Even France, where the
Salic law prohibited the accession of a woman to the throne, was ruled for
a year by Louise of Savoy while King Francis was held captive by Spain.
True, the reign of the one female ruler in England's history, the Empress
Matilda in the twelfth century, had been characterized by a disastrous civil
war. But that had been part of a complicated power struggle in which her
gender was only one of several factors. There was no indication that the
English people feared Mary would become another Matilda, or that other
contenders for the throne would instigate a civil war if she reigned.

The second aspect of the problem was perhaps more difficult. However competent a female ruler might be, there remained the question of
her husband. It was essential that she marry, or the dynastic line would end
with her. But God's law commanded that she obey her husband. Thus, to
allow a woman to succeed to the throne implicitly meant placing the
country in the hands of her husband. The female rulers of Henry's experience had been in situations that bypassed this problem. Margaret of Austria was only the regent, accountable to the nephew in whose name she
governed, however much autonomy he permitted her. Isabella co-ruled
with Ferdinand in a marriage that had united two contiguous kingdoms.
If Mary came to the throne, the question of her marriage would be para-
mount. Various betrothals were negotiated over the years, but each held
the obvious pitfall: if she married a French prince, France would rule England; if she married her cousin Charles, Spain would rule England.

But there was another cousin, James V of Scotland, with whom Mary
might well have replicated Isabella and Ferdinand's success. Scotland, as
Henry VII had known when he gave his daughter Margaret to James IV,
was the lesser kingdom. If the two united, it would probably be swallowed
up by England, ending years of border disputes and wars. Henry VII had
considered the possibility of his daughter inheriting the throne of England,
and its implications for her marriage to the Scottish king. He had found
the idea perfectly reasonable: "What, as God forbid, if all my bairns be

dead; if Margaret justly succeedeth . . . Scotland will come to England." In 1516 Henry VIII had briefly pondered a marriage between Mary and James V, and then inexplicably dropped the idea.

If fear of England's being dominated by a foreign king, even a Scottish one, stood in Henry's way, there was yet another possibility of a match for Mary that, curiously, no one seems to have thought of. Mary had an English cousin, Henry Brandon, Earl of Lincoln, the son of the French Queen and her hard-won husband, Charles Brandon. It seems odd that no match was suggested. Perhaps the boy was already sickly: he died in 1534, soon after his robust father's fourth marriage. But in his own right, young Brandon seems to have been viewed as a possibility for the succession: Chapuys wrote that his death pleased the Scottish ambassador because, "though of the younger sister, his being a native would have made him a formidable contender of the Scotch king." (James, as Henry VII's grandson, was also in the line of succession.)

There were precedents in Europe for a sonless king to marry his daughter to the likely heir to the throne. Henry's onetime brother-in-law, Louis XII of France, had had two daughters—which was why he had been so anxious, on the death of Anne of Brittany, to marry Henry's young sister Mary. But he had been a realist as well, and had married his elder daughter, Claude, to the cousin who would inherit the throne, thus ensuring that a king of his bloodline, if not his name, would continue to rule France. He had not attempted to get rid of Anne when she failed to give him a son. (Admittedly, such an effort would have been tricky: years earlier he'd dumped his first wife to marry Anne and acquire her holdings in Brittany.)

There was yet another throne he might have looked to for an example of creating a workable succession through a daughter: Ferdinand and Isabella had managed it. When their only son, Juan, died without children, they focused on the sons their daughters would bear. The eldest son of Juana and her husband Philip the Handsome, Charles, became heir to both Spain and the Holy Roman Empire. The Spanish sovereigns enthusiastically embraced their grandchild as the future king of Aragon and Castile.

It was obvious, then, that women were not incapable of exercising political leadership, and it was also clear that a king could judiciously choose his daughter's husband in a way that enabled a smooth succession. By the standards of the day, such solutions were a sad necessity, and anyone, including Catherine herself, would sympathize with Henry's intense desire for a son to succeed him. Allowing Mary to succeed was fraught with peril for a country that had only recently emerged from dynastic civil strife.

The peril of such a course was not nearly as great as that of the path Henry ultimately chose, however—and his fanatic persistence in adhering to that path when it became apparent just how destructive it was suggests a different, and less political, motive. It was neither a conviction of the frailty of women nor the fear of throwing England into turmoil that lay behind Henry's determination to rid himself of Catherine of Aragon. Nor was it the charms of the elusive Ann. It was rather the greatest force in Henry's life: the monstrous ego that had until now gone unchallenged, and thus unnoticed. When the Spanish ambassador suggested to Henry that perhaps God had ordained that the succession should continue through Mary, Henry had angrily cried out three times, "Am I not a man like others?" But of course that wasn't what he meant. There were other men— even kings like Louis XII—who did not have sons to inherit their domains. As Lawrence Stone reports in *Crisis of the Aristocracy,* among the nobility of Henry's generation, 19 percent of first marriages were barren and 29 percent failed to produce living sons. Surely not all those sonless fathers had invoked God's wrath by marrying their dead brothers' wives. Nor did remarriage alleviate the problem, since second marriages proved even less fertile: 48 percent of second marriages in the sixteenth century were barren and 58 percent sonless. Like Henry, "other men" often had no male heirs. But some men did, and Henry was incensed that anyone should have something he could not. He did not want to be a man like other men, a man on whom God for his own mysterious purposes might visit inexplicable deprivations. He was a man *unlike* other men, better than other men, a man chosen by God to have everything he wanted. How then could he allow another man's son to accede to England's throne? He could not—any more than he could allow a pretty young woman to reject him. He must have what he wanted.

This was the essence of Henry's mind, his ego, and his stunning conception of the relationship between God's will and his own. Behind the tortuous explications of the Bible, the years of scholarly, legal, and religious debate, the slow destruction of Catherine of Aragon and the swift legal murder of Ann Boleyn lay one simple and pathological concept: God wanted Henry VIII to have whatever he wanted. Martin Luther had defected from Rome when his spiritual agony over his own unworthiness convinced him that human beings could not merit salvation: Henry merited not only salvation in the next life, but complete gratification in this one. Whereas his wife strove desperately to link her will to God's, Henry strove equally hard to link God's will to his.

Thus it was also crucial that he be right in his pursuit of what he wanted. He could not be a man who lusted as other men did; he could not be a man who yearned in vain for sons as other men did. His longings must all be gratified, because by definition they were noble longings. To allow Mary's succession would be to admit that he was indeed a man like others, subject to imperfection and to the humbling sufferings God imposed on his creatures.

If God saw Henry's needs as crucial, it was obvious God wanted Henry to have his son. Henry simply had to find out what he had done to prevent God's acquiescence to his wishes. It wasn't hard to guess. The marriage to Catherine of Aragon had required a papal dispensation since she was his brother's widow and canon law, based on the book of Leviticus, prohibited sexual relations with the wife of one's brother. He and the pope had been wrong all those years ago. God was displeased by the marriage, and had failed to bless it with sons. Another book of the Bible, Deuteronomy, actually said that a man should marry his brother's widow, to maintain his brother's line—but Henry didn't want to think about Deuteronomy. Leviticus was more interesting.

It's worth looking at the wording of the passage from Leviticus that Henry embraced so belatedly and so wholeheartedly: "And if a man shall take his brother's wife, it is an unclean thing; he hath uncovered his brother's nakedness; they shall be childless" (Lev. 20:21). Henry was not childless. Not all of Catherine's pregnancies ended in stillbirths: their first son had survived nearly two months. Even more important was the existence of the full-grown, healthy Princess Mary. Leviticus did not specify gender.

At some point, probably in 1526 or early in 1527, Henry secretly discussed his doubts with Cardinal Wolsey, who, if he and Henry are to be believed, was appalled. "I have often kneeled before him in his privy chamber on my knees, the space of an hour or two, to persuade him from his will and appetite: but I never could bring to pass to dissuade him therefrom."

However, Wolsey had little choice but to cater to the king's "will and appetite." On May 17, 1527, in his capacity as papal legate *a latere,* he set up a secret court in his palace in Westminster, ordering the king to answer the charge that he had spent the past eighteen years living in sin with his brother's widow. He cited the passage in Leviticus. So secret were the proceedings that Henry's partner in sin, Catherine, was kept in the dark.

Incredibly, Henry and Wolsey seemed to have thought that if they could rush the proceedings through, get the pope to rubber-stamp them, and then present Catherine with a fait accompli, she would cheerily concede that she had inadvertently been a whore for most of her adult life and birthed a bastard daughter.

The hearing was conducted with great solemnity and every trapping of legality. Together, Wolsey and William Warham, the Archbishop of Canterbury, were to rule on the case, with Richard Wolman acting as prosecutor and Dr. John Bell as Henry's not overly convincing defense. Had it gone according to plan, Warham would have accepted Henry's evidence, told him he was living in sin, pronounced the dispensation of Julius II invalid, and then announced the finding to the current pope, Clement VII. Further secret sessions were held on May 20, 23, and 31. Things didn't work out as Henry wanted, however. The court decided that more theological expertise was needed to bolster his position.

Then it became clear that it would take more than theologians to persuade Clement VII to dissolve Henry's marriage. As the English learned on June 1, hostilities between the Holy Roman emperor and the pope had taken a devastating turn. Charles V's troops, largely mercenaries, had sacked Rome, slaughtering lesser clerics and holding the pope prisoner in the Castel Sant' Angelo. Charles, though protesting his horror at the overzealousness of his troops, kept a tight rein on his captive, and Clement was in no position to offer a grave affront to the emperor's aunt Catherine.

If Henry imagined that he could keep his wife in ignorance for long, he seriously misgauged both her intelligence and the loyalty much of his court felt toward her. Catherine had learned of the clandestine hearing within hours of the first session. She was aghast. If Henry left her and married another woman, he would not only destroy her and her daughter's happiness; he would endanger his own immortal soul. She acted instantly, contacting the Spanish ambassador, Don Iñigo Mendoza, to tell him what was happening. The emperor and the pope, she wrote, must be told at once, and the pope must inform Wolsey that under no circumstances could the case be tried in England.

Henry apparently didn't realize that Catherine knew what he was up to, and on June 22 he finally decided to confront her with the news of his qualms of conscience. When he came to see her in her apartments, he said that he had been advised by learned and pious men that their marriage was in truth no marriage at all. He asked her to choose a place to retire to since they could no longer live together as husband and wife. The usually self-possessed queen burst into a storm of tears. Weeks of knowing secondhand about her husband's perfidy had not prepared Catherine for the blow of hearing it from his own lips.

Her first emotional outburst over, Catherine wasted little more time weeping. If Henry was truly going through with his insane plan, she must do all she could to stop him. She was not a woman much given to subterfuge, but when it was called for, she knew how to use it. It was crucial that she get a message to the one ally she could count on, her nephew Charles V. She knew Henry would have all messages from Mendoza seized. Among her most beloved servants was a Spaniard who had been with her since her arrival in England, Francisco Felipez. She conferred with him, and he agreed to take part in a dangerous plot. Felipez was to ask Henry's permission to visit his dying mother in Spain. The queen, he was to say, had refused his request, bitterly accusing him of using his mother as an excuse to desert her now that she was no longer in the king's favor.

Henry saw through the ruse, as Catherine must have known he would, but she also knew that it was too good an opportunity for the king to pass up. If one of Catherine's servants were caught smuggling messages out of the country at her behest, it might tarnish her saintly reputation among the people, and perhaps also give Henry useful information about the strategies she had in mind. He provided Felipez with the necessary passport and a show of sympathy for his dying mother. Then he issued secret orders for the man's arrest as soon as he reached Calais.

Felipez bypassed Calais. By the end of July, he was talking privately with the emperor in his palace near Valladolid, presenting Catherine's plea. Charles must demand that Henry drop his effort to annul their marriage. He must also insist that the pope revoke Wolsey's legatine authority and forbid the case to be tried in England. If the trial were in Rome, she was sure she would win. Charles promptly complied. He could be certain that Clement, at least, would heed his wishes. The blood had not yet dried in the streets of Rome.

With Catherine inexplicably refusing to collaborate in the destruction of her own marriage, Henry became increasingly aware of the need to garner support for the annulment and for his remarriage. At whatever stage the idea of marrying Ann Boleyn had entered the picture, it was definitely Henry's plan now. But his official stance was that he hoped only to confirm his daughter's legitimacy, and to learn that his marriage to his beloved Catherine was indeed valid. It was on these terms that he would approach the pope.

The support Henry sought was both ecclesiastical and political, and he sought it both at home and abroad. On July 22, Wolsey took himself off to France with a great entourage. The ostensible reason for his trip was to cement a new Anglo-French alliance. But from Henry's perspective the most important of Wolsey's tasks was to gain Francis's support for the annulment. This support was crucial in a situation that, at best, would greatly antagonize the third great European leader, Charles. Wolsey himself hoped to procure a French bride for Henry, who apparently managed to keep the extent of his feelings for Ann Boleyn secret from his chief minister.

Wolsey's trip abroad was a failure, and while he was gone Ann Boleyn and her coterie were able to solidify their influence with the king. When the cardinal returned to England in September, he found that Ann had supplanted not only Catherine of Aragon, but Thomas Cardinal Wolsey, in the king's affections. Riding straight to Richmond, Wolsey sent word to Henry of his return, asking where he might see him. But the king was with Ann, and she spoke for him. "Where else should the Cardinal come?" she asked grandly. "Tell him he may come here, where the King is." With a sinking heart, Wolsey did so. He had never liked Catherine of Aragon's influence over her husband. Now he saw that Catherine had been replaced by a woman who had even less affection for him—a woman who held the deadly weapon of Henry's utter infatuation.

Goaded on by Ann, Henry no longer trusted the man who had run his country for him while he played soldier-king. The reason for his turning against Wolsey is unclear. Perhaps it is true that Wolsey had begged him not to pursue the annulment, thus committing the unpardonable sin of telling Henry he couldn't have everything he wanted. Possibly Ann had convinced Henry that Wolsey was their enemy. Or maybe Henry had simply grown tired of Wolsey, as he had grown tired of Catherine. Catherine hadn't given him a son; Wolsey hadn't gotten him an annulment. Both were dispensable. With God on his side and Ann in his bed, Henry could begin again.

The king had started to undermine Wolsey while the cardinal was in France, sending the much less able diplomat William Knight to the pope, first with a preposterous plan, quickly abandoned, to ask for a dispensation to commit bigamy if Clement found Henry's marriage to Catherine valid; then with a request for a dispensation to marry any woman, regardless of whether she was already related to him in any of the ways prohibited by canon law, in the event that the first marriage was annulled. This was the earliest acknowledgement, however indirect, of his intention to marry Ann, whose sister had been his mistress, and of course it underscores the hypocrisy of his piety since canon law prohibited marriage with the sister of a wife or mistress.

Clement reworded the bull to eliminate any suggestion that the marriage to Catherine *was* invalid, thus making it worthless. Henry could marry Ann, in spite of his previous affair with her sister—but only if Clement found his marriage to Catherine invalid. He ignored the suggestion about bigamy. The pope was playing for time. But no one knew exactly what he wanted to do with that time.

Chapter 4

THE COURT OF TWO QUEENS

SIR THOMAS WYATT

This brilliant poet was a friend and reputed lover of Ann Boleyn,
later ending up in the Tower but not on the block.

enry was growing increasingly impatient with Clement's foot-dragging. An annulment wasn't such a hard thing to provide: an assiduous crew of canonists could always find some biblical byway. Louis XII had gotten an annulment; Charles Brandon had gotten two of them before marrying the lovely Princess Mary.

Even Henry's other sister, Margaret of Scotland, was trying, with every indication of ultimate success, to end her marriage to the Earl of Angus. Her battle with the Scottish lords to retain her regency had grown more bitter and more urgent. Along with living in open adultery with his mistress, Angus had joined forces with his wife's enemies. Sexual betrayal might be overlooked, but treason was another matter. Margaret could not survive politically with Angus as her husband, and she had found another man whose loyalty she was certain of, Henry Stewart, later the Earl of Methven. So she looked around and discovered, conveniently, that Angus had been contracted to someone else at the time of their marriage.

Henry was outraged by Margaret's behavior. The fact that Margaret had already chosen her next husband increased his fury. Taking time from his own spouse-shedding efforts, he dictated a scathing letter, reminding her that "the divine ordinance of inseparable matrimony" was first instituted in paradise. "What charge of conscience, what grudge and fretting, yea what danger of damnation" she was subjecting herself to! "Relinquish the adulterous company of him that is not nor may not of right be your husband." Her daughter—"so goodly a creature, so virtuous a lady"—would be perceived as a bastard.

One wonders if Ann Boleyn was with him when he dictated this letter to Wolsey—sitting on his knee, perhaps, or watching from a corner, smiling quietly to herself. One wonders as well if she spared a thought, as Henry did not, for Henry's own goodly and virtuous daughter.

Unimpeded by her brother's moral suasions, Margaret got her annulment in December 1527—having added to her suit the ludicrous suggestion that her first husband hadn't really been killed at Flodden Field but rather died sometime after her second marriage. It must have seemed to Henry that if his sister, acting out of mere self-interest, was able to get her marriage annulled, he, acting on God's behalf, could surely get his. Perhaps, if the timing had been better, or if Catherine had come from a less powerful family, he would have.

But the pope was in no position to grant Henry the annulment he willingly gave Margaret. For one thing, Henry's marriage itself had been the result of a papal dispensation granted by Julius II, and the basis of his suit was that the dispensation had been wrongly granted. For another, although Clement had fled Castel Sant' Angelo for the somewhat safer town of Orvieto, the emperor's power over him remained firm. Furthermore, he wasn't convinced that Henry's lack of a son meant God frowned on his marriage. The pope would need strong canonical proof that the union was invalid if, as seemed inevitable, Catherine and her nephew fought the annulment. All of Christendom would be watching the trial— and the papacy. Clement did not want to alienate Charles, he did not want to alienate Henry, and he did not want to undercut papal authority as represented by his predecessor. His greatest hope was to drag the matter out until the problem somehow solved itself.

Henry's tactics offered him a way to do that. The king was claiming, publicly and loudly, that it was not an annulment per se that he wanted, but simply an investigation into the legality of his marriage. Clement could not have believed him. By now, everyone in Europe knew of Henry's involvement with Ann. But the pope could pretend to take Henry at his word. He would give Henry his investigation, and he would, against Catherine's wishes, allow it to take place in England. But not with Wolsey running the show. Instead, Wolsey would merely be the assessor, the secondary judge. For the chief judge he chose one of the most intriguing figures in the murky history of what was now being called "the king's great matter."

Lorenzo Cardinal Campeggio had come late to the priesthood, a widower with grown children who had been a professor of canon law before taking holy orders. Since then he had become one of the most distinguished canonists in Europe and risen quickly up the clerical ranks. Like Clement, he was worldly and sophisticated. He had old connections with England. He had spent a year there in 1518, during which time the king had given him a palace and the lucrative bishopric of Salisbury. Henry might well have believed that Clement chose Campeggio as papal legate to England to preserve a semblance of objectivity while giving his friend the king exactly what he wanted.

But Campeggio was the pope's man, not Henry's, and the pope wanted delay. Campeggio's health was poor—he suffered from severe gout—and he was not looking forward to a long journey culminating in what could only be distressing confrontations with the impatient king and his injured wife. Wolsey had demanded that the pope sign a promise to comply with any decision reached by the court in England. Clement signed the decree, but secretly took two steps to assure its uselessness. First he ordered Campeggio never to allow it to leave his hands. Then he told him to take no action on the hearings until he got word from Clement himself.

A virulent outbreak of the sweating sickness hit England in July 1528, shortly before the legate was scheduled to begin his long journey. To Campeggio and Clement, the epidemic was a blessing. What a relief it would be if one of the three principals in the king's great matter were to die! Campeggio waited in Rome until the epidemic ended.

Henry was terrified. Caught in his self-spun fantasy about God's anger, he must have wondered if this was a divine judgement. One of Ann's ladies was struck, and Henry promptly ordered his beloved to stay at Hever Castle while he and his court, including Catherine, frantically sped from one residence to another in an attempt to outrun the disease. Ann caught the sweats. Henry sent her one of his physicians, Dr. William Butts, while remaining with the woman he insisted was no longer his wife.

Ann survived. Her brother-in-law, the cuckolded William Carey, was less fortunate. His death left the king's old mistress Mary Boleyn destitute. Ann wrote Henry, asking for his help. The king exerted pressure on Ann's father to help out the family black sheep, and extended to Mary an annuity of £100. Typically, Henry could not resist moralizing about his former mistress, whom he characterized as a sinful Eve. If Ann had any doubts about the wisdom of withholding her favors from Henry, his cavalier attitude toward the sister he had once used must have dispelled them.

On October 9, Campeggio arrived in London, his gout torturing him so badly that he was bedridden for two weeks before he could see the king. When he did so, it was to try to convince Henry that the verse from Leviticus didn't apply to his marriage. But Henry was adamant, and he had organized his arguments with great efficiency. Campeggio was impressed with Henry's knowledge of canon law, but not with his conclusions. They quickly reached a stalemate.

Unable to move Henry, Campeggio turned to the disagreeable task of dealing with Catherine. Clement had instructed the legate that, if Henry refused to give in, he should propose to the queen that she enter a convent. Canonical precedent would in that case permit the pope to dissolve her marriage, with no reference to the original dispensation. It would have been a graceful, pleasant way out for the queen. She was religious and ascetic already, and a wealthy convent would offer her as much comfort as she required. The vow of chastity would prove little burden to a wife whose husband's distaste had long since forced celibacy on her. Her daughter's legitimacy would not be questioned, and Mary would remain in the line of succession, second only to whatever son followed in the wake of her father's second marriage.

Catherine would not consider it. She had no religious vocation. It was common practice for women and men to enter the religious life for worldly reasons, as Wolsey had done. But for the truly pious, this was sacrilege. The concept of vocation has always been an integral part of Catholicism: one is called to the religious life or the married life, and one honors that call. Catherine told Campeggio firmly "that she intended to live and die in the estate of matrimony to which God had called her." Henry, Wolsey, Campeggio, the pope himself could juggle canonical texts to make them conform to their own wills, but Catherine could not.

She could, however, see the irony of the suggestion. Blandly she told Campeggio that she would consider taking vows as a religious—provided Henry followed suit. Campeggio missed the bitter humor, and took her remark at face value. He wrote to Clement seriously suggesting that Henry might take a temporary vow of chastity with the promise of a future dispensation. Clement, with more perspective, ignored the suggestion.

There was no hope, then, for an amicable resolution. There would have to be a trial.

❧ It's harder to feel sympathy for Ann during these months of waiting than it is for Catherine. Yet Ann too was trapped, in a situation she had only partially chosen. Henry had been confident that he had only to let Catherine and the pope know about his doubts and the marriage would be annulled. Ann, unfamiliar with the complexities of canon law, had been swept up in his confidence.

Like Henry, she may have assumed that Catherine would go along with the annulment. One can hardly blame her. Ann had not lived with Catherine for twenty years, as Henry had. Probably she reasoned that

Catherine would do what she herself would in that situation—take the most comfortable path. Ann's own spiritual leanings were taking her further and further from the Catholicism that for Catherine was the core of her being, and someone who had no feeling for the religious life would be unlikely to understand the queen's revulsion toward abusing it. Nor did she share Catherine's concern for Henry's soul. She did not love him—probably not at all, and certainly not with the deep devotion that twenty years of marriage had instilled in her rival. She may even have convinced herself that Catherine would be better off without the husband who no longer loved her.

Catherine didn't see it that way, and without Catherine's cooperation, the pope was in an increasingly difficult position. Though she disliked Wolsey, Ann realized that he still had some influence on the king, and probably on the pope. She set out to court him, flattering his epicurean skills and hinting that she would be grateful for a gift of carp from his famous fishponds for her lenten meals. She wrote him a friendly letter in July 1528, and demanded that Henry add a postscript. The cardinal responded in kind, and for a time the two enemies appeared to be the best of friends.

Meanwhile, Ann found herself shifted back and forth between court and country. Henry wanted her with him at all times, but it wasn't practical. When they got the news that Campeggio was on his way to London, it was important that Henry maintain his facade of concerned inquiry, which was hardly possible if the woman Henry planned to marry was conspicuously by his side. In September 1528 he sent Ann to Hever Castle while he stayed at court, where Catherine remained. Ann recognized the wisdom of this, but it must have been unnerving, especially when she heard that he had publicly announced his love for Catherine to a group of London citizens. The queen, Henry told his eager audience, was "a woman of most gentleness, of most humility and buxomness, yea and of all good qualities appertaining to nobility, she is without comparison. . . . If I were to marry again, if the marriage be good, I would surely choose her above all other women." He followed this impassioned speech with a visit to Ann at Hever, destroying the possibility that Campeggio or anyone else would believe him.

Shortly afterward Ann returned to London, where she lived in a suite of apartments at the palace at Greenwich. At least Henry had the taste not to reinstate her as a lady-in-waiting to Catherine, but the picture of all three living together at court is an unattractive one.

To the outside world, it must have appeared as though there were two queens at Greenwich—Catherine holding her usual low-key court, Ann holding a gayer one with visitors and festivities. Henry was constantly giving Ann ornate gifts, which she took no effort to hide. She even began distributing "cramp rings"—rings blessed by the monarch that were believed to alleviate painful cramps. Campeggio wrote to Clement that Henry "cannot do without her for an hour" and was constantly "kissing her and treating her as though she were his wife."

Catherine too appeared cheerful at first. Ironically Henry took exception to this. Whereas earlier he had been upset by her tears, he was now affronted by her smiles. He sent messengers with a list of grievances to her. One stated that His Majesty was "persuaded by her behavior that she did not love him. She exhorted the ladies and gentlemen of her court to dance and make merry pastime, though it would be better for her to exhort them to pray that God would send some good end in this matter. She shows no pensiveness in her countenance, nor in her apparel nor behavior." Presumably rejection by Henry called for an air of perpetual gloom.

Sadly for Catherine, her gaiety was all show. She did love Henry, and losing him was the greatest personal sorrow of her life. But she was a princess, and her personal emotions were never her chief concern. As a woman she suffered, but as a queen she must go about her business. At the moment, that business was the struggle to preserve her title.

The calm efficiency with which Catherine pursued her task was far more threatening to Henry than her display of cheerfulness. From the beginning the queen had insisted that since her marriage to Arthur had never been consummated, it was not a true marriage. Any secondary substantiation of her marriage's validity would, however, be useful to her case. In the spring of 1528 information had come into her hands that could be used if the legatine court refused to accept her word. Her nephew the emperor had been busy investigating the original dispensation. The son of the former Spanish ambassador Roderigo de Puebla had given to Charles his father's private papers. Among them was a second brief issued by Pope Julius II, with the same date as the first, but with significant differences in phrasing. For one thing, it assumed that the marriage to Arthur had been consummated; for another, it added that there were "other reasons" besides those already given for granting the dispensation. At the very least, the document invalidated the bull Clement had so reluctantly sent with Campeggio to England, since that bull had been drawn up on the basis of the original dispensation alone. Charles sent a copy of the document to his aunt.

Advisers had been appointed to help Catherine with her case, all English and all handpicked by Henry. (The one Spaniard, her old friend Juan Luis Vives, had shown himself too much her advocate and had been sent back to Flanders.) She handed over to them all the documents for her defense, including the new brief. They promptly told the king about it.

Wolsey claimed the document a forgery, and demanded that the original be sent to England. He had Catherine's counselors present her with a letter demanding that she write to the emperor, asking him, "for her sake and her child's," to send the document to Henry. At first she demurred, but later the council, charging her with disobedience to the king, forced her to write a letter its members dictated. She was also forced to swear that she would write no other letter.

Fortunately, in extracting their vow from a woman who, unlike her husband, honored vows, the counselors didn't think to make her swear she would send no oral message to her nephew. Her access to Mendoza was by now severely limited, but she managed to get word to him, and he showed up in her apartments in disguise. Once again, they called on the brave and loyal Francisco Felipez, but this time he was caught by Wolsey's spies, who beat him badly enough to break his arm. Since he carried no letter, the spies found nothing to incriminate him, and he was allowed to go free.

Catherine and Mendoza had to find another messenger. Henry had determined that her letter should be borne by one of her chaplains, the English priest Thomas Abell, whom she distrusted. But accompanying Abell was a Spanish interpreter, Juan de Montoya, whom Catherine believed dependable. She gave him her verbal message to Margaret of Austria, who continued to serve as the Hapsburg regent in the Netherlands, telling her to ignore Catherine's letter and under no circumstances to let the document out of her hands.

At some point in their journey, Montoya told Abell of the queen's secret message. We don't know what Abell's views about the annulment were before this. Wolsey trusted him and Catherine didn't, so if he had any reservations about Henry's actions, he was presumably quiet about them. Now, however, he revealed himself to be the queen's staunch champion. Horrified that a messenger would reveal crucial information to someone other than its intended hearer, Abell took over the job of communicating the queen's case to Margaret. He repeated Catherine's message, adding his own adamant agreement, and told the regent that Charles could offer instead a notarized copy, which would be valid in an ecclesiastical court. Returning to England, he resumed his chaplaincy and in his spare time wrote a book against the king's case. His support of the queen remained unwavering, and he spent the last six years of his life in the Tower, leaving it only for his execution in 1540.

Henry was becoming increasingly aware that neither his knowledge of canon law nor his moral righteousness was going to make ridding himself of Catherine easy. If God wanted Henry out of his sonless marriage, he evidently wanted him to work for his freedom. Fiercely Henry demanded that the trial begin. Campeggio, suffering a renewed attack of gout and dearly wishing he'd never come near England, began the proceedings. "God help me," he wrote wearily to Clement.

The court opened on June 18. Henry sent a proxy. Catherine appeared briefly, to formally protest the hearings and appeal her case to Rome.

Three days later the court met again, in a scene so magnificently dramatic even Shakespeare hardly improved on it. It was, says Cavendish, "the strangest and newest sight or device that ever was read or heard in history . . . a king and a queen should be convented or constrained to appear in court as common people." The king was seated on the right, on a dais, with the queen next to him, but her chair lower. Campeggio and Wolsey sat below Henry, resplendent in their red robes and huge gold crosses. The judges, the bishops, the great nobility crowded the courtroom, while outside the common people thronged, some sympathetic to the king, some to the queen, some simply curious about this unprecedented trial.

"King Henry of England, come to the court," called the crier.

Henry responded loudly, "Here, my lords."

"Catherine, Queen of England, come to the court."

Catherine did not answer. Instead she rose slowly, and walking to her husband, knelt at his feet. "Sir, I beseech you, for the love that has been between us, and for the love of God, let me have justice and right, take of me some pity and compassion, for I am a poor woman and a stranger born out of your dominion. I have here no assured friend, and much less indifferent council. I flee to you as to the head of justice within this realm." The pain at his betrayal rang through her words: "Alas sir, where have I offended you, or what occasion of displeasure have I deserved against your will or pleasure?"

The king said nothing. What could he say? She had offended him by not having the sons she had wanted as much as he had; she had offended him by growing old. Proudly, she went on. "I take God and all the world to witness that I have been to you a true, humble, and obedient wife." Then she answered, indirectly, his use of Leviticus, implicitly reminding him that God had not, in fact, punished the couple by making them childless. "By me you have had divers children, although it hath pleased God to call them from out of this world."

Then she went on to address the question of her marriage to Henry's brother. She had not truly been Arthur's wife, she told Henry in front of the court, because the marriage had not been consummated. "When ye had me at the first, I take God to be my judge, I was a true maid, without touch of man. And whether this be true or no, I put it to your conscience." Henry said nothing. "If there be any just cause by the law that you can allege against me, either of dishonesty or any other impediment, to put me from you, I am content to depart, to my great shame and dishonor. If there be none, I must lowly beseech you, let me remain in my former estate." She spoke a few minutes longer, then rose, curtsied to the king, and slowly moved toward the doors of the great hall.

Startled, the crier called, "Catherine, Queen of England, come to the court." She ignored him.

Her gentleman-usher Griffith said to her, "Madam, ye be called again."

"It matters not," she said. "This is no indifferent court for me. I will not tarry."

After an awkward silence, Henry rose and publicly agreed that Catherine was as good a wife as any man could want, that he had no displeasure "in the queen's person or age," and that he would like nothing better than to stay with her, if only their marriage weren't forbidden by God. After all his machinations, including the proposal of a legally bigamous marriage, and with Ann Boleyn continually by his side or on his lap, the words rang hollow.

The king's speech was followed by Wolsey's begging him to tell the court that the annulment was his own idea and not the cardinal's. "Nay, my Lord Cardinal," Henry said, a little too emphatically for Wolsey's comfort. "Ye have been rather against me."

So ended the first session. Catherine did not attend the next two, and perhaps it was just as well. The first point the court addressed was the consummation of her marriage to Arthur. Witnesses were called to swear that the prince had made references to his sexual prowess after his wedding night. "It is a good pastime, Sir, to have a wife," he had supposedly boasted, and had called for ale, thirsty because he had "been in Spain this night." Several of the noblemen reminded the court that Arthur was not too young to have consummated a marriage, since they themselves "did carnally know and use a woman" at the same age.

These impressive recollections completed, Archbishop Warham read out the names of all the bishops who had endorsed the annulment. When Warham got to the name of the holder of the see of Rochester, Margaret Beaufort's old confessor Bishop Fisher startled the court by rising from his seat and angrily crying, "That is not my hand nor seal!" Warham sputtered, then claimed Fisher had agreed that Warham could sign for him, and affix the seal himself. Icily Fisher replied, "There is no thing more untrue."

The trial dragged on for weeks, getting nowhere. At one point Campeggio, pressed by Henry, went with Wolsey to visit Catherine. Both men once more asked her to retire to a convent, and she once more refused. Then on July 23, the day the courts recessed for summer in Rome, Campeggio suddenly declared that as this was a Roman court, it would recess until October. By then, of course, it could not be continued, as the cardinal well knew. Clement had secretly decided to revoke the case to Rome.

Campeggio remained in England through the summer, finally leaving in October—the month when the court was supposed to have reconvened. At the customs house in Dover, several of the king's agents ransacked his luggage, searching, apparently, for the decretal bull Clement had sent with him. They found nothing but "old hosen and old coats"; the bull had long since been burned. On October 26, with what must have been a great sigh of relief, Cardinal Campeggio left England behind him forever.

Catherine may have hoped that, with the case moved to Rome, Henry would realize his annulment was a lost cause. But it was not in Henry's makeup either to reconsider his conviction that God wanted him rid of Catherine, or to cut his losses. Furious at being thwarted, he now wanted revenge.

Catherine was too popular for Henry to harm her without antagonizing his people. But there was someone else he could take his frustrations out on, someone the people hated. Wolsey had brought Campeggio back to England with him; Wolsey represented the church, the pope, the forces that were keeping Henry from marrying Ann. It made no difference that Henry himself had dictated the strategy Wolsey had reluctantly used for getting the annulment. It mattered even less that Wolsey had been his loyal servant for twenty years, running the country while Henry played crusader. Wolsey had outlasted his usefulness.

Moreover, Ann hated Wolsey for having destroyed her relationship with Henry Percy years before. She was angry, frustrated, and scared, and she took it out on the still-besotted king. There were stormy scenes.

Henry did not love her, she cried. He was keeping her from a respectable marriage, and soon she would be too old for a husband and children. She screamed; she fled from him, and returned weeping, telling Henry that Wolsey was the source of their inability to wed.

The king could simultaneously appease his beloved and vent his own ire on his prelate. At first he settled for petty insults—refusing to see the cardinal, openly ridiculing him in meetings of the king's council. On the day Campeggio went to court to request permission to leave England, Wolsey went with him. Court was at Grafton in Northamptonshire, and Wolsey, after taking Campeggio to his rooms, asked where his own were. He was told that there were no rooms for him. Only one person had the courage to offer kindness to the snubbed cardinal. Henry Norris, the king's groom of the stool, told Wolsey that the smallness of the house probably explained the king's oversight, and offered his own rooms to the cardinal until better could be found.

There was little beyond such small courtesies that anyone could do to help Wolsey. A month later Henry took the chancellorship from him. Heartbroken, Wolsey retired, on the king's orders, to the small palace of Esher, close to the magnificent Hampton Court, the residence he had built for his own glory and later given to Henry. Shortly afterward he was sent to York to take up his duties as archbishop—duties he had not thought about in fifteen years. But exile from court and the politics that had been Wolsey's life was not enough for Henry. On November 4, 1530, the cardinal was arrested on trumped-up charges of treason. The official charge was praemunire—a long-unused prohibition of appealing to a foreign legal authority any plea that should be tried in the king's courts. Since the pope was a foreign ruler, praemunire was a potent weapon against the clergy. The fact that Wolsey had appealed to Rome on Henry's orders was conveniently overlooked.

On the way to London, Wolsey was struck with a severe stomach ailment, and he died before he reached Henry. He had, in his own words, served his king better than he had served his God. His king had repaid him as he would many others.

In one of his efforts to placate Henry, the cardinal had given him York Place. Renaming it Whitehall, Henry renovated it and gave it to Ann, who made certain there were no lodgings there suitable for Catherine. From now on, when Henry came to see her, he would see her alone. Shortly after Ann moved to Whitehall, Henry made her father Earl of Wiltshire and her brother George Viscount Rochford. In celebration he gave a banquet at Whitehall. Ann, now Lady Ann Rochford, sat by the king's side, and she was given formal precedence over all the other ladies at court, as though she was already the queen.

But Henry continued to visit Catherine and to maintain an amiable public relationship with her. Meanwhile, a figure appeared on the scene who would become one of Catherine's staunchest allies. Eustache Chapuys, the new imperial ambassador, is one of history's more engaging minor characters. "A footnote to English history," as Catherine's biographer Garrett Mattingly dubbed him, he provided Catherine with the support she so desperately needed in her long, lonely battle. His letters to the emperor, loaded with rich detail and pungent wit, have given us much of what we know about the years following the first annulment efforts, the reign of Ann Boleyn, and its aftermath. Chapuys was fiercely partisan, beyond the requirements of his master, for Catherine and her daughter seem to have brought out the strong streak of chivalry in this otherwise cynical diplomat. His affection for Catherine and Mary was matched only by his contempt for Ann. Even after her coronation, he would refer to Ann at best only as "the Lady"; in his less polite moments, she was "the concubine." He soon had a rich spy network reporting to him on every aspect of court life, and he especially reveled in anything negative he heard about Ann. Despite his obvious bias he was able to establish a good relationship with Henry, for he knew how to flatter the king, with whom he affected an air of virile camaraderie in the face of irrational womanhood.

Unfortunately for Chapuys and for others loyal to Catherine, another figure appeared on the scene that same autumn. Thomas Cranmer was a timid, unprepossessing cleric at Cambridge, whom two of Henry's advisers on ecclesiastical law, Stephen Gardiner and Edward Fox, happened to meet in their lodgings near the court at Waltham. Conversation over dinner turned to the annulment, and the quiet scholar offered the observation that it was theologians, not experts in canon law, who could provide the answer the king sought. The remark changed his life, pulling him out of the satisfying obscurity of Cambridge and into the dramatic world of Henry's court.

Fox reported Cranmer's remark to Henry, who was thrilled to learn of any possible way out of the stalemate. Henry summoned the cleric and was impressed by his logic and the scope of his knowledge. Cranmer, whose religious sympathies were close to Lutheran, proposed that the decision about the annulment should be made not by the pope with his army of canonists, but by the divines in England's universities. If they agreed the marriage was invalid, then the Archbishop of Canterbury could officially dissolve it and Henry could remarry. The king was charmed. Immediately he gave Cranmer two jobs: to write a treatise expounding his views, and to serve as the Boleyn family's chaplain.

Henry had threatened Clement with a break from Rome, but until now it had been bluster. The bluster had failed; with the adjournment of the court at Blackfriars, it was extremely unlikely that Henry would get his annulment from the pope. Now here was a way to turn the threat into reality. Henry, the Defender of the Faith who had vociferously championed the pope against Luther and other heretics, had found a respectable voice to suggest that he didn't need the pope after all.

Ann had probably been making similar suggestions herself. Her progressive beliefs fitted nicely with her ambitions, and she must have welcomed Cranmer, with his objectivity and his air of academic disinterest, as the perfect ally. She had been reading William Tyndale's *Obedience of a Christian Man,* which eloquently set forth the idea that the king ruled by divine right and must be obeyed in everything. No matter that Tyndale was a heretic living in exile; no matter that Ann was breaking the law by reading his book, which Henry had banned—his work was now useful to Henry. According to the Protestant author of the Book of Martyrs, John Foxe, Ann lent Henry other "heretical" books, and there seems little doubt that she used her position with the king to foster her own evangelical Christianity. Ann had become an intellectual as well as an emotional influence on Henry.

She had also become increasingly demanding. The scenes, the tantrums escalated.

Occasionally Henry still spent time with Catherine, visiting her apartments, having her mend his shirts as she had in the old days. She too was angry, adamantly refusing to accept the premise, as she sat stitching his shirts and talking about their daughter, that she had never been his wife.

Some biographers paint a sympathetic picture of Henry at this stage, henpecked by two domineering women, unable to escape hysterical diatribes wherever he went. The sympathy misses the point. Both women had reason to complain, and both were wholly in his power. It was Henry who had created the conditions about which Catherine and Ann so bitterly complained. It is not the king who warrants our sympathy, fleeing from one set of apartments to another in search of a peace he would sacrifice nothing to attain.

As he tried to have it both ways with Ann and Catherine, Henry also tried, for a time, to have it both ways with the pope. He was still appealing to Clement to grant an annulment, sending a petition signed by all the peers of the realm as well as a group of bishops and abbots. At the same time, Cranmer's ideas were slowly being implemented. Edward Fox put together an extensive list of all the scriptural and historical arguments by which Henry could declare his marriage null without the pope's approval and gave it to the king in the summer of 1530. Called the *Collectanea satis copiosa,* it proved a valuable tool in the king's startling new effort.

Henry's next step was to put together a plan, to be proposed to the upcoming Parliament, that would empower the Archbishop of Canterbury to decide on the validity of the king's marriage. Since God wanted Henry to free himself of Catherine and the pope wasn't helping him to do so, God no longer spoke through the pope. Unfortunately for Henry, God didn't seem overly anxious to speak through the Archbishop of Canterbury either. Archbishop Warham, who 20 years earlier had opposed Henry's marriage to his brother's widow, could not now bring himself to support its dissolution. But he was old and ailing. Having destroyed Cardinal Wolsey, Henry was reluctant to throw Archbishop Warham into the Tower. He waited.

Meanwhile a third major newcomer had emerged—a clerk who had been in Wolsey's employ. Thomas Cromwell entered the king's service in January 1530, and by the end of the year was on the king's council. Like Wolsey, he knew how to read Henry, and like Wolsey, he was a brilliant politician. Unlike Wolsey, he saw no need to flaunt his rise from the lower classes. Quietly he gained Henry's confidence. By 1533 he was chancellor of the exchequer. A brilliant administrator and a shrewd politician who had been influenced by Machiavelli, Cromwell knew how to flatter, how to insinuate ideas into Henry's mind, so that the king would believe them to be his own. It was Cromwell who first seems to have introduced the notion that Henry could declare himself head of the church of England.

All this was taking a long time, and the strain was beginning to show on the would-be queen. On New Year's Day 1531 Ann was saying, in Chapuys's hearing, that "she cared not for the queen or any of her family, and that she would rather see her hanged than have to confess that she was her queen and mistress." Both Parliament and the convocation of the clergy met that month and were accused of praemunire, but were able to buy a pardon for £100,000. Chapuys wryly noted, "Of this writ of Praemunire, there is no one in England who knows anything. Its whole basis is in the imagination of the king, who comments and amplifies it at pleasure, connecting it with any case he chooses."

Parliament was also faced with a list of demands, chief of which was that Henry be styled "protector and only supreme head of the English Church." The clergy responded by adding a clause that weakened the title considerably: Henry was head of the church "as far as the law of Christ allows"—a formula that kept the pope very much in the picture. It was only a mild defeat for Henry, and he was encouraged to continue to separate the church of England from the Church of Rome. He still wanted the pope's approval, however, and spent much time and effort trying to get Clement to agree to try his case somewhere other than Rome. Months were passing; years were passing. Catherine still held the title of queen, and Ann, though she apparently continued to avoid Henry's bed, was still the concubine.

And she was losing supporters. The Duke of Suffolk had originally backed Henry, although his wife, Henry's sister Mary, was staunchly behind Catherine. Forced to deliver many of Henry's hostile messages to Catherine, Suffolk never relished the task. Now he began to pull away from Ann and to express his own views openly, if cautiously. In the spring of 1531 he told Henry that Catherine would obey Henry only after two others. Henry asked who the others were, presumably expecting them to be the pope and the emperor. Suffolk answered, no, they were God first and her conscience second. Henry ignored his friend; enamored as he was of his own conscience, the king never acknowledged anyone else's.

The Duchess of Norfolk also withdrew her support for Ann, her husband's niece. She had always been fond of Catherine, and her fondness was probably strengthened by Henry's behavior, for Elizabeth Howard was herself not only a betrayed wife but a battered wife. In 1526 the duke had taken as mistress Bess Holland, a laundress in the Norfolk household, and the relationship lasted for years. When his wife quarreled with him over it, he attacked her with a dagger, pulled her out of her bed by the hair, and, as she later reported, "set his women to bind me until blood came out of my fingers' ends, and pinacled me, and set on my breast til I spit blood." She had cause to identify with the queen. The duchess sent Catherine a gift of oranges, in one of which she had hidden a secret message; soon she was sending more information about Henry's tactics. Her usefulness as a spy was weakened by her open hostility to Ann, however, and she was banned from court in the spring of 1532.

Others were demonstrating their hostility in uglier ways. A nasty cartoon drawing found its way into Ann's chambers, depicting a man labeled *H* and two women, *K* and *A*. *A* had no head. Ann showed it to her waiting woman Ann Gainsford. "Come hither, Nan, see here a book of prophesy; this he saith is the king, this the queen, and this is myself with my head off."

Ann Gainsford shuddered. "If I thought it were true, though he were an emperor, I would not myself marry him with that condition."

Defiantly, Ann answered, "Yes, Nan, I think the book a bauble, yet by the hope I have that the realm may be happy by my issue, I am resolved to have him, whatever might become of me."

The situation was tense for both Henry and Ann, and they fought constantly, following their quarrels with penitent, passionate reconciliations. Henry was still enraptured by his alluring virgin, and increasingly angry with Catherine.

On Friday, July 14, he took one more step away from the queen. Until then they had still lived together at court, wherever that happened to be. Now, as he left with Ann on his summer progress, he ordered Catherine to stay at Windsor. Henceforth, though they would attend state occasions together, he would not live with her, but with Ann. Shortly afterward he had the council send Catherine an order to move to the More, one of Wolsey's old houses—without Mary. The last condition was sheer spite, and the best punishment he could have come up with, for the only person Catherine loved as much as her husband was her daughter.

Henry continued to send deputations to harass Catherine. One arrived at the More in October. After the usual round of fruitless and by now wholly familiar arguments, they warned her that if her obstinacy continued Henry would send her to a yet more distant manor. That was fine, she told them. She would go anywhere her husband ordered her—even the stake, if he so commanded. It was only when his will countermanded God's that she would resist him.

At the More Catherine continued to put on a good face, so the Venetian diplomats who visited her in November found her in comfortable and seemingly contented state. They reported to their master that the English people loved her "more than any queen who ever reigned," and uniformly opposed the divorce.

Ironically, Henry and Ann's efforts to simulate cheerfulness were less successful, and the chronicler Hall mournfully notes that during the Christmas festivities at Greenwich "there was no mirth because the queen and her ladies were absent." Ann could act like a queen, but everyone knew she wasn't one, and might never be. On New Year's Day 1532 Henry did not give Catherine a gift and ordered his courtiers to follow his example. He returned her gift of a gold cup, commanding her to send him no more presents.

Meanwhile, Ann's anger at the pope and her evangelical sympathies had intensified. Henry was no evangelical, but his hostility to the papacy was certainly keeping pace with Ann's, and he was willing to use a cautious flirtation with the reformers to advance his own cause. But it must have been difficult for the man who had gotten a pope to dub him Defender of the Faith to sever that bond. (Ironically, Martin Luther opposed the divorce.) Henry was becoming what he had once despised: a schismatic—in fact, a heretic. Ann, Cromwell, and Cranmer were pushing him into a radical stance that he would never in his heart wholly embrace.

Had there been no other disaffection for the papacy in England than Henry's own, his efforts to overthrow papal power in his country could not have succeeded. But there was plenty of anger to coalesce with his, for, in addition to withholding Henry's annulment, the church had genuine abuses to answer for. Cromwell knew how to use these to the king's advantage. After Parliament convened in January 1532, the Commons, under Cromwell's subtle guidance, presented Henry with the Supplication against the Ordinaries (bishops or their deputies who acted as judges in the spiritual courts), listing a range of grievances against the church. Most important among these was that the clergy "daily make divers and many fashions of laws, constitutions and ordinances concerning temporal things . . . not having . . . your most royal assent."

The convocation of the clergy was given an opportunity to respond, for Henry always liked the trappings of fairness to attend his most tyrannical actions. As he had suddenly discovered Leviticus eighteen years after his marriage, so he now discovered something else—"the prelates at their consecration make an oath to the pope clean contrary to the oath they make to us, so that they seem his subjects and not ours." They had made this oath for centuries; it was odd that a monarch who prided himself on his mastery of theology and canon law had only just noticed it.

Months of wrangling followed, with Stephen Gardiner persuasively arguing for the church's independence from the king. Gardiner had supported the annulment—he had no investment in the king's marriage to Catherine—but now his own privilege as a churchman was in danger. His eloquence earned him a stinging rebuke from Henry, and he quickly pulled back, offering Ann his luxurious estate at Hansworth by way of apology. On May 15, the clergy backed down completely. With the Submission of the Clergy, Henry was given virtual control over the church of

England. The next day Henry's onetime friend Thomas More resigned the chancellorship. Henry eventually gave the post to his lackey Thomas Audley.

Catherine, isolated at the More, continued her lonely fight to retain her title, with the support of a few loyal friends and the imperial ambassador. Emotionally, her greatest support came from her oldest friend, Maria de Salinas, now the widowed Countess Willoughby, who had been her lady-in-waiting since they had arrived together from Spain as young girls. Marriage and motherhood had not separated the lady from her mistress.

With Maria's encouragement and Chapuys's help, Catherine continued writing to pope and emperor. Charles was now at war with the Turks, who were invading Hungary. Catherine, knowing what a threat the "infidel" was to Christianity, warned him that heresy in England was equally threatening. Her language is sad and significant: "I see no difference in what these people are attempting here and what the Enemy of our Faith aims at where you are," she said.

"These people" were Ann Boleyn, Cromwell, Cranmer—everyone but Henry. Catherine would always see Henry as a victim, misled by the machinations of others: never would she face the fact that her fate was his doing. The Henry of her dreams was the gentle prince who had rescued her more than 20 years before, not the self-centered tyrant who had created the hell she lived in now. After warning the emperor that the annulment carried with it the certainty of heresy taking over England, she ended poignantly, "What goes on here is so ugly and against God, and touches so nearly the honor of my lord, the King, that I cannot bear to write it."

In the summer of 1532 Warham died. Both Catherine and Chapuys realized that Henry would replace him with Cranmer, whom Chapuys described as "being devoted heart and soul to the Lutheran sect." It was perhaps an exaggeration, but Cranmer was certainly a reformer, and no friend of the papacy. His consecration (ironically, ratified by the pope) as Archbishop of Canterbury in the middle of the following year hastened the end of Catherine's hopes.

On September 1, Henry took an important but ambiguous step toward regularizing his relationship with Ann. In a grand ceremony held at Windsor Castle, bejeweled and with her long hair flowing about her shoulders, Ann was invested with the title Marchioness of Pembroke. It was the first time a woman was given such a title in her own right and not simply by virtue of being the wife of a marquis. Significantly, the title was to pass to "heirs male of her body," and the usual phrase "lawfully begotten" was absent from the wording of the investiture. Perhaps Ann was planning to begin sexual relations with Henry before the marriage that always seemed a step beyond her reach. Or she may have been providing for the possibility that the king might tire of her and pass her on to some appropriate nobleman. Whoever fathered her future sons, and whether in or out of wedlock, Ann was looking after their interests.

Shortly after Ann's investiture as marchioness, an emissary from Henry approached Catherine, demanding that she give the king her jewels, the official property of the queen of England. She refused, sarcastically observing that to do so would be to disobey her husband, who at New Year's had ordered her not to send him any more gifts. Only if he directly commanded her to relinquish the jewels would she comply. The next day the messenger returned with the king's written command. Heartsick, Catherine obeyed.

With Catherine's jewels, Ann felt ready to take Catherine's place. A meeting between Henry and Francis I, with Ann as a formal participant, would display her in a reputable light as the imminent queen. Francis had been Henry's ally from the first, writing frequently to the pope in support of the annulment. The royal meeting was arranged for September, to be held first in English-held Calais and then in French Boulogne, but there was a hitch. Francis might be a great womanizer, but he liked the proprieties, and Ann was as yet only Henry's mistress—for Francis could not believe that the relationship had remained unconsummated. Politely, he told the English ambassador that his own wife, Eleanor (whom he had married shortly after the death of Claude), would not be able to receive Ann. Eleanor was Spanish, and Catherine's niece: surely Henry would find "the sight of a Spanish dress as hateful as the devil himself." Well, then, perhaps Francis's sister, Ann's old friend Marguerite, now queen of Navarre, might come with Francis. Marguerite, it turned out, was ill. Rumor spread quickly that, disapproving of the annulment, she had refused to meet with the king's concubine. Francis then offered the Duchess of Vendôme, probably smiling inwardly, for the duchess was notorious for her sexual escapades. Henry, of course, refused. Rejection by the woman she had once deeply admired must have hurt Ann, who later wrote to Marguerite that the only thing marring the meeting with Francis was "the want of the queen of Navarre's company." A year later she wrote to Marguerite that her "greatest wish, next to having a son, was to see you again."

The compromise was that no ladies would be present at the official meetings. Ann would stay in Calais while Henry went to Boulogne, and

Francis would pay a friendly visit to Calais after official business was completed. This plan turned out to be very successful. Henry gave a great banquet, outdoing himself in ostentation. Hangings of cloth of gold and cloth of silver covered the walls of the banquet hall, which was decorated with jewel-encrusted gold wreaths. The sumptuous banquet was followed by a masque, led by Ann and six other "gorgeously apparelled" ladies. Francis gallantly danced with Ann, and later the two spent some time in private conversation. There were others at the banquet, less conspicuous, but nonetheless important. Ann's brother George, Viscount Rochford, almost certainly was there, since he was one of Henry's favorite courtiers and knew Francis well; his wife, Jane, was among Ann's attendants. One of Henry's squires of the body was also present, a talented, ambitious young diplomat named Edward Seymour, who watched Ann and her brother with interest. George Boleyn had risen far since his sister had caught the king's fancy. Edward Seymour also had sisters.

Around this time—speculations vary—Ann decided that virginity was not the useful tool it had been for the past seven years. Henry needed something now to push him to marry her at any cost, and that something could only be the imminence of the son he wanted. Perhaps too she sensed that her mystique was fading, and that passion long ungratified might eventually turn itself elsewhere. The visit to Francis would certainly have reminded her of Wolsey's plan of a French marriage. In any case, the time was right.

By January 1533, Ann's goal had been accomplished: she was pregnant. She hoped the child she was carrying was a boy. Henry was certain of it, since his special relationship with God made it inevitable. He had no choice but to marry her quickly. On January 25, in great secrecy, they were married.

It was not a secret Ann permitted to be kept for long. Henry might have hoped to keep a discreet silence for a time, but that was not to his new wife's advantage. She was queen, and she wanted that fact to be public knowledge. If the child was a girl, or if she miscarried, the secret marriage could evaporate into the ether. On February 15 she told her uncle that if she were not pregnant by Easter she would make a pilgrimage to pray to the Blessed Virgin. A week later it was clear that sacred intervention was no longer needed. Chatting with her old friend Thomas Wyatt amid a crowd of courtiers, she loudly asked him to send her some apples. "I have such a longing to eat apples!" she laughed. "Do you know what the king says? He says it means I am with child! But I tell him no. No, it couldn't. No!" And still laughing, she left the room.

For years Ann had lived with the stigma of being perceived as the king's mistress, a stigma that remained until Henry chose to admit that they were married. The public hints of pregnancy forced Henry to acknowledge that Ann was his wife, Clement or no Clement. A week later, at a banquet Ann held in her rooms, Henry invited the dowager Duchess of Norfolk to admire the sumptuous plate and tapestries that he had given Ann, and said that Ann had made a good marriage and had a fine dowry. After Cranmer's investiture on March 30, Ann's household was formed. On Easter Sunday, at a mass attended by a regally attired Ann, the priest prayed publicly for Queen Ann.

Chapter 5

ANNA SANS TÊTE

THOMAS CROMWELL

An obscure clerk and Machiavellian politician, Cromwell rose to power helping Henry get rid of two wives he no longer wanted. His role in helping to choose the king's fourth wife brought about his downfall.

ith Ann now officially on the throne, the marriage between Henry and Catherine had to be legally annulled—by someone. Before his consecration as Archbishop of Canterbury, Cranmer had taken a secret oath that he would obey the pope only insofar as such obedience did not clash with the will of the king. Immediately after his installation the archbishop wrote begging Henry to permit him to investigate once more the question of his first marriage. Henry consented, and Cranmer held a short trial, summoning Catherine, who of course refused to come. On May 23, 1533, to no one's surprise, Cranmer found that the marriage was null and void, based on the text from Leviticus.

Henry had not even waited for Cranmer's verdict to declare his first marriage void: once Ann had made his second public, he had little choice in the matter. On April 9 a deputation led by the gleeful Duke of Norfolk and the reluctant Duke of Suffolk called on Catherine to tell her that she might no longer call herself queen. As Arthur's widow, she must once again be known as the Princess Dowager of Wales. If she submitted, Henry would be generous. If not, she would remain at Ampthill in Bedfordshire as the king's prisoner, with her former chamberlain, Lord Mountjoy, as warder, and her household seriously reduced. Those who remained would have to swear to address her as Princess Dowager.

Catherine remained adamant. The size of her household was unimportant, though she hoped the king would see fit to leave her with her confessor, her physician, and two maids. If not, she would fend for herself. But whoever did remain would have to address her by her rightful title: she was not the princess dowager; she was the queen.

Not anymore, Norfolk told her. Perhaps the news had not reached her, but Henry had married Ann two months ago.

If he'd hoped that learning of the marriage would shatter Catherine's determination, he was mistaken. Grimly she prepared to move her household, whatever part of it the king left her, to wherever he decided she was to live. And grimly she began to plan the next move in the battle to reclaim her title.

As the one queen prepared for a life of drab obscurity, the other readied herself for her greatest and most ostentatious moment of triumph. Ann's coronation was one of the most brilliantly theatrical events in an increasingly theatrical court. Henry wanted to provide his discombobulated people with a spectacle that would both enchant them and reinforce the new queen's regality. Four days of no-holds-barred ceremonies were planned, beginning May 29 with the queen escorted by river to her temporary quarters in the Tower of London, and culminating on June 1 with the coronation itself.

On Thursday at 1 P.M. fifty great barges accompanied by a host of smaller boats set out from Billingsgate, decked in gold foil and packed with musicians. At their head was a light wherry with a flame-belching mechanical dragon, and huge wildmen who uttered fearsome cries and threw fireworks into the water. Then came the barges of the mayor and the various guilds, all done up in cloth of gold and silver. One barge sported a large representation of a golden tree on which perched a white falcon, the symbol Ann had chosen for herself. About the tree stood several virgins, "singing and playing sweetly." Eventually came Ann's own barge, magnificently decorated. She was dressed in cloth of gold and attended by the most important of her ladies. Then followed Henry's equally gorgeous barge. Along the shores were minstrels and fireworks; cannon saluted the royal entourage.

The next day was reserved for court ceremonies at the Tower, which included the investitures of eighteen new knights of the bath. Saturday was Ann's procession to Westminster, and again, it was spectacular. But it was only the prologue to the most important event of all, the coronation itself.

The procession began early in the morning at Westminster Hall. Once again, all the important nobility, clergy, and the mayor of London walked before their queen in solemn ceremony. This, at least, was a shorter stretch—seven hundred yards between the dais of the hall and the high altar of the abbey, all carpeted with blue cloth. Then came Ann, in purple velvet and ermine coronation robes, a gold canopy held over her head and her long train carried by the Dowager Duchess of Norfolk, Ann's step-grandmother, the highest ranking noblewoman among her supporters. The abbey was equally resplendent, cloth of gold being prominent, and the king had a special stand covered with a latticework screen which allowed him to watch the ceremonies without his presence distracting attention from the central figure of Ann.

After a solemn high mass, Ann prostrated herself at the feet of her friend the Archbishop of Canterbury, who offered formal prayers for her. She rose; then Cranmer anointed her and placed the crown on her head and the scepter in her hand. The service was finished with more ceremony, after which the new queen returned to Westminster Hall to rest briefly until the banquet, to which eight hundred guests had been invited. There were three courses and a total of eighty dishes, as well as "subtleties," elaborate sculptures of sugar and plaster, including "wax ships" that especially impressed the guests. Finally, an exhausted and triumphant Ann was able to retire. Her rest was short-lived, for the following day was taken up with jousts, dancing, and another banquet.

For seven years Ann Boleyn had waited for this day. Now she was queen: England and the world knew it. Her bulging belly, obvious even under her stately robes, proved she had the right to her crown. In three months she would give Henry the son who was the reason for all the ceremony and splendor, all the work and frustration and suffering of the past seven years. And she could rejoice in the knowledge that though she had powerful enemies, she also had powerful friends. Henry's sister the French Queen might reject her, but his other sister, the Queen Dowager of Scotland, did not. Margaret was going out of her way to offer her support to Ann, referring to her in a letter as "our dearest sister" and persuading her son, the young Scottish king, to acknowledge Henry's new marriage.

The fact that Henry was able to put his time and energy into his new queen's coronation and preparations for the birth of their child, rather than into fighting a defensive war against the Holy Roman Empire, was in large part due to the decency and good sense of his first wife. The months immediately before and after the coronation were dangerous ones, for much of the population of England was outraged at Henry's treatment of the woman they still loved as their queen. A bad harvest in 1533 and 1534 was seen as a sign of God's displeasure with the new marriage. Taverns were full of rebellious mutterings. Chapuys was doing all he could to exploit this anger. On April 10, he had written to Charles that "considering the injury done to Madame, your aunt, you can hardly avoid making war now upon this king and this kingdom." It would be good timing, he added, "for the king has neither horsemen nor captains and the affections of the people are entirely on the side of the Queen."

Some of the northern barons were coming to Chapuys with suggestions that the emperor's intervention would be welcome. Lords Darcy and Hussey approached the ambassador, as did the influential Marchioness of Exeter. Henry himself was all too aware of the power Catherine held over the nobility and peasants. Later he told his council that if Catherine so chose, "she could quite easily take the field, muster a great array, and wage against me a war as fierce as any her mother Isabella ever waged in Spain."

Chapuys had other plans as well: Catherine and Mary were to be smuggled out of England to safety until the war was successfully completed, after which, presumably, they would return home triumphantly to rule England.

But Catherine would have nothing to do with it. She had grown fond of Chapuys, whom she called her *especial amigo,* and she usually relied on his advice. But she refused to instigate a war against the husband she still loved. "I shall not ask His Holiness for a war," she said firmly. "That is a thing I would rather die than provoke." Nor would she flee, for that "would be a sin against the law and against my lawful husband." Chapuys was frustrated. The very determination he so admired made her impervious to his efforts to help her.

Soon after Ann's coronation, yet another deputation from Henry appeared at Catherine's doorstep. She was ill, and received the king's messengers from her bed. But physical debility did not dampen her dignity. She insisted that her servants remain in her bedchamber as the men, headed by Lord Mountjoy, read the king's demands—the same demands he had been making all along. In turn, she gave the same answers she had always given. If the pope declared her marriage invalid, she would accept his judgment. Otherwise she was still queen. When Mountjoy showed her the list of demands, she read it, striking out the phrase "princess dowager" wherever it occurred, her pen cutting holes into the paper as she slashed out the repulsive words. Mountjoy said she would be prosecuted for treason. She challenged him to prove it. All she had done was refuse to slander herself by confessing that she had been "the King's harlot these four and twenty years." Mountjoy left, having gained nothing. He could hardly have expected anything else after all these years.

Cromwell, on hearing Mountjoy's report, could not hold back his praise for the woman he was trying to destroy, paying her the highest compliment he could imagine. "Nature wronged the Queen in not making her a man," he said. "But for her sex she would have surpassed all the heroes of history."

But that virile spirit would have to be broken. In July, Catherine was ordered to move to the small, remote palace of Buckden in Huntingdonshire, her suite of servants once more cut. Among those who remained were a handful of ladies-in-waiting, her physician, two chaplains (one of whom was the ever-loyal Thomas Abell), and, thankfully, her old friend

Francisco Felipez, who had suffered so many wounds in her service. Maria de Salinas, the friend she "loved more than any other mortal," did not go with her—forbidden to do so, we must assume, by the king.

The journey from Ampthill to Buckden was cheering, for the roads were lined with people, who shouted blessings at their Spanish queen as the humble entourage passed by. Henry had forbidden her giving alms to the people, fearing that her usual generosity fueled their rejection of his new marriage. But they cheered the impoverished queen as though the smiles she bestowed on them were golden coins.

Catherine suffered another loss in the weeks following Ann Boleyn's coronation. Her old friend Mary Tudor, the French Queen, died on June 24. To the end, Mary had remained loyal to Catherine. She had been in London for the wedding of her daughter Frances to the Marquis of Dorset shortly before Ann's coronation. Her health failing, she nevertheless braved the trip home rather than obey her brother's summons to the coronation.

Three months after Mary's death, her husband married their young ward, Catherine Willoughby. Catherine had lived in the Suffolk household for years, and the transition from ward to wife was probably a smooth one in an age when it was not unusual for middle-aged men to marry teenage girls. Along with his child bride, the duke had acquired a formidable mother-in-law, for Catherine Willoughby was the daughter of Maria de Salinas.

Around Christmas 1533, Suffolk was sent with yet another delegation to harass the queen. He was to force Catherine's servants to take an oath that they would address her only as Princess Dowager and to dismiss those who refused; he was then to move Catherine and what was left of her suite to the unhealthy, isolated castle of Somersham in the middle of the Fens. Probably Henry—or Ann, or Cromwell—hoped the already ailing queen would take a chill and die in the dank fen country.

Suffolk hated the task; Maria told Chapuys that the duke had said he wished an accident would befall him on the road to prevent him from fulfilling it. The story is interesting for two reasons. It demonstrates how far Suffolk had come from his early, unquestioning support of the king's annulment, and it shows that Maria de Salinas was actively in league with Chapuys. The duke's marriage was proving useful to the queen; she now had a spy in the enemy's camp, and anything the king's best friend knew of Henry's plans would find its way, through his mother-in-law, to the Spanish ambassador.

Sadly for Suffolk, no accident overcame him on the road to Buckden. Once again he faced Catherine, repeating Henry's bribes and threats.

Once again Catherine reiterated that she would not betray herself and her husband by denying their marriage, and would not be served by any who called her Princess Dowager. Nor would she go willingly to Somersham. Its climate would kill her, and it would be a sin to consent to her own death; they would have to take her by force. Then she turned her back on Brandon and locked herself in her chambers. The queen's servants were equally vehement. None would take the oath, and the exasperated duke had them locked in the porter's lodge, hoping to frighten them into submission.

The next morning Suffolk and the rest of the deputation again argued vainly with Catherine, shouting through the door. Outside the castle, groups of farmers and peasants milled about with unconvincing casualness. Exasperated, Suffolk wrote letters to Henry, Cromwell, and Norfolk, explaining desperately that there was "no other remedy than to convey her by force," a step he could not take without the king's orders, and begging them to send instructions instantly.

Henry was too busy with his Christmas celebrations to answer, and Brandon spent a gloomy holiday staring at a locked door. Finally, on the last day of the year, he gave up. He had to do something, if only to save face and to convince Henry that he had discharged his duty. Dismantling such rooms as he had access to, he took away Catherine's hangings and furniture, loading them in the courtyard. He ordered her servants freed, but, for form's sake, arrested a few. Among them, sadly, was Thomas Abell, who was taken to the Tower.

⁂ If Henry was escalating his cruelty toward his former wife, there were reasons. Things had not gone as well for him as he had been certain they would at the time of Ann's coronation. To begin with, the pope, on hearing the news of Henry's marriage and his pregnant wife's coronation, finally took action—though it was limited. On July 11 he declared their marriage null and void and said Henry would be excommunicated if he hadn't separated from Ann and returned to Catherine by September. He did not, however, formally declare Henry's first marriage valid. Still, it was the first time in many years that an English king had been directly threatened with excommunication.

Henry was stunned. But he knew that in September, when the threat was to be carried out, Ann would give birth to his son, and the pope would see that Henry had been right all along.

On August 26, Ann "took to her chamber." Isolated from the world of men, the queen remained in a special bed of state, and all the duties usually performed by her male servants were taken over by her ladies until after the baby's birth. Eleven days later Ann's child was born. As the queen lay spent and exhausted after her hours of labor, the unsettling news reached Henry. Once more, he was the father of a healthy baby girl.

The birth of Princess Elizabeth was a shock. All the court astrologers had assured Henry he would have a son. He had worked out the details for the joust that would be held to celebrate his birth. He had had an official announcement made up for the public, announcing the birth of a prince, with no alternative document if the child turned out to be a girl. It was left to Ann's chamberlain to squeeze a hasty, tiny *s* next to the word *prince.*

If there had been any sincerity in Henry's belief that his lack of a living legitimate son was proof of God's displeasure with his first marriage, he would have had to view Elizabeth's birth as a sign either that he had misinterpreted the divine will or that he'd erred badly in choosing the sister of a former mistress as his consort. At the very least, some self-questioning was in order. But Henry wanted Ann, and that meant God wanted him to have her. The birth of Elizabeth must be accepted as a dress rehearsal for that of the son to come. The jousts were canceled and the celebrations scaled down to the level customary for the birth of a girl, but the christening on September 10 was as grand as anyone could wish. If Henry recalled the day he had smiled at his other infant daughter with the certainty that "by God's grace, sons will follow," he hastily dismissed the thought. This time, sons *would* follow.

Henry's passion for Ann did not abate. However much she had failed him by producing a daughter, he needed her now more than ever, to prove to himself and to the world that he was right. They were more than lovers; they were allies, fighting Catherine and her supporters, fighting the pope, who dared to speak for God. Henry desperately needed to believe himself right. He had risked too much, hurt too many other people. Shakespeare's portrait in *Henry VIII* is flat and unconvincing, but he captured the essence of the man in his description of another power seeker, the usurping duke in *The Tempest,* who

> *made such a sinner of his memory,*
> *To credit his own lie, he did believe*
> *He was indeed the duke.*

Henry had to believe he and not Clement spoke for God: to sustain this belief, he had to sustain his passion for Ann, and his faith that, finally, she would give him the son that would vindicate him in the world's eyes.

For her part, Ann needed Henry's belief in her just to survive. Because of this, she shared his obsession with attacking papal power. But she had other reasons as well, religious reasons. Ann's challenge to traditional religion went deeper than Henry's. The Defender of the Faith challenged the pope only because the pope challenged him, but Ann had a genuine sympathy for reform, and had she lived might eventually have become a full-fledged Protestant.

In 1531, Eustache Chapuys had dubbed Ann "more Lutheran than Luther himself." But Chapuys was a passionate Catholic, and his hatred for Ann naturally led him to hurl at her the nastiest epithet he could think of. Early in the Reformation, *Lutheran* was used loosely to describe an adherent of any of the numerous brands of religious dissent that were emerging, though some of these were wholly at odds with the teachings of Martin Luther. However radical Ann's ideas might have become if she had lived longer, during the brief years of her reign she was clearly an evangelical, not a bona fide "heretic." Given her sustained interest in and affection for Marguerite of Navarre, whom she had known so well during her years in France, this is hardly surprising. Marguerite's religion was not only radical; her religious writings strongly spoke to the importance of womanhood in interpreting divinity.

However, there is no record of Ann ever denying, or questioning, the doctrine of transubstantiation, one of the central Protestant concerns. And she clearly believed that good works could assure a place in heaven—a soundly Catholic belief in direct opposition to the Lutheran insistence on justification by faith, which held that only belief in Jesus Christ could bring salvation. Shortly before her death Ann told her jailer she "would be a saint in heaven, because I have done many good deeds in my days."

But if she was not a Protestant, in her brief reign Ann showed a great affinity for those who were. E. W. Ives insists, with good evidence, that Ann "was not a catalyst in the English Reformation; she was an element in the equation." She used her influence with Henry to get appointments for a number of reforming bishops, including the militant Hugh Latimer, who would be forbidden to preach later in Henry's reign. She chose her own chaplains from among the reformers. These included William Latimer, who later wrote a colorful paean to her reformism, and Matthew Parker, who became Elizabeth's first Archbishop of Canterbury. Ann appointed Parker to the collegiate church of Stoke by Clare near Sudbury and provided patronage for his reforms there, which included regular preaching, scholarships, and the appointment of a lecturer on the Bible.

Apart from her acceptance of the royal supremacy, which was too self-serving to offer any sense of whether she really believed in it or not, the most important of Ann's reformist beliefs was in the centrality of scripture. She owned at least one copy of Tyndale's translation of the Bible, which Henry had banned because of its Lutheran prologues. William Latimer said that she kept another English Bible on a lectern in her chambers, to be read by her ladies.

Ann extended her support for the vernacular Bible beyond the court itself. A year into her reign she learned about Richard Herman, who had been expelled from the society of English merchants in Antwerp because he "did both with his goods and policy, to his great hurt and hindrance in this world, help the setting forth of the New Testament in English." She intervened, and was able to get him reinstated. Others who suffered religious persecution found a friend in Ann. She helped a French refugee known only as Mistress Mary, who had fled to England, and tried to help another French Protestant, John Sturm, get a passport out of France. The French reformer Nicholas Bourbon had been arrested and deprived of all his possessions—including, poignantly, his pet nightingale. When word of his plight got to England, William Butts, the court physician who had helped Ann through the sweating sickness, asked for Ann's assistance, and she persuaded Henry to intervene with Francis. Bourbon came to England, and Ann paid for his lodgings. In a poem written sometime later, he specifically credited Ann with his rescue: "For no crime, but through a false charge . . . / I was shut up in prison. . . . / Then your pity lighted upon me from the ends of the earth / Snatching me in my affliction / Anna, away from all my troubles. / If this had not happened, I should be chained in that darkness, / Unhappily languishing, still under restraint."

Ann's compassion extended beyond religious exiles. Perhaps influenced by Hugh Latimer, whose advocacy for the destitute often got him in trouble with the nobility, she showed concern for the sufferings of the lower classes and the poor. She gave her staff standing orders that all poor petitioners be promptly helped, and if the staff overlooked a petitioner she personally intervened. On progress, she and her ladies distributed to the poor the clothes they had spent so much of their time sewing. In addition the poor were given a shilling each; pregnant women were given a pair of sheets and two shillings. In one instance, she gave £20 to one of Hugh Latimer's parishioners whose husband's cattle had recently died.

It's nice to have these images of a caring, thoughtful Ann Boleyn to juxtapose with the more common picture of her that emerged during the three years of her marriage, that of the vicious shrew. It's true that she was often nasty to Henry, but her irritability doesn't deserve censure. Whatever Henry suffered in his new marriage he had brought on himself, and the power in the relationship was all his. There were others to whom Ann was cruel—though this cruelty was shared by Henry, and it was Henry who had the power to implement it.

If this point seems overemphasized here, it is only because historians have often echoed contemporaries who blamed Ann rather than Henry for the evils that occurred in the wake of the annulment. The image of the cruel seductress who entranced the weak but innocent man and mistreated his daughter is a potent one still, and Ann has been trapped in it. But Henry was far from innocent, and far from weak, and what he did he wanted to do. Ann was both his accomplice and his victim. We tend to overlook the latter aspect in our distaste for the former.

Ann wasn't always nice. She used her influence over Henry, running roughshod over anyone who stood in her way. She had gambled everything on the promise that she would give Henry a son. Knowing that others would see Elizabeth's birth as proof that her marriage to the king was wrong, she could only hope that Henry would not agree with them. Everything she did must reinforce her queenly image, her right to be on the throne. Until she had a son, the face of that aging, rejected woman incarcerated in the palace at Buckden would haunt her, for in a few years the face might be hers. And it would be worse for Ann than for Catherine. Once in 1530, while quarreling with Henry, she had recalled that "it is foretold in ancient prophecies that at this time a queen shall be burnt." She could not have forgotten the drawing she had found in her chambers, showing her headless.

Even without the aid of prophecy, the reasonably predictable reality was bad enough. If Ann's marriage were annulled, she would not become a princess dowager, with all the social and financial benefits that such a position conferred, though the title of Marchioness of Pembroke would guarantee her some income. She would be a member of the nobility who had disgraced her family, a cast-off mistress like her sister Mary, except that, unlike Mary, she was hated by much of the country, and would be unable to make a good marriage. Probably she would not be able to marry at all. If Henry got this marriage annulled, it would almost certainly be on the basis of a precontract to Henry Percy. There had been ominous rumblings in the summer of 1532 about her relationship with Percy, whose wife tried to get out of her miserable marriage by claiming that Percy had already been betrothed to Ann. The king investigated the charge and was satisfied with Percy's oath that there was no precontract. But he could always change his mind.

Ann knew too that she had enemies at court. Nicholas Carewe, one of Henry's favorite gentlemen of the privy chamber, disliked her. Her uncle Norfolk, who preferred his womenfolk to be docile, had realized that his niece was not his puppet, and he too had grown hostile. By now Suffolk, like his wife, despised her. Then there were the Marchioness of Exeter and Margaret Pole, Countess of Salisbury, close friends of the old queen. These and others would hide their hostility as best they could and bide their time, sniffing out any gossip that might work against her.

And perhaps there were enemies she didn't yet recognize—or people who might turn on her if they found any advantage in it. She herself had not been Catherine's foe in the beginning; she had simply been an ambitious lady-in-waiting, until the king pursued her. There were other ladies-in-waiting; there were other ambitious people at court.

Outside of court there were more people to be feared. Elizabeth Barton, known as the Nun of Kent, was a mystic who had achieved some fame as a prophet and healer. She had been happy to remain in obscurity until, like Joan of Arc, she heard holy voices whose bidding she felt bound to obey. In 1527 her voices had demanded that she speak out against the annulment. Henry would die within a month if he contracted a second marriage, she declared publicly. The Nun herself had no political motives; she told the world only what her angel voices had told her. Alone, she could be dismissed as a madwoman, or as an agent of the devil. But she attracted the attention of others who opposed the annulment and the marriage with Ann Boleyn. In 1533 she was arrested, along with five of her followers. All were executed in April 1534. Her martyrdom was blamed on Ann.

On March 24, 1534, Clement finally gave his verdict on the marriage of Henry and Catherine: it was valid in the eyes of God and the church. The decision came too late to do any good for Catherine, but it still gave fuel to Ann's enemies.

So did Henry's escalated persecution of anyone who stood in his way. These included not only people like Bishop Fisher, who publicly spoke out against the new marriage, but also those who quietly followed their own consciences. Elizabeth I's famous distaste for seeking "windows into men's souls" was not inherited from her father. Thomas More, who said

DIVORCED, BEHEADED, SURVIVED

nothing against the annulment but who refused to declare support for it, was arrested in April of 1534. He was followed a few weeks later by Fisher. In the summer they were joined in the Tower by a group of Carthusian monks who, like More, had refused to sign the Oath of Succession but said nothing against it or against Henry's marriage. Increasingly, Ann was blamed for these persecutions, but there is no evidence that she initiated them. Even Chapuys, always on the lookout for any opportunity to attack Ann, didn't attribute them to her. It was Henry whose royal supremacy these challengers were threatening, and Henry who decided their fates. Relieved though Ann might be by their deaths the next year—especially that of the outspoken Fisher—she must have been at least a little alarmed by them as well. Fisher had been Margaret Beaufort's dearest friend, and Henry had known him all his life. More had been Henry's own cherished companion. A man who would kill his friends wasn't the safest of husbands.

Still, for the moment there was nothing Ann's enemies could do to harm her, because she was again pregnant. Once more Henry began making preparations: a silver cradle, baby clothes made of cloth of gold. Then in late July, she miscarried. A far less imaginative woman than Ann would have found her position frightening, and perhaps even a kinder woman would have been tempted to lash out at anyone who threatened her position as queen.

Ann lashed out. Sadly but predictably, the two chief objects of her hatred were the woman she had replaced, and that woman's daughter. Chapuys reported that Ann had sworn she would not be contented "until both the queen and her daughter had been done to death by poison or otherwise." He was doubtless exaggerating, since if Ann planned to poison her rivals she would want their deaths to appear natural and would not broadcast her intentions. But she did demand that Henry have both Catherine and Mary put to death legally, since they had not signed the Oath of Succession, which declared Elizabeth heir to the throne if the marriage produced no sons.

There was, in truth, no right way Ann could treat Catherine and Mary. Her very existence as Henry's wife was the greatest harm she could do them. She had made a few clumsy efforts to befriend Mary—based on the condition that Mary acknowledge her as queen, which Mary was no more likely to do than Catherine was. Only when these overtures failed did she turn to threats.

There are no other examples of real cruelty on Ann's part, though there are some unkindnesses. In 1534 her sister Mary secretly married William Stafford, a soldier she had met during the trip to Calais in 1532. Ann was furious, and, with the support of the rest of the Boleyn clan, had Mary sent from court. This action is puzzling, since Ann had treated Mary, the family black sheep, extremely well until then. She had used her influence to try to get the sister of Mary's first husband appointed abbess of the wealthy convent of Wilton; she had obtained financial support for Mary when William Carey died of the sweating sickness, leaving her destitute; she had included Mary in the retinue of ladies who accompanied her to Calais; and she had made Mary one of her ladies-in-waiting when she became queen. But now Ann desperately needed the trappings of queenly dignity, and her sister's marriage to a man below her station threatened that dignity.

There may have been another reason for Ann's resentment. In a letter to Cromwell, begging him to use his influence to get permission for her to come back to court, Mary wrote eloquently of how Stafford had rescued her from great unhappiness. "I was in bondage," she wrote, "and glad I was to be at liberty. . . . I saw that all the world did set so little by me, and he so much, that I thought I could take no better way but to take him and forsake all other ways, and to live a poor honest life with him." She knew that she "might have had a greater man of birth, but I assure you I could never have had one that loved me so well. . . . I had rather beg my bread with him than be the greatest queen christened." It's unlikely that Ann ever saw the letter, but if Mary was indiscreet enough to commit such sentiments in writing to Cromwell, she was probably indiscreet enough to speak them to Ann. She must have realized that Ann herself had married not for love, but in the hope of becoming the "greatest queen christened." The irony of their positions would not be lost on either sister. Mary, who had submitted to Henry when he first desired her, had found personal happiness. Ann, holding on to her chastity, had been trapped first by Henry and later by the ambition that had taken the place of hope. Ann might have resented her sister's happiness.

Dismissing Mary was a foolish move. The number of Ann's enemies at court was growing daily, and she could ill afford to lose any friend, even as unimportant a friend as her sister. Ladies-in-waiting were useful allies, and they could be dangerous antagonists. They could easily be bribed, and their intimate knowledge of the queen's daily behavior could prove valuable to enemies.

It is unclear what Ann's relationships with her other ladies were like.

We don't have the stories of deep friendship and intense loyalty that emerge from the reigns of Catherine of Aragon and Katherine Parr. All we have are a few spare, tantalizing glimpses that, put together, suggest pleasant but distanced relationships with a queen who treated her ladies well but always remembered that she was above them. There are pictures of Ann and her ladies sewing together, both sumptuous court decoration and clothing for the poor, and once dancing together along with Henry's courtiers. We have the somber image of the four unnamed loyal ladies who walked with her to the scaffold at her execution. Ann Gainsford had been alarmed for Ann when she saw the crude cartoon of the headless queen. Even years later, Gainsford, now Mrs. Zouche, spoke affectionately of her former mistress, so perhaps there was some closeness between them. The queen also had some affection for Elizabeth Browne, for after her arrest, when she had problems of her own to occupy her mind, she fretted about her former attendant's possible miscarriage. But Browne ended up testifying against her, so we can't assume a particularly close friendship.

It would be interesting to know what Ann's relationship was with Bess Holland, the mistress of her uncle Norfolk. Holland's birth was apparently more gentle than her earlier occupation as laundress suggested, for she was distantly related to Lord Hussey. Still, from laundress to royal lady-in-waiting is a big jump, and with Ann's exaggerated sense of royal protocol, it's hard to know what to make of her taking Holland into her circle, especially since she had never had any fondness for her uncle. She might have felt some affinity toward another despised "other woman." Unfortunately, we have no records of the relationship between the two.

Ann's need for friends grew after her miscarriage. The death of that unborn son was also the death of Henry's obsession with Ann Boleyn. It is amazing that it had lasted so many years. Henry, as his treatment of Catherine and of Thomas More had shown, was not capable of love. His great passion was for himself, and his attractions to others were all based on the image they reflected back to him. Ann had challenged that image, and he had pursued her, falling in love with the pursuit itself. But the very qualities that had intrigued him when they pulled Ann beyond his grasp— the fierce independence, the wild gaiety, the self-assertion that at times seemed to match his own narcissism—palled after he captured her. Probably Henry was bored long before he allowed it to show, maybe even before their marriage. But he needed Ann to justify his actions. He couldn't allow anyone, least of all himself, to know that his great love had been merely a sensual attraction, no different from that of other men for numerous women—no different from Norfolk's passion for his laundress. As long as it seemed likely that Ann would give him a son, Henry had to believe he loved her.

Ann believed it too. As early as the summer of 1533, according to Chapuys, she was "full of jealousy—and not without reason." Henry apparently had a new mistress, and Ann confronted him with "words . . . which he did not like." He told her she would have to close her eyes and put up with it, "just like others who were worthier than she." He reminded her that it was he who had raised her to her present status, and that he could as easily deprive her of it. They made up after that quarrel, and Henry told Ann that he loved her so much he would go begging in the streets rather than part with her.

In the autumn of 1534, after Ann's first miscarriage, Chapuys reported Henry's involvement with one of the queen's maids of honor. Catherine had been saddened by Henry's affairs, but as long as they remained in the background she accepted their inevitability. But Ann misinterpreted Henry's feelings for her, confusing intensity with depth, and she could not believe that the man who had sacrificed so much for her could now interest himself in other women. She demanded that Henry dismiss the woman, but he angrily refused, reminding her again that "she should remember where she came from." Determined to break up the affair, she plotted with Jane Rochford, her sister-in-law, to make the lady's life at court so unpleasant that she would leave of her own accord. Henry discovered the plot and angrily dismissed Lady Rochford instead.

The unnamed lady was soon replaced in Henry's bed by Ann's cousin Madge Shelton, but this too proved a transient affair. Transient or not, however, these affairs threatened Ann. We do not have to believe that she was in love with her husband to see why his infidelities would shake her far more than similar affairs had hurt Catherine. Until Henry's belated attack of conscience, Catherine had believed that her position as Henry's wife was unassailable. Ann had good reason to know that hers wasn't. Unlike Catherine, Ann couldn't afford an unfaithful husband—at least, not until she had a son.

Eventually the time came when the new affair wasn't a casual fling, when Ann's worst fears were realized. Henry believed himself to be in love again, with a woman who was as dissimilar to Ann as Ann was to Catherine.

Ann had known Jane Seymour for some time. Jane had been a lady-in-waiting to Catherine of Aragon, coming to court about 1529. Like

Ann, she had had a love affair thwarted by social snobbery—though in her case there was no lustful king orchestrating the breakup. Jane had formed an attachment to young Will Dormer, son of the highly placed Sir Robert and Lady Dormer. Her cousin, Francis Bryan, approached the Dormers on her behalf. But even Bryan's intimacy with the king failed to impress them. A Seymour wasn't good enough for a Dormer, and that was that. Will Dormer was provided with a more appropriate wife, and Jane was sent to court.

But here the similarity with Ann ends. If Jane's heart was broken, we have no record of it. There is no one on whom she swore revenge, as Ann did—no fury, no rebellion against those who controlled her fate. Jane simply did as she was told.

She might have left court in the summer of 1533 when Catherine's household was cut, but if so she was back before the beginning of 1534. She appears in financial records as one of Ann's ladies-in-waiting who received a New Year's gift from Henry.

Also at court was her brother Edward, a squire of the body who had been to Calais with Henry and Ann. Friendly to Ann, and like her sympathetic to the reform movement, Edward was shrewd, intelligent, and ambitious. At this stage, his highest aim for his sister had probably been realized, for being a lady-in-waiting to the queen was the greatest political plum a woman could dream of. But he was observant, and when Henry's eye turned toward Jane, he was ready.

That appears to have happened in early September of 1535. Henry and Ann were on progress, and one of the places where they stopped was Wolf Hall, home of Jane's father, Sir John. Jane may have already been at her father's house, or she may have been in Ann's entourage, but her presence in any case seems to have been conspicuous. Possibly Edward saw to it that the king noticed his modest sister in the comfortable domesticity of her father's house. In any case, Henry was soon openly courting this quiet, colorless lady.

As with his early courtship of Ann, the king did not at first seem to have contemplated marriage. He was in even less of a position to do so than he had been in the early days of his lust for Ann: his juggling two wives had been greeted with a mixture of horror and derision throughout the Continent, and most of his own people were still hoping he would discard Ann and return to Catherine. To repudiate her and marry yet another woman would invite both scandal and civil war—and make him the laughingstock of Europe.

Only his first wife's death could release him from his second. Catherine was aging and ill, but she stubbornly survived. Shortly after the pope's declaration that her marriage was valid, Henry once again sent a delegation to harangue her, this time led by Edward Lee, Archbishop of York, and Cuthbert Tunstall, Bishop of Durham. The king's emissaries read her the Oath of Succession, reminding her that it was treason to refuse to sign. Contemptuously, she told them that she was the queen of England. "By right the king can have no other wife, and let this be your answer," she said coolly. As to the penalties for so-called treason, she was ready to face them—but she demanded a public execution. Much as Henry would have cheered her death, his henchmen knew as well as he did that executing Catherine would incite revolt.

As Suffolk had done a year and a half earlier, Lee and Tunstall turned to her servants. One by one, they refused the oath. A handful of her Spanish servants had not yet been interviewed at the end of the first day, and they consulted with Catherine when the deputation left for the evening. The next day they agreed to take the oath, but only in their native language. Lee and Tunstall didn't argue: a concession was a concession. But the servants took advantage of the similarity in the sounds of very different Spanish words, so that instead of swearing that Henry should be (*sea hecho*) head of the church, they swore that he had made himself (*se ha hecho*) its head. Thus Catherine managed to keep some of her dearest servants with her, including the indispensable Francisco Felipez.

Soon afterward, Henry had Catherine moved from Buckden to Kimbolton Castle, also in Huntingdonshire. This was allegedly a favor, for she had written asking for a drier residence. Her request offered him an opportunity to appear compassionate while removing her even farther from court and from the people. Kimbolton had a wide moat and thick walls, making it a more effective prison than Buckden. Sir Edmund Bedingfield was appointed steward and Sir Edward Chamberlayn, appropriately enough, chamberlain. In fact both were her jailers. They were sworn to address her only as Princess Dowager, to which she steadfastly refused to respond. The result was that for over a year she lived with them without ever speaking with them directly. Instead, she and a handful of attendants remained sequestered in her apartments, emerging only for an occasional walk in the walled garden outside the chapel.

Catherine was permitted no visitors. Chapuys applied frequently for permission to see her, and was refused each time. Somehow she managed to get a note to him, asking him to please visit her: it was clear she had something to say to him. Again he applied for permission to see her; again he was turned down.

Finally he came up with an ingenious plan. He was going on a pilgrimage to Our Lady of Walsingham, he announced, and since he would pass Kimbolton on the way, he would visit the queen. He invited some Spanish merchants to join him, and they set off with a huge, liveried entourage, complete with musicians and a fool, and carrying on as if they were making a miniature progress. Midway to Kimbolton a messenger from the king overtook them, with a command from Henry that they were not to visit Catherine. Chapuys was polite but noncommittal, and the messenger rode on to Kimbolton. Soon another messenger came, this time from Catherine. It was Francisco Felipez, coming to tell Chapuys that, since the king forbade his visit, Catherine would not see him. The ambassador nodded. He would, of course, obey the queen's wishes, he told Felipez, but surely she could not object if his party rode nearer the castle to see where Catherine was staying; he himself would remain behind. Felipez offered no objection.

Once outside the castle, the Spaniards decided to put on a show for the castle's residents. As Catherine's and Bedingfield's servants looked on, the musicians played, the young Spaniards sang and made their horses perform tricks, and the fool danced and turned somersaults on the edge of the moat until he lost his footing and fell in. He was hauled out by the Spaniards, much to the merriment of everyone on both sides of the moat, and the Spaniards bantered with each other in their own language about the fool's plight. Whatever information Catherine needed to know or to give was thus exchanged in a volley of laughter.

It's a wonderful story, that complicated, *Mission Impossible* communication between Catherine and Chapuys, and it makes a charming picture, combining fun and a small triumph over Henry. There was little laughter or triumph in the rest of Catherine's life, as Henry grew increasingly cruel. The worst punishment was her separation from Mary. She knew that her daughter was as much a prisoner as she was, and that Mary would be made to suffer for not admitting the validity of the annulment.

Catherine had written to Mary shortly before her removal to Kimbolton, warning the princess of the king's intention to make her sign the Oath of Succession, and tacitly admitting that she might die for her refusal. She should obey Henry "in everything save only that you will not offend God and lose your own soul; and go no further with learning and disputation in the matter. . . . Speak you few words and meddle nothing." Good, practical advice. Like Thomas More, Catherine did not seek martyrdom either for herself or for her daughter. Mary was not to argue about the annulment, or to express her anger about Ann Boleyn. Only in the instance when obedience to her father jeopardized her immortal soul was she to defy him—and then only passively, by refusing to sign the oath. What pain those calm words cost Catherine we can only guess. She was urging her child to risk death.

Catherine was not alone in thinking Mary's life, and her own, were in danger. Rumors continued to abound throughout England that Ann was plotting to poison both women. Neither Catherine nor Mary doubted that it could happen. In the spring of 1535, Mary fell seriously ill with nausea and weakness, probably brought on by extreme stress. Chapuys, Catherine, and possibly Henry himself thought it resulted from poisoning. Henry sent his own physician to see the girl. Dr. Butts, alarmed, sent for Catherine's physician, Miguel de la Sá. Both doctors suspected poison, and warned Mary's terrified waiting woman that the penalty for poisoners was to be boiled to death in a cauldron of oil.

Catherine wrote Chapuys a desperate letter, asking him to plead with Henry on her behalf. "Desire him for me to be so charitable as to send his daughter and mine to where I am. . . . There is no need for anyone to nurse her but myself. . . . I will put her in my own bed in my own chamber, and watch with her when needful. . . . "

Henry's response was typical. At first he simply refused, then seemingly made an allowance: Mary could be moved to a house thirty miles from Kimbolton, near enough that de la Sá could visit her, provided Catherine would not try to see her.

Catherine again wrote Chapuys, asking him to thank Henry "for the goodness he shows his daughter and me," and promising to refrain from trying to visit her daughter. But she added that she had wanted to be with the girl because "the comfort and mirth we should have together would be half her cure." Her request, she said bitterly, "was so just and reasonable, and touched so nearly the honor and conscience of the King, my lord, that I did not think it would be denied me."

Catherine could have saved herself and Mary at any time, had she been willing to betray Henry. But her admonitions to Mary, and her own assertions to the various emissaries from Henry who tried to bully her into submission, were sincere. Henry was her husband, Mary's father, and the king of England. In everything that did not violate their duty to God, he was to be obeyed. So when Chapuys, time and again, begged her to allow him to organize a rebellion against Henry, she refused. She also refused to flee the country. Chapuys organized plans for both contingencies, keeping in constant touch with Henry's enemies at court and throughout the country, ready at a moment's notice to pull together the growing, disparate forces of discontent in England. But Catherine would have none of it, even when she was convinced that her husband meant to kill her and their daughter. The idea was no less repugnant to her than the idea of acquiescing to the annulment.

As 1535 progressed she became more and more discouraged. The executions of More, Fisher, and the Carthusians shook her. England was coming closer and closer to heresy. Souls were endangered, the souls of the people she had come to know and love, and for whom as queen of England she bore some responsibility. After much prayer and soul-searching, Catherine took a step that was the closest she would ever come to rebelling against her husband. On October 15 she wrote a letter to the new pope, Paul III, asking him to implement the bull excommunicating Henry. England must be laid under an interdict, to be enforced by the emperor at the head of an army. "If a remedy be not applied shortly," she wrote, "there will be no end to ruined souls and martyred saints. The good will be firm and suffer. The lukewarm will fail if they find none to help them, and the greater part will stray away like sheep without a shepherd." She wrote a similar letter to Charles. Chapuys had long been urging such a move.

It was too late. The complicated political scene in Europe had shifted, and a war between France and the empire seemed imminent. Charles wanted Henry to be his ally, not Francis's. It was one more defeat for Catherine, and she was tired. She fell ill again in November, confined to her bed with severe attacks of pain and nausea. By early December she had rallied enough to write Chapuys, asking him to petition Henry for a little money to buy Christmas presents for her servants—and, as always, thanking the ambassador for all his efforts on her behalf. She made out her will, leaving Mary the few treasures she had left—her old furs and a gold collar.

Catherine's recovery was short-lived, and on December 29 Dr. de la Sá sent Chapuys a blunt message. The queen was dying; if he wished to see her again, he must come at once. Frantically, Chapuys rushed to Henry and begged for permission to visit Catherine. Henry was in a generous mood. Since the princess dowager was dying, Chapuys could see her one last time.

What about Mary? Chapuys asked. Wouldn't Henry let the girl see her dying mother? But Henry hedged. He'd have to ask the council about that.

Despairing, Chapuys left the king. If he argued too hotly for Catherine's need to see her daughter, Henry might grow angry and withdraw his own permission.

He arrived at Kimbolton on the second day of the new year, 1536. An old friend of the queen was already there. Maria de Salinas had been living comfortably and quietly in London when news of Catherine's deteriorating health reached her. For months she had been imploring Henry to let her visit Catherine, and for months her petitions had been ignored. Like Chapuys, she knew this was her last chance to see Catherine. In the dark early hours of the new year's first morning she stole out alone, mounted her horse, and headed for Kimbolton Castle, nearly sixty miles north of London. It was a bitter cold night, and she was an aging woman used to traveling with a retinue of servants. On the way her horse stumbled, throwing her into the mud. She remounted and continued on, arriving at nightfall.

At first the steward, Bedingfield, refused her admittance to the castle because she lacked the king's consent. Pointing to her muddied clothes, she told him of the fall from her horse. The king *had* given his consent, she said, but the papers had been lost when she fell. There was so little time left for the princess dowager. Surely Bedingfield could honor the king's wish and let Catherine see her old friend before she died? Bedingfield gave in, and Maria was allowed to enter Catherine's rooms. Once there she locked the door behind her and did not come out again. "We saw neither her nor her letters anymore," reported the rueful steward.

Together Catherine's two dear friends, the lady-in-waiting and the ambassador from Spain, brought comfort to her dying. Chapuys lied shamelessly, telling her all she wanted to hear. The pope would issue the bull of excommunication, he assured her, and when that happened Henry would come to his senses, leave the whore, and restore Mary to her proper place as heir to the throne. More honestly, he told her that the king was tiring of Ann; he did not mention that yet another woman had captured His Majesty's fancy.

Chapuys stayed for three days. Catherine seemed to get better, and she urged him to return to London: he had much work to do, she reminded him. He left reluctantly, promising to return shortly.

Catherine was not better, and she knew it. The next day she wrote a letter to Henry, telling him that she pardoned him for all the wrongs he had done her, asking him to see to the welfare of her remaining servants and to be a good father to Mary. The letter ended, "Lastly I make this vow, that mine eyes desire you above all things." She signed it "Catherine,

Queen of England." In those last words she captured the essence of her life, the two strongest forces that, along with her deep piety, had given her the strength to carry on through the grim years. She loved Henry, deeply and passionately, and nothing he did could ever change that. And she was the queen of England. Nothing he did could ever change that, either. The next day she died, in the arms of her oldest and dearest friend.

When Catherine's body was cut open for embalming, the undertakers discovered that her heart had turned black, with a hideous growth on the outside. De la Sá was certain she had been poisoned, and the accusation was later used against Ann Boleyn. But no one had access to the queen except for her most faithful ladies. Modern medical historians are certain she died of cancer. It's interesting in the light of current "new age" thinking about the relationship between the illnesses people get and their emotional condition: Catherine of Aragon died of something very close to a broken heart.

The news of her death was brought to Henry, who crowed, "God be praised, the harridan is dead!" Ann too rejoiced. But her joy must have been mixed with uneasiness. Catherine's timing, like the pope's, was bad. Five years earlier, when Henry's passion for Ann was fresh and his confidence that God meant her to bear his son was unshaken, the death of the old queen would have been an unmitigated benefit for the woman who replaced her. But things had changed. Ann was no longer the enchanting creature fresh from the exotic courts of France and breathing an air of exquisite, unattainable sexual delights. She was an arrogant, temperamental wife, alienating Henry from his people, and a bedfellow whose novelty had worn off in three years. With Catherine dead, the king's options had expanded infinitely.

Ann had only one hope now, but it was the greatest hope a king's wife—especially Henry's wife—could have: she was pregnant. Whatever affairs the king indulged in, whatever his feelings toward Ann herself, she was safe if she bore his son.

If. The goal that had once seemed a given was now "if." Catherine too had once been certain that she would bear the prince who would succeed Henry as king. She had miscarried, as Ann had. She had borne a daughter, as Ann had. She had been thirty when that child was born, and after Mary there were only more miscarriages, and then nothing. Then Henry had realized that God frowned on his marriage.

Ann was no younger now than Catherine had been when Mary was born. The dead queen was very much alive in Ann's mind, in those early weeks of 1536. If Ann failed Henry this time, would he continue to hope for a son, or would his conscience and his concupiscence once more unite to persuade him that some other lady was the queen God really intended for him?

On January 29 Catherine of Aragon was buried. On the same day Ann Boleyn, in the chilling phrase of her daughter's biographer, J. E. Neale, "miscarried of her saviour."

Chapter 6

THE VESSEL

JANE SEYMOUR

Henry's third wife chose the motto "Bound to Serve and Obey,"
which she did. She became the mother of his only legitimate son.

Died

or Henry, the loss of a male fetus was infinitely more tragic than the death of the woman who had been his wife for twenty years. It proved to him that Ann would not bear him sons—that, like Catherine, she was not really his wife.

It's possible, as Retha Warnicke argues in her fascinating study of Ann's reign, that the fetus was deformed, and that Henry believed this was a sign of witchcraft. Chapuys did, in fact, hear rumors that Henry had told one of his courtiers that Ann had lured him into marriage through "sortileges and charms." Intriguing as Warnicke's argument is, however, there is no proof that the fetus was abnormal. The fact of a second miscarriage, on top of the birth of a girl, would be enough for a man of Henry's ego to bandy about words like "witchcraft" and decide to rid himself of his second wife as he had of his first.

It was certainly enough to inspire singular cruelty. Coming to his wife's bedside, he said coldly, "I see that God will not give me male children." Stung, Ann blamed the miscarriage on her husband's flirtation with Jane Seymour, and on the shock she had gotten a few days earlier when Henry had suffered a near-fatal fall from a horse.

Ann's jealousy of Jane was interpreted romantically by her ladies: "her too great love," they called it. But it's hard to believe that shrewd, savvy woman really loved the obvious lout that Henry had become. Catherine's love makes sense, for she had known him in his early years, and the Henry she loved was always the boy who had courted and rescued her. Ann had known Henry first as a predator, then as a self-deluding hypocrite. Possibly she loved him anyway: she would not be the first intelligent woman to love a contemptible man. But it is equally likely that her jealousy came from a realistic appraisal of the danger she was now in.

Before the miscarriage, Henry might have enjoyed an asexual flirtation with the maidenly Jane Seymour, or he might have hoped to win her over as he had a number of other women. But until Ann's child was born, he could not think of marrying Jane. The miscarriage changed all that. Now Henry wanted to be rid of Ann, and he wanted to marry Jane.

What Jane wanted, if indeed she wanted anything, is hard to ascertain. Among all the women Henry married—among all the major figures of that dramatic era—Jane is the only one whose personality never clearly emerges. In popular mythology she's close to a saint, the perfect foil to the temptress Ann Boleyn. It's an ironic image, since she did exactly what Ann had done. Having attracted the king's interest, she refused his advances without removing herself from his presence. Then, as the efforts to rid himself of his current wife got under way, she accepted her role as that wife's replacement. There are two differences, neither of which is to her credit. The first is that Ann, unlike Catherine, was still young enough to conceive again when Henry threw her over. The second is that at some point it became clear to Jane that Ann was not to be merely discarded, but killed.

One nineteenth-century historian who didn't accept the saintly image of Jane was Agnes Strickland, whose multivolume *Lives of the Queens of England* has preserved for us much of our information about the era and its women. She bitterly decries Jane's "shameless conduct in receiving the courtship of Henry VIII," blaming her for Ann's downfall. A number of recent historians agree. Ives accuses Jane of "dangling her virtue as a public bait." Hester Chapman describes her as maintaining a "perfectly calculated and exquisitely sustained" pose.

While most accounts in her own time extol her great virtue, they are notably lacking in detail. Despite the praise, the figure that emerges in contemporary accounts is neither saint nor villain, neither virtuous nor calculating. Nothing as defined as malice or ambition or compassion or warmth or coldness comes through in the descriptions of Jane. In all the events in which she took part, Jane as an individual seems puzzlingly, almost eerily, absent. Her brother pushed her at the king, and she, in Strickland's apt word, "received" Henry's advances. Acting as a virtuous woman was supposed to, and as Henry seems to have wanted her to, she held out for marriage, passively watching the horrifying process of Ann's destruction. Did she believe in Ann's guilt? Was she angry with Ann for betraying Henry? With Henry for killing Ann? Was she frightened at the thought of marrying a man who had humiliated one wife and was about to kill another? Did she ever turn to her brother and say, "Get me out of this"? We don't know. We don't even have enough material to make an educated guess.

Perhaps it is this very lack of a self that has caused her to come down to us as Henry's "good" wife. She is Snow White to Ann Boleyn's wicked witch, the embodiment of the qualities Andrea Dworkin describes in *Woman Hating.* "For a woman to be good," Dworkin writes, "she must be dead, or as close to it as possible. . . . Cinderella, Sleeping Beauty, Snow-white, Rapunzel—all are characterized by passivity, beauty, innocence, and *victimization*. They are archetypal good women. . . . They never think, act, initiate, confront, resist, challenge, feel, care, or question. . . . First they are objects of malice, then they are objects of romantic adoration. They warrant neither."

Jane's contemporary Eustache Chapuys, predisposed to like the woman who was helping to destroy "the concubine," tried hard to praise her. "She is of no great beauty, so fair that one would call her pale," he admitted. "The said Seymour is not a woman of great wit, but she may have good understanding."

As queen, she would take as her motto "Bound to obey and serve." In the early stages of Henry's courtship, the man Jane obeyed and served was her brother Edward. He played chaperon at all the king's visits with his sister, for if Jane was to be Henry's next wife there could be no suggestion of impropriety in their premarital relationship. Probably it was Edward who decided that she should refuse to be Henry's mistress but allow herself to be persuaded to become his wife, and who choreographed her responses. Chapuys was certainly convinced that someone told Jane what to do, and wrote home that she had been instructed "not in any wise to give in to the king's fancy unless he makes her his queen."

By this time, Henry was open about his courtship of Jane. He gave her a locket, which Ann saw and, in a jealous rage, tore from her neck. The locket, presumably, was an honorable gift; a purse full of money wasn't. When Henry sent such a purse to Jane, along with a letter, Jane kissed the letter but refused to read it. Handing it back unopened, she fell to her knees and besought the startled messenger to "ask the king on her behalf to consider carefully that she was a gentlewoman, born of good and honorable parents and with an unsullied reputation. She had no greater treasure in the world than her honor which she would rather die a thousand times than tarnish." If Henry wanted to give her money, he could do so when she made a good match.

Henry was charmed. Cromwell's rooms at Greenwich had a private passage to the king's apartments: Henry ousted the lord privy seal from the rooms and gave them to Edward Seymour and his strong-minded wife, Anne Stanhope. There, safely chaperoned, Henry might visit with Jane to his heart's content. As reward for furthering the king's relationship with his sister, Edward was made a gentleman of the king's privy chamber.

Although Henry didn't know it, Edward Seymour was probably doing a great deal more than giving him access to Jane. Approached by Princess Mary's supporters on the Privy Council, he had become an active member of the plot to overthrow Ann Boleyn. He and the others told Jane how to behave with Henry, and she complied. Along with ostentatiously preserving her chastity, Jane was to speak against Ann to Henry, always in the presence of supporters among the nobility, who would then agree with her. She was to emphasize "how much his subjects abominate the marriage contracted with the concubine and that no one considers it legitimate." Again, Jane went along—gladly? sadly? Or indifferently doing as she was told?

It had not taken Cromwell long to realize that a simple annulment was not enough to satisfy Henry's needs, or his own. For one thing, Ann would not accept the repudiation of her marriage and her daughter's legitimacy any more than Catherine had. She had neither Catherine's deep religious belief in the sanctity of her marriage nor her great love for Henry, but she had as much pride and as much love for her daughter. Like Catherine, she would have vastly preferred to have a son to inherit the throne, but if she didn't, no other woman's son would take the throne from Elizabeth. There would be a fight; Henry's will would come into question.

Above all, it was crucial to give Henry what he wanted in a way that would allow the king to persuade himself that it was not his will but divine justice at issue. Cromwell understood the king, probably better than anyone. It was not simply that Henry no longer loved Ann Boleyn. He hated her.

He had not hated Catherine of Aragon when he decided to rid himself of her. She was simply no longer of use to him. He probably even had some affection for her, and had she agreed to the annulment, he might well have maintained a warm and cordial friendship with her. He came to hate her later because she defied him. With Ann it was different. Henry had been wholly besotted with her. There is nothing quite as embarrassing as the recollection of an obsessive infatuation when it's over. Every excessive gesture, every pathetic plea, lives in the memory—the terrible feeling of "Did I really do *that?*" The overly extravagant gifts, the mawkish letters—how those "pretty dukkys" must have haunted Henry now!

For a healthy or even a mildly neurotic person, such embarrassment finds expression in rueful self-deprecation. For Henry there was no such outlet. He could not admit he had been the dupe of his own shallow passion. He could cope with the humiliating emotions Ann had once stirred in him only by disowning them. He had not been foolish; she had made him foolish.

Ann's failure to bear a son had done two things. It had intensified Henry's hatred for her, because it had intensified the degree to which she'd made him look foolish. At the same time, it allowed him to rid himself of her. With a son, Ann would have had an absolute weapon against his hatred. He would have to go on living with her, acknowledging her as his queen, even bedding her in the hope of producing other sons should this one die. He could be cruel to her, within limits; he could have mistresses. But he could not get rid of her. Without a son, he could.

Henry loathed Ann, and he wanted a son. He needed to be rid of her for the second reason, but he needed her killed for the first. Above all, as Cromwell realized, Henry must be protected against knowing his own motives. He must always be able to think himself righteous. He must be deceived. Not deeply deceived—only enough to allow him to deceive himself. Cromwell looked for something that would justify Henry's hatred for Ann, something that would allow his accommodating conscience to countenance her death. Adultery might work, Cromwell thought. It was not a capital crime in itself—but a queen with a lover probably dreamed of marrying that lover, which she could do only if her husband was dead. Deliberately envisioning the death of the king was treason.

Plain, garden-variety adultery, however, might backfire. People would pity the king and wonder about his virility. He would be the talk of the taverns—Henry the cuckold. Maybe that was why he couldn't have a son—he couldn't even keep his wife satisfied! Comparisons would be made between the king and his supposed rival, and the king would lose. If the rival was young, well then, she'd turned away from the tired old king to a younger, lusty man: poor old King Hal, not the man he once was. If the rival was older, less attractive than Henry, it was worse yet: poor old Hal, got his horns from *that* bag of bones!

But suppose Ann had more than one lover? Two, three, even more? And not all of them noblemen, either. Better if she betrayed her position with one of the more common servants she was frequently in contact with. Even better, what if another lover were her own brother? Lord Rochford had become very powerful during Ann's reign, and everyone knew how close the brother and sister were. The queen, Cromwell had decided, must be a monster of insatiable and unnatural lust. No one could smirk at the king then. He had been bewitched by a woman of more than human evil.

The plot was formed. Now Cromwell had to gather his confederates.

Many he had probably been working with already—Nicholas Carewe, the Seymour brothers. Others he could enlist. There was Jane Rochford, George Boleyn's wife, who had been one of Ann's ladies. Lady Rochford had once plotted with Ann to drive one of Henry's mistresses from court, but her affection for the queen had cooled, perhaps because she felt excluded from the close bond that knit Ann and her brother. The taste for plotting Lady Rochford had shown in the incident with the unknown mistress could now be turned to Cromwell's use. Testimony from Ann's sister-in-law would help make the story he was concocting look plausible.

There were other ladies-in-waiting as well, among them Ann Cobham and Lady Worcester. Patiently, Cromwell and the others watched and waited. Ann was bound to say or do something, innocent in itself, that could be usefully interpreted. As Henry had needed Leviticus to help him construct his belief in the sinfulness of his first marriage, he would need something to convince him of Ann's licentiousness so that he might without qualms have her executed.

Shortly before April 30, Ann was talking with Henry Norris, the king's groom of the stool. Norris was an influential courtier who was also one of her friends. He had long been betrothed to one of Ann's ladies-in-waiting, Madge Shelton, and Ann asked him why he had not yet married her. He answered that he "would tarry a time." For some reason this offended Ann: possibly she thought his waffling was due to her own disfavor at court. She raged at him, accusing him of hoping to marry her. "You look for dead men's shoes," she cried, "for if aught came to the king but good you would look to have me."

Norris was astounded, and probably terrified. Vehemently he denied such a thought, and the two quarreled, loudly and publicly. When they calmed down, Ann realized the damage she had done, for witnesses might conclude that they were lovers. One of these was probably John Skip, her almoner, for she asked Norris to go to Skip and "swear for the queen that she was a good woman." Unfortunately for them both, Norris agreed. The man who had been so kind to the doomed Wolsey seven years earlier was now being dangerously kind to the doomed Ann Boleyn.

Cromwell continued his search, and soon found another victim. On the Saturday before May Day, Ann had seen the young court musician Mark Smeaton looking sad and downcast. Borrowing the affectation of the wounded swain, he dolefully replied that it did not matter. Ann rebuked him for assuming this role: the game of courtly love was not proper for one of his station. "You may not look to have me speak to you as I should to a nobleman," she told him, "because you are an inferior person." Humbly, he answered, "No, no, madame, a look sufficeth."

It sufficed Cromwell too. Smeaton had evidently been infatuated with the queen for some time, or else had been misled by her enjoyment of his music into attempting a flirtation with her. In any case, the next day he was arrested, taken to Cromwell's house at Stepney, and interrogated for nearly twenty-four hours. There were rumors that he was tortured to obtain his confession. He may simply have been threatened with a traitor's death, which meant he would be hanged and, while still alive, disemboweled. Noblemen usually escaped this fate, being given the cleaner punishment of beheading, but men of Smeaton's class found guilty of treason suffered the full penalty. He told his interrogators what they wanted to hear and was then taken to the Tower and put in irons.

The next step was to get Norris arrested. Cromwell went to the Privy Council with Smeaton's confession, and then to Henry, telling him about the confession and about Norris's quarrel with Ann. Henry waited to confront Norris until the May Day tournament, in which Norris and Rochford were jousting. At the end of the joust, Henry abruptly rose, leaving Ann, and demanded that Norris ride with him to Westminster. He accused Norris of adultery with Ann, charges the astonished courtier denied. By dawn the next morning, Norris was in the Tower. Now it was Ann's turn. She was arrested a few hours after Norris and was accused of adultery with him, Smeaton, and another unnamed man. Henry had her sent to the Tower rooms where she had lodged three years earlier, the night before her coronation. It was better than the dungeon she had feared, and the combination of relief and horror caused her to burst into hysterics. "It is too good for me," she cried. "Jesu have mercy on me!" Then she knelt down and began to sob, "and in the same sorrow fell into a great laughing," reported her jailer, Sir William Kingston.

Ann's babblings turned out to be useful for Cromwell, and Kingston faithfully reported them all. Her brother had been arrested shortly after she was, and she must have been given some hint of this, for she demanded to know where he was. When Kingston gave an evasive answer, she repeated, "Oh, where is my sweet brother?" Then she began talking about the men she was supposed to have committed adultery with, wondering what they had said of her. "Oh, Norris," she cried, "hast thou accused me? Thou art in the Tower with me, and thou and I shall die together. And Mark, thou art here too." In her hysteria, Ann realized what she would later try to deny—that she was doomed, that her guilt or innocence had nothing to do with her fate. "Mr. Kingston," she said, "shall I die without justice?"

Primly, Kingston told her that "the poorest subject the king hath, hath justice." "And therewith," he later told Cromwell, "she laughed."

With good reason. Ann knew Henry and his justice. Bitterly she looked around her. There were four women to attend her, all her enemies—including her aunt Lady Shelton and Lady Kingston. "I think it much unkindness in the king to put such about me as I never loved," she told Kingston. It was not unkindness; it was strategy. Cromwell could count on these four to report anything she said to Kingston. Kingston would in turn report to Cromwell, and Cromwell would, selectively, report to Henry.

One of the things Kingston reported was something Ann, in her first outburst, had said to demonstrate her innocence of any involvement with Norris. A year before she charged Norris with wanting to marry her she had had a similar, though much lighter, exchange with Francis Weston in which she rebuked Weston for flirting with Madge Shelton, Norris's betrothed, and neglecting his own wife. Weston answered that Norris came to Ann's chambers more to see Ann herself than Madge, and added coyly that he himself loved "one in her house better than" either Madge or his own wife. With equal coyness, Ann had asked who it was; he replied, "It is yourself." It was standard courtly flirtation, which no one could take seriously—but it served Cromwell's purposes to take it seriously now.

Francis Weston was arrested the next day, as was William Brereton, a groom of the privy chamber and a Boleyn sympathizer. Why Cromwell chose him is unclear, but it added to the list and made Ann's sexual appetite look all the more monstrous.

With Ann safely in the Tower, Henry cheerfully pursued his courtship of Jane Seymour, who had moved from Greenwich to Sir Nicholas Carewe's house in Beddington. In the days that followed, the king visited her so openly and so frequently that public sympathy for Ann, rare during her reign, began to emerge. So overt was this sympathy that Henry felt obliged to warn Jane about it. He sent a letter telling her that "there is a ballad made lately of great derision against us, which if it go abroad and is seen by you, I pray you to pay no manner of regard to it." He promised to search for the author of the "malignant writing" and punish him severely. Fortunately for the author, he (or perhaps she) was never found; sadly for us, the ballad has disappeared from history.

We do not know if the ballad frightened Jane or if she scorned it, as Ann had once scorned a similar attack from the populace. Nor do we know if Jane had any feelings of compassion for the woman in the Tower, whose death would mean her own ascent to the throne.

One person at least did feel sadness for Ann, and he came close to telling Henry that he might be making a mistake. Archbishop Cranmer's letter is painful to read even today. The struggle between his concern for Ann and his fear for himself shows in every line. "I am in such perplexity that my mind is clean amazed; for I never had better opinion in woman than I had in her; which maketh me think that she should not be culpable," he wrote, then quickly added, "I think your Highness would not have gone so far, except she had been surely culpable." Next to Henry himself, he was "most bound unto her of all creatures living," and he hoped "that she may declare herself inculpable and innocent." But if she was guilty, "there is not one that loveth God and his gospel that will ever favor her, but must hate her above all other. . . . "

Poor Cranmer! He must have known that Cromwell was lying, and that Henry was accepting the lie for his own purposes. How could he let Ann die, knowing she was innocent? Yet how, knowing Henry's desire to believe in her guilt, could he argue? He liked his position as Archbishop of Canterbury, and he liked life. He could not risk being accused as a conspirator in her purported treason.

Henry made certain none of Ann's other friends could reach him with pleas—or information—that might tempt him to reconsider. John Husee, the London agent for the governor of Calais, excused his failure to bring one of the governor's requests to the king by explaining that "I can hitherto find no ways to come to the King's presence. His Grace came not abroad (except it were in the garden, and in his boat at night, at which times it may become no man to prevent him) these fourteen days."

Husee's letters give a sense of the confusion felt by the average Londoner during this time. "Here are so many tales I cannot well tell which to write," he says on May 13. "For now this day some saith young Weston shall 'scape; and some saith that none shall die but the Queen and her brother . . . and the saying now is that those which shall suffer shall die when the Queen and her brother goeth to execution." His own opinion was that "I think verily they shall all suffer. . . . "

Adding to everyone's confusion, Richard Page and Thomas Wyatt were arrested on May 8 for their support of Ann, a move the public reasonably but incorrectly assumed meant they too were accused of being her lovers. Both were later released.

There was no chance that Ann would receive a fair trial, but as ever, Henry liked to put on a good face. There were to be two grand juries, for Ann and her brother, as queen and viscount, were tried separately from the four men of lower station. The first grand jury was called on May 9, with Giles Heron, son-in-law of Ann's old enemy Thomas More, as foreman. The second grand jury quickly followed, and both decided that there was indeed reason to send the cases to trial. Three days later the trials of Smeaton, Weston, Norris, and Brereton began.

Smeaton, who had confessed to Cromwell, again confessed to adultery but not to treason. The others pleaded not guilty to all the charges. There is no record of the trial, but we can assume the jurors heard the testimony that would soon be used against Ann and her brother. The four men were quickly found guilty and sentenced to be drawn and quartered.

Accounts of the second trial do survive. The grand jury had charged Ann with adultery and treason, and the wording is interesting. Ann had wooed her lovers "by means of indecent language, gifts, and other acts"; the men "by the said queen's most vile provocation and invitation became given and inclined to the said queen." Having become "inflamed by carnal love for the queen," all four men "did satisfy her inordinate desires." Thereafter she and her lovers had "compassed and imagined the king's death," after which she had promised to marry "some one of the traitors" after Henry died.

A constant theme in the language of the accusations is Ann's aggressiveness. The adultery was initiated by Ann, driven by her "inordinate desires." It was no simple adulteress who had turned Henry into a cuckold, and she was not drawn by the superior wooing of a younger man. The aggressiveness itself was a sign of her wickedness. It is ironic that Henry would choose to believe this, since it had taken him seven years of courtship to get Ann into his bed. It's also worth noting that though she was being tried for both treason and adultery, at the time of the trial only treason was a capital crime.

A final, bizarre charge was added to the rest. The king, on learning about Ann's crimes, "had been so grieved that certain harms and dangers had happened to his royal body." Just what the jury was expected to make of this is difficult to say. Did Henry go into a swoon when he heard the hideous tale? Did he tear his hair and bang his head against walls, or try to kill himself? There are no other indications that poor Henry was dying of heartbreak like a hero in Boccaccio: as Ives notes, the "supposedly enfeebled monarch" was in lusty and public pursuit of Jane Seymour. But it's consistent with Henry's bloated sense of self-importance. Surely no jury could excuse a woman who had made him suffer.

The charges in this lurid trial were just the beginning. Ann's uncle Norfolk was quickly appointed lord high steward—a nice sadistic touch. Norfolk had little affection for his niece and nephew, but their condem-

nation would be a great stain on the family honor. The duke thoughtfully exempted his brother-in-law, Ann and George Boleyn's father, from the
jury, though he had no need to fear that that miserable opportunist would
risk defending his children. He was less kind to the man Ann had once
loved, Henry Percy, now Earl of Northumberland: the wretched, ailing
earl was forced to sit on the jury.

The trial took place in King's Hall in the Tower, with two thousand
spectators avidly watching. The official record of the trial is as brief as the
record of the first, but there are other sources—Charles Wriothesley wrote
about it in his contemporary chronicle of Henry's reign, and Chapuys collected all the reports he could and sent them to Spain.

Ann entered the courtroom coolly, and remained calm as Cromwell
read the charges to her. The witnesses to the accusations had signed each
of the charges, but they themselves did not come forth. As each charge
was read, she denied it. To the original grand jury charges had now been
added the accusation that she had poisoned Catherine and planned to poison Mary: no, she said, she had done no poisoning. Her answers, says
Wriothesley, were "wise and discreet . . . as though she had never been
guilty to the same."

Norfolk read the verdict: the jury found her guilty. His niece was to
die, by burning or beheading, at "the king's pleasure."

Ann listened with the same dignified composure she had maintained
throughout the trial. She regretted only that innocent men must die with
her, and that she had not always "borne toward the king the humility
which I owed him." That was as close to a sneer as she could allow herself. Henry had now found himself a woman of absolute humility to
replace his self-assured queen.

As she left, Henry Percy, weak from a deadly illness and drained by
the ordeal of passing false judgement against the woman he had once
loved, collapsed and had to be taken out of the courtroom. He died soon
afterward.

As soon as Ann was condemned to die, Henry sent a messenger to
tell Jane the good news. It's an unappetizing picture, the rush to assure his
new love of the old one's imminent execution, and Henry compounded
the ugliness by running off that same afternoon to visit Jane in person.
One wonders if they laughed together, envisioning Ann's death—or did
Jane chastely console the king in his elaborate charade of betrayed
husband?

Rochford's trial came next. Cromwell read out the charges of incest
and treason, and George Boleyn denied them. Then—in what would have

been comical in a less tragic context—Cromwell solemnly accused Rochford of joining with his sister in making fun of Henry's poetry and clothing. Rochford refrained from pointing out that such behavior, while rude, was hardly a capital crime. He simply denied the accusation. Then Cromwell handed him a piece of paper, instructing him not to read it aloud. Rochford read it aloud. It was an allegation that Ann had told her brother Henry was impotent. Rochford denied it, and was then asked if he had told other people that Elizabeth was not Henry's child. Was she perhaps Rochford's own daughter? Again, Rochford denied the charges. He too was found guilty.

Had the jurors been interested in knowing whether or not the allegations were true—as opposed to accepting that their king wanted his wife and her companions dead—they would have asked one or two questions of their own, and searched their memories, for on eleven of the occasions when Ann was supposedly committing adultery, either she or her alleged lover was somewhere other than the place in which the couple were accused of meeting. One of the sexual encounters with Mark Smeaton was said to have taken place three weeks earlier, April 26, at Westminster—though court was then at Greenwich. Surely, as a number of historians have noted, the jurors, all peers of the realm and many at court themselves, would remember that.

But memory is selective. Henry himself was now "remembering" a few things. He recalled that Ann had not been a virgin when he first had intercourse with her. He also declared that she'd had more than a hundred lovers since their marriage.

On May 17, Cranmer declared that Ann, condemned for adultery, had never been Henry's wife. The relevant papers have been lost, so we don't know the grounds of the annulment—perhaps Ann's precontract with Percy, perhaps Henry's affair with her sister. Henry's minions could easily find something for him. Ives suggests that they decided the papal dispensation to marry his mistress's sister had been "contrary to the law of God," which certainly sounds like Henry.

On the same morning the marriage was annulled, the five men accused with Ann were executed. Smeaton repeated his confession before he was executed, perhaps afraid that even at the last he might be drawn and quartered instead of beheaded. The other four all died as people were expected to die on the block: they refrained from accusations of injustice, instead making general statements about the sinfulness of their lives, as good Christians did when facing death. They did not acknowledge the charges against them.

Ann believed that she would die the next day, and according to Kingston, she was sorry not to, for she "thought to be dead this time, and past my pain." Her moods varied wildly: one moment she was sure Henry would remit her sentence and send her to a nunnery; the next she was imagining the scene of her death. She told Kingston she was sure it would not rain until after she was released. She then said that the people were praying for her and a disaster from heaven would take place after she died. Sometimes she would laugh merrily, and declare that her new nickname would be Anna Sans Tête. More and more, however, she spent her time in prayer, receiving comfort from the religion that had meant much to her in her reign. "I have seen many men and also women executed," said Kingston, "and they have been in much sorrow, but this lady hath much joy and pleasure in death."

That death came on May 19. Henry, in what no doubt seemed to him an act of great charity, had not only decided against having her burned at the stake, but had sent to Calais for a swordsman to execute Ann—a sword would be quicker than the customary ax. Kingston explained kindly that the execution would not be painful. Ann put her hands to her throat and laughed. "I heard say the executioner was very good, and I have a little neck."

Her address to the crowd was dignified and predictable, though it must have galled her to say that Henry had been "a good, a gentle, and sovereign lord." She admitted no wrongdoing, specific or generic, and she said that she "accused no man," which might suggest that there was a man, Henry, to be accused. More than that, she could not defy the conventions of execution. She tucked her hair into her cap, put on her blindfold, and knelt. "To Christ I commend my soul," she said, and the executioner struck.

Her ladies put her body and head in a small chest that had contained arrows, and she was buried in the little chapel in the Tower. Few had believed her guilty, even her enemy Chapuys, and there was much shock and bitterness at her death. Her cousin and friend, Thomas Wyatt, witnessing the trials and executions of Ann and the five innocent men, spoke for many when he wrote, "These bloody days have broken my heart. . . . "

On the morning of the execution the king was, appropriately enough, surrounded by his huntsmen and hounds when the news that Ann was finally dead reached him. The hunt finished, the prey slaughtered, he rode off to meet Jane. The following day their betrothal was formally announced.

Henry married Jane with little fanfare in the small chapel at White-hall a week and a half later, on May 30. Strickland writes bitingly that "the wedding cake must have been baking, the wedding dinner providing, the wedding clothes preparing, while the life blood was yet running warm in the veins of the victim whose place was to be rendered vacant by a violent death."

Henry made no pretense of grief either for the woman he had pursued for seven years or for the sorrow she had allegedly heaped on him. Chapuys cynically remarked that he had never seen a cuckold wear his horns so cheerfully.

The cheery cuckold indulged in a bit of public hypocrisy that must have broadened Chapuys's smile. It was not enough for Henry that his marriage to Jane seem acceptable; it had to appear downright altruistic. Thomas Audley, now Chancellor of England, proclaimed in Parliament that Henry, having suffered "great anxieties and perturbations" in his first marriage and "perils and dangers" in his second, might well prefer to avoid marriage again. "Yet this, our most excellent prince, again condescendeth to contract matrimony, and hath, on the humble petition of the nobility, taken to himself a wife this time whose age and fine form give promise of issue." Many a nobleman present must have wished the king would grant some of their other petitions with as much alacrity as he had honored this one.

In July, less than two months after the marriage, Chapuys was reporting rumors that Henry had postponed Jane's coronation until he was certain she was not barren. A month later Henry told Cromwell that he felt he was growing old and did not think he would have children by Jane. Ironically, he said then that he planned to make Mary his heir. That bizarre reversal of attitude seems not to have lasted, however. Perhaps he had simply found himself more bored with his colorless new queen than he had anticipated, and had a difficult time performing his conjugal duties. Or maybe the ghosts of the two queens he had destroyed were coming between him and his new bride. If so, it must have alarmed Jane and her brothers. If she failed to inspire Henry's sexual appetite for too long, God might find a reason for his protégé to rid himself of his third queen.

Henry's brief bout with self-doubt soon passed, and he and Jane seemed happy enough together. One courtier, John Russell, wrote enthusiastically in a letter to Arthur Plantagenet, Lord Lisle, that Jane was "as gentle a lady as ever I knew, and as fair a queen as any in Christendom. The King hath come out of hell into heaven, for the gentleness in this, and the cursedness and the unhappiness in the other." Sir John may have been exaggerating, and his next words suggest a shrewd knowledge of the king, for he suggests that Lisle should write to Henry, congratulating him for being "so well matched with so gracious a woman as she is, wherein you shall content his Grace in so doing." The word was out: if you wanted Henry's favors, you raved about his new queen.

For the conservatives at court, Jane must have been a huge relief. Ann had been close to the Protestants and had, perforce, been the mortal enemy of both Catherine and Mary. But Jane retained her sympathy for them, and her religious inclinations, such as they were, seemed to be with the old beliefs, in spite of her brother Edward's reformist propensities.

The radicals were less pleased. In Germany, Martin Luther wrote to a friend that Jane "was an enemy of the gospel," and he was concerned that Henry's return to conservatism would cause harm to his friend, the English Protestant Robert Barnes.

In fact, Jane didn't affect policy in any way. On the one occasion when she tried to, she was soundly rebuffed. This was during the Pilgrimage of Grace, that complex series of religious and economic rebellions in 1536 that began in Lincolnshire and spread to Yorkshire. Henry, always fearful of rebellion, now found himself faced with the reality. As J. J. Scarisbrick describes them, the risings "were so complex, were sprung of so many different motives in any one area and varied in structure and character from one region to another so widely as to almost defeat generalization." In part, especially in the north, they resulted from anger of the old feudal aristocracy at losing its prerogatives under an increasingly centralized political system. In the northwest, by contrast, it was the poorer classes who were suffering even more than in the past by various agrarian changes and by the loss of the systems of dispensing charity built into the old church structure. In places like Lincolnshire, the focus was the reinstating of pre-Reformation religious institutions. One of the rebels' many demands was the restoration of the monasteries that had been destroyed in the process of Henry's break with Rome.

While Henry was busy quelling the rebellion, his meek new wife surprised him by throwing herself on her knees and begging him to restore the monasteries. Henry stormed at her, ordering her not to meddle in affairs of state and ominously reminding her of what happened to the last queen who had so meddled. To Catherine, who had been her husband's regent and political adviser, such a command would have seemed ludicrous; to Ann, used to openly asserting her will, it would have seemed outrageous. But Jane was neither a Catherine of Aragon nor an Ann Boleyn, and we hear no more of her "meddling."

We see one instance of gratuitous kindness in which Jane perhaps merits her reputation for goodness: her championing of the princess Mary. Henry had never forgiven his daughter for her failure to embrace her own bastardy and the humiliation of her mother. Public opinion had placed the blame for Mary's treatment on the vicious machinations of the witch-wife Ann Boleyn. But Ann was dead, and Mary remained in disgrace. Jane, timid though she was, risked Henry's wrath by imploring him to let Mary return to court. According to one version, however, it wasn't generosity but social snobbery that motivated Jane. "Now that it hath pleased Your Grace to make me your wife," Jane said, "there are none but my inferiors to make merry withal, Your Grace excepted—unless it would please you that we might enjoy the company of the Lady Mary's grace at court. I would make merry with her." In the best bluff King Hal tradition, Henry replied, "We will have her here, darling, if she will make thee merry."

Before Mary was allowed to "make merry" with the new queen, Henry demanded a heavy penance from his daughter. Through Cromwell, he let her know that only a complete capitulation would satisfy him. She had already written to Henry, congratulating him on his marriage and daily praying that God would "send your Grace shortly a Prince." The letter did not suit Henry. His daughter must fully abase herself; she must admit that he was supreme head of the church, and that her mother's marriage was invalid. Badgered by Cromwell and Henry's other henchmen, fearing that she would be poisoned, advised even by Chapuys to submit to the king, Mary finally broke down. She signed, without reading, the document Cromwell placed before her. Even so, she could hardly avoid noticing some of its phrases. She knew she was agreeing to "utterly refuse the Bishop of Rome's pretended authority." Above all, the last sentence of the document, right before her final signature, read, "The marriage heretofore had between His Majesty and my mother, the late Princess Dowager, was by God's law and man's law, incestuous and unlawful."

"The late Princess Dowager." Catherine's daughter was acquiescing to the title her mother had so proudly rejected all those years. It was a capitulation Mary Tudor would regret all her life.

Mary was back at court early in the summer of 1536. If the Spanish Chronicle, a contemporary account of Henry's reign, is to be credited, the first day of her return was one of high drama. Frightened and timid, Mary entered the Presence Chamber, where the king and queen awaited her. Falling to her knees, Mary begged her father's blessing. Henry raised her to her feet and kissed her, then brought her to her new stepmother, who also embraced her. Then, glowering broadly about him, he snarled, "Some of you were desirous that I should put this jewel to death."

Mary flinched, and the queen hastened to intervene. "That had been great pity, to have lost your chiefest jewel of England."

Henry had not married Jane to provide a stepmother for Catherine of Aragon's daughter. Patting Jane's belly, he replied, "Nay, nay. Edward . . ." Later he told his daughter that she was safe, since "she who did you so much harm and prevented me from seeing you for so long hath paid the penalty." Mary was only too willing to believe, as her mother had, that the fault was all Ann Boleyn's. The witch had caused poor Henry to act against his own gentle instincts: all the ruthlessness had died on the block a few weeks earlier. The story must be taken with a grain of salt, as must all of the material in the Spanish Chronicle, but Henry's manner is true to form: lavish gestures, simultaneously embracing and threatening his daughter; his defiant public assumption that Jane, not yet even pregnant, would give him his son; his casting the blame for his mistreatment of Mary on Ann Boleyn. In any event, Jane's kindness to Mary is undisputed, and for the brief remainder of her reign, she continued to be Mary's friend and patron.

There are a few incidents in Jane's life that suggest a less charitable side to her nature, but like her positive attributes, her faults seem almost negligible. Shortly before Christmas 1536, her father died at Wolf Hall. One might have expected a queen so invested with all the womanly virtues to have rushed to her mother's side and mourned at her father's funeral. But Jane remained at court, participating in a holiday pageant and showing no signs of grief. Perhaps Jane's seeming indifference wasn't her fault, however. Henry hated the thought of death and mourning, and he may have ordered his wife to ignore her loss. If so, she obeyed with characteristic placidity.

Another incident suggests a snobbery and self-assertion surprising in a woman of Jane's apparent temperament. One of her ladies-in-waiting was Ann, daughter of the ambitious Lady Lisle, whose husband was the governor of Calais. Jane was unhappy with Ann's continental clothing. Lady Lisle's chief friend at court, John Husee, wrote her that "the queen's pleasure is that Mrs. Ann shall wear no more her French apparel. So that she must have provided a bonnet or two, with frontlets and edge of pearl, and a gown of black satin, and another of velvet . . . she must have cloth of smocks and sleeves, for there is fault founden that their smocks are too coarse." It's possible that Jane was demonstrating an authentic commitment to the dignity of the crown, or even that this was a flash of egotism, a sense of self-importance now that she was queen of England. It seems more likely that she was acting under the influence of her imperious sister-in-law Anne Stanhope, who had an overbearing belief in the importance of station. She was as naturally domineering as Jane was placid, and her husband would certainly have encouraged her demands that a Seymour queen make her ladies-in-waiting dress the part to the hilt.

We catch only a few other glimpses of Jane during her reign. In February 1537 she stood godmother to Edward and Anne's child. It had been a cold winter: in January she and Henry, with the entire court, had crossed the frozen Thames on horseback, a feat Strickland sarcastically dubs "the most remarkable of this queen's proceedings." But from Henry's perspective, Jane didn't have to do anything remarkable; all she had to do was bear a healthy son. And by then she was pregnant.

Henry was particularly solicitous of Jane during the months she was carrying their child—remembering, no doubt, the sons his previous wives had miscarried. He decided to remain close to court to make certain she was doing well, canceling a trip to preside over the Council of the North. He explained in a letter to the Duke of Norfolk that although Jane seemed well and was provided with everything she wanted, "being just a woman" she might become upset by "displeasant rumors and bruits"—which could "engender no little danger or displeasure to the infant with which she is now pregnant."

Jane seemed to enjoy her pregnancy. She constantly craved, and was given, quails—*fat* quails. "My lord, the king commanded me to write you for some fat quails, as the queen is very desirous to eat some but here be none to be gotten," wrote John Husee to Lord Lisle. To get more of his daughters into court, the letter urges, Sir Arthur should send some quails at once. "But they must be very fat."

Gorging on her fat quails and dictating her ladies' wardrobes, Jane appears to have to passed the months of her pregnancy comfortably and happily. Yet surely through those long months upon whose outcome so much depended, she remembered the pregnancies of other queens—their stillbirths, their miscarriages, their daughters. Like any pregnant woman, she must have feared death in childbirth. She could control the wardrobes of her women; she could control the food she ate. But she could not, any more than Henry could, control her child's or her own health.

On October 12, after three days in labor, Jane Seymour had her baby. She had done her work well; the child was a boy, healthy and strong. The streets of London were filled with bonfires, clanging bells, and conduits gushing ale and wine.

As the people rejoiced and the court planned for the christening of Henry's heir, the woman who had borne that heir lay weak and exhausted. But her work wasn't finished—she had to play her part in the elaborate christening ceremonies. Sitting in her state bedchamber, she formally greeted three or four hundred honored guests. The ceremony lasted for five hours, after which the guests marched in great array to the chapel. Their weary queen was left to lie in bed, listening to the trumpets proclaiming her tiny son Edward a true member of the Christian community, and smile at her success. The ghosts of Ann and Catherine could rest now. Jane would not be dismissed or destroyed for failing to give the king his son.

Three days later she fell ill; within a week she was dead of puerperal fever. Henry grieved, and gave her a splendid funeral. Jane Seymour had been the perfect wife, docile and submissive, giving him his son and then dying before he grew bored with her. The men she had served and obeyed—Henry, her brothers, the son who would never know her—would always remember her fondly, when their few moments of leisure allowed them to remember at all.

Meanwhile, Henry made preparations for his heir's upbringing as he went on with affairs of state. And almost immediately, he began to search for yet another wife.

Chapter 7

THE FLANDERS MARE

ANNE OF CLEVES

Henry commissioned Hans Holbein to paint this picture of the German princess, and was entranced by the portrait's beauty. Oddly, he was less entranced by his fourth wife in the flesh, calling her "a great Flanders mare."

Divorced

I n the Louvre in Paris, upstairs in a tiny room far removed from the hall where people crowd to see the *Mona Lisa,* is a small painting of another woman, Anne of Cleves. Her lips show only the faintest trace of a smile, and her large eyes look pensive and a little frightened. While the world wonders endlessly why Leonardo da Vinci's famous beauty is smiling, it is not hard to imagine why Hans Holbein's Anne of Cleves is not. For Holbein was painting the German princess in order to show her portrait to her suitor, the English king, and the prospect of being married to Henry VIII was nothing to smile about.

In the long run, though, Anne had the last laugh. If the stories of his first two marriages are high tragedy, with Henry as the ruthless destroyer of two strong but ultimately helpless women, that of his fourth is broad comedy—the narcissistic buffoon foiled by a woman with common sense.

It took three years for Henry to find a wife after the death of Jane Seymour. Few women wanted to risk marrying him, and few monarchs were willing to endanger the lives of sisters or daughters by offering them to a man with an alarming capacity for shedding unwanted wives.

As soon as Jane died, rumors began to spread that when she was giving birth the midwife had said that either Jane or the child must die, and Henry told her to save the child since he could always get another wife. The tales had no foundation, but their quick acceptance shows how distrusted Henry was.

The king apparently had no idea how unpopular he had become. Before Jane was even buried, the grieving widower began trying to decide whom to marry next. No pretty lady-in-waiting had stirred his romantic inclinations or evoked the voice of God during Jane's brief tenure, so Henry was, for the first time in his life, in the position of having to search for a bride. The Privy Council, always on hand to beg Henry to do what he wanted to do, entreated him to find a new wife for the sake of the realm. Cromwell promptly put out feelers at the courts of Europe. Sending the news of Jane's death to the French ambassador, he added that though Henry was loath to marry again, "yet his tender zeal to his subjects hath already overcome his Grace's said disposition."

In spite of this altruism, Henry wanted to make certain his wife-to-be was beautiful. He seemed unaware that he himself was not. The golden prince who had awed Erasmus and the Venetian ambassador nearly three decades before had coarsened over the years. Portraits done around this time show the Henry we know—beady-eyed and corpulent. European diplomats were talking about how he had "waxed fat." By the 1530s he had acquired running sores on his legs that the doctors were unable to cure. He was in his late forties, old by the standards of the era, and aging less well than contemporaries like the still attractive Duke of Suffolk.

If Henry's person was no longer seen as beautiful, neither was his character. Mary, sister of Charles V and regent of the Netherlands since Margaret of Austria's death, resented Henry's treatment of her aunt Catherine of Aragon. Furthermore, though she had been hostile to Ann Boleyn, she believed that Henry had invented the charges of adultery. "I suppose that when he is tired of his new wife, he will find some occasion to quit himself of her also," she said when she heard the news of the marriage to Jane Seymour. "Our sex will not be too well satisfied if these practices come into vogue."

Henry's methods of wooing shocked even those of his own sex. He would like to marry a French noblewoman, he told the ambassador of Francis I, but first he wanted to see all the eligible ladies, from whom he would pick the most appealing. Would the king kindly send a bunch of France's greatest beauties to Calais so Henry could inspect them?

He would not. Womanizer though he was, Francis was appalled. Frenchwomen, he replied coldly, were not to be brought to market, "like horses trotted out at a fair."

Henry was disappointed, but not discouraged. If he couldn't see the women in person, he would do the next best thing. Hans Holbein, the brilliant Flemish portraitist, had been in England since 1532, and had painted a number of people connected with the court. Henry was impressed with his work, and by 1536 Holbein was officially "the king's painter," having painted Jane Seymour as well as a montage of Henry, Jane, Henry VII, and Elizabeth of York. Henry decided to use Holbein's skill in a different way: he sent the artist running around Europe to do portraits of the various ladies the king was considering marrying.

Among these ladies was Marie of Guise, daughter of one of the most powerful families in France. She was a tall woman (how tall we don't know, but her daughter, Mary, Queen of Scots, was five eleven). Henry, six feet tall himself, found that enticing. He told the French ambassador that "he was big in person and had need of a big wife." But Marie wasn't interested. A story, perhaps apocryphal, is told that Henry's ambassador repeated the king's remark to Marie, who replied that although she was very tall, her neck was very small. Marie and her family opted instead for Henry's nephew, James of Scotland, who had only one dead wife behind him.

Henry plowed ahead. If a marriage alliance with France wasn't feasible, there was always the Holy Roman Empire. Charles had a lovely young niece, sixteen-year-old Christina, the widow of the Duke of Milan. Christina didn't find the idea any more attractive than Marie of Guise had, and reportedly said that if she had two heads, she would gladly give His Majesty one. The sources for this comment are later than Henry's reign, but contemporaries quoted remarks that, if less witty, were equally negative. The English ministers, Christina said, need not waste their time negotiating a marriage, for "she was not minded to fix her heart that way." "Her council," snickered the reformer George Constantine, "suspecteth that her great aunt [Catherine of Aragon] was poisoned, that the second was innocently put to death, and the third lost for lack of keeping her childbed."

One of Henry's negotiators, the smarmy Thomas Wriothesley, wrote to the king that he personally had questioned the young widow, who assured him of her willingness to do whatever her uncle the emperor wanted. But it seems likely that whatever she said to Wriothesley, she was only trying to be tactful, and that she wanted no part of Henry. She was at this time living in Brussels with her aunt Mary, the Hapsburg regent, and must have known Mary's opinions about Henry as a husband. Whatever political games they were willing to play with Henry, neither Charles nor Mary wanted to sacrifice their niece to the man who had destroyed their aunt.

For his own political purposes, Charles now interfered in the marriage negotiations between Henry and Christina until Cromwell cried, "I never heard so many gay words, and saw so little effect ensue of the same." The farcical negotiations continued until the following January, when Wriothesley wrote to the king that the cause was hopeless. One pleasant relic of Henry's ill-fated courtship remains. Holbein's portrait of the lady—who refused to sit for him for more than three hours on a project she knew was pointless—is the only one of his paintings of pretty princesses to survive except for Anne's. It hangs in the National Gallery in London, the knowing eyes looking directly and calmly at the viewer, with no false modesty or feminine self-deprecation. Christina knew what she wanted, and it wasn't the king of England. Several years later she married the less powerful but also less menacing Duke of Lorraine; widowed again, she would become an influence in the reign of her cousin Philip of Spain.

Meanwhile, relations between the Catholic powers France and Spain had become alarmingly cordial. Moreover, in December 1538 Pope Paul III had finally put into effect Clement's bull excommunicating the English king. Henry was worried, and the Protestant faction at court played on his fears. He had become increasingly conservative in his religious views since his disenchantment with Ann Boleyn, and though he persecuted anyone who supported the pope, he was equally severe toward genuine reformers. In June 1539, perhaps in an effort to placate the pope, Henry had Parliament pass the controversial Act of Six Articles, which its opponents quickly dubbed "the whip with six strings." All its tenets upheld traditional church teachings; central and most dramatic was the affirmation of the doctrine of transubstantiation, the belief that the bread and wine of the Eucharist become in reality the body and blood of Christ. Anyone who denied the "real presence" in the elements was to be burned at the stake.

If Henry married a Catholic-leaning wife, she would bring conservative friends to court, and they would influence the king. Cromwell, Cranmer, and the other reformers convinced Henry that the Franco-Spanish alliance spelled danger for England, and Henry's councilors scouted around for an ally in the terrifying event that the two Catholic enemies would unite to war against the apostate king. Henry began to flirt with the Protestant states—and the Protestant princesses. The German territory of Cleves was governed by a duke of mildly Protestant sympathies who had connections with the anti-imperial Schmalkaldic League, and who also had two unmarried sisters, Amalie and Anne. In August 1539 Holbein was once more on his way to the Continent, to paint the sisters' portraits.

There was reason for Henry to be concerned about the appearance of the sisters, particularly of Anne, who as the elder was the more likely candidate for his consort. One of his emissaries, John Hutton, had early warned Cromwell that "I hear no great praise, either of her personage nor beauty." But Cromwell soon got other reports from the men employed to negotiate the marriage contract. Christopher Mont was impressed with Anne, whose beauty "every man praiseth . . . as much for her face as for her person." Nicholas Wotton, another of the marriage commissioners, approvingly described Holbein's portrait as "very lively [lifelike]," though he added information that might have given Henry pause. Anne enjoyed doing needlework, but she was lacking in the range of courtly accomplishments expected of an English noblewoman—playing a musical instrument, singing, dancing, and the ability to converse wittily in at least one or two languages besides English. Though literate in German, Anne knew no other languages. Neither could she sing or play any instrument, "for they take it here in Germany for a rebuke or an occasion of lightness that great ladies should be learned or have any knowledge of music." To Henry, who loved music and was an accomplished musician himself, this should have caused concern.

Anne was intelligent, however, and Wotton was sure she would quickly learn English "whenever she putteth her mind to it." She had been briefly betrothed to the Duke of Lorraine, but the precontract had been formally renounced and Anne was free to marry where she willed—or rather, where her brother willed. (Anne's early betrothal to the man who later married one of Henry's other choices gives an interesting example of the intricate and almost incestuous world of sixteenth-century European royalty.)

Henry didn't object to the precontract—former betrothals came in handy when one's wife failed to produce sons. And he was enchanted by Holbein's "very lively" portrait. On September 4, 1439, the marriage contract was signed. Anne of Cleves was about to leave her homeland forever, to become the bride of the man who rumor declared had killed three wives before her.

It was a grueling journey from Cleves to England, made more difficult by the inevitable round of ceremony that went with the voyage of a royal bride-to-be. Anne was first to travel by land to Calais, accompanied by 263 attendants and 226 horses. There she would be met by a committee of high-ranking English noblemen who would escort her to Dover, and from there by stages to London. She left in mid-November, averaging five miles a day, finally reaching Calais on December 11. She was greeted by Sir William Fitzwilliam, Earl of Southampton, the Lord High Admiral; the Lord Deputy of Calais; and several hundred other aristocrats, all done up in velvet and cloth of gold, along with two hundred yeomen wearing the king's colors of red and blue. Among these gentlemen were a pair of smooth, handsome young men who were rising rapidly in Henry's favor: his brother-in-law Thomas Seymour and Thomas Culpeper, a distant cousin of Ann Boleyn's. The king's ships, the *Lion* and the *Sweepstake,* were as decorative as his gentlemen: dozens of banners of silk and gold waved in the cold, rough wind, and 150 guns greeted Anne with a salute that caused "such a smoke that one of her train could not see another."

The smoke cleared, but the weather didn't. For two weeks the combined German and English entourage waited in Calais as storms raged. Anne used the time to good advantage, persuading Southampton to teach her some of the card games she had been told Henry enjoyed, and shock-

ing the staid lord admiral by inviting him and his gentlemen to sup with
her one evening. In spite of such informality, Southampton enjoyed her
company, and wrote to Henry praising her manner and, significantly, her
"excellent beauty." Probably she also began learning English. She spent an
anxious Christmas in Calais, but on December 27 the winds died down
and she sailed to Dover, accompanied by a convoy of fifty royal ships, in
only five hours. Once again Anne was greeted with great ceremony, this
time led by the Duke of Suffolk and his young wife, Catherine Willoughby, daughter of the stalwart Maria de Salinas.

There were more storms at Dover, and the land journey to Canterbury
was wet and cold. She braved it well, however, and from Canterbury went
on to Rochester, where she lodged at the bishop's palace. By now it was
New Year's Day. Soon she would be in London, where she would meet
Henry for the first time. Meanwhile she could catch her breath and begin
to get accustomed to her new land and its strange language and ways.

Henry had other plans. Years earlier he had been the handsome
prince who had rescued the fair, sad Princess Catherine. Now he would
take on a similar role—the lusty young bridegroom impatient to sweep his
lovely bride into his arms and carry her away. It did not occur to him that
the Henry of 1509 was much better suited to this role than the Henry of
1540. In his own mind he was still the magnificent young prince. He rode
grandly and impetuously to Rochester, disguised as a messenger, and burst
in on Anne, who was gazing out the window at a bear-baiting in the
courtyard. She managed to maintain her composure at the unexpected
intrusion of a fat, bedraggled, and boisterous stranger, but when he returned shortly afterward and announced his true identity, she was faced
with the horrifying knowledge that this boor was her new lord.

We don't know what occurred during that bizarre meeting since only
Henry and Anne were there. But Henry wasn't happy. Leaving Anne's
chambers, he sent for the lords who had brought her from Calais, berating
them for failing to tell him about what he decided was her lack of beauty.
"I see no such thing as has been shown me of her by pictures or report," he
ranted. "I am ashamed that men have praised her as they have done, and I
love her not." Henry was clearly claiming that Holbein's portrait of Anne,
as well as the ambassadors' descriptions, had been grossly inaccurate.

The royal party returned to Greenwich, where Henry continued his
tantrum, this time focusing his anger on Cromwell and Southampton,
who, he yelled, had saddled him with "a great Flanders mare." In a three-
way wrangle that reads more like a vaudeville routine than a royal confer-
ence, Cromwell tried to blame Southampton, who had described Anne as

beautiful. When he realized the princess was less attractive than accounts had suggested, the earl should have held her in Calais until he could tell the king what she really looked like. Southampton retorted that his job had been to bring the lady to England, not to send bulletins about her looks to the king—an argument that would have been more convincing if he had not done just that, taking it on himself to assure Henry that the princess was as beautiful as she had been said to be. As the lord high admiral and the lord privy seal tried to shift blame to one another, the petulant monarch demanded that his ministers release him from this suddenly repellent engagement.

Historians have tended to accept Henry's word that he found Anne ugly—and most have decided that since Henry thought she was ugly, she was. But there are problems with both these ideas. There is no doubt that Henry had quickly convinced himself that Anne was ugly. What Henry wanted to believe, he believed. The man who had persuaded himself that Catherine of Aragon wasn't his wife and that Ann Boleyn had been a multiple adulteress would have little trouble believing in the hideousness of still another wife. Beyond that, however, his version of what went on in that chamber in Rochester is questionable.

In the reports Henry got before Anne came to England, there is only one suggestion that she was unattractive—the memo from Hutton. At least three others gave a contradictory opinion: those of Mont, Wotton, and Southampton. All other references to her unattractiveness come after Henry's dissatisfaction was known to everyone, and thus can be largely discounted. It would have been worse than foolhardy to argue with the enraged king, and no one cared enough about the foreign bride to suggest to Henry that maybe she wasn't really all that bad-looking.

The French ambassador, Charles de Marillac, had a hard time deciding what he thought: in one letter he described her as tall, thin, and "of middling beauty," but later complained of her "want of beauty." Then again, she was Protestant, and as such to a jaundiced Catholic eye could not have seemed in any way lovely. We are entitled to be a little skeptical about his opinion when he adds that all her ladies, "twelve or fifteen damsels, are even inferior in beauty to their mistress." The Duke of Cleves might have tried to pawn his dog of a sister off on Henry, but he would hardly bother scouring the land to find a dozen ugly ladies to accompany her.

The differing judgments of Hutton and the others remind us that beauty is after all a subjective concept, and that Henry might truly have found Anne unattractive. If he did, his attitude toward her would be distasteful enough. He had had no difficulty in forcing his exquisite sister

Mary to marry a king universally considered repulsive. His demands on himself were far less stringent: as Francis I had observed, Henry thought women, like horses, should be inspected before buying.

But Henry *had* inspected his Flanders mare. He had sent Hans Holbein to paint her portrait, and he had liked the picture. He liked it well enough to agree, on the basis of it, to marry her.

We are then left with the possibility that Holbein's painting was inaccurate—that Nicholas Wotton had lied when he told Henry it was "very lively." But why would Wotton lie? And equally important, why would Holbein lie? He could not have inadvertently misrepresented Anne. He was a brilliant portraitist, which is why Henry employed him. If his depiction of Anne was inaccurate, it must have been deliberately so. He knew Henry well, and he understood why the king had commissioned him. He must have known of Henry's request to Francis to look over the French noblewomen; he must have understood precisely how crucial it was to Henry that he do his job well.

Three suggestions have been put forth by historians for Holbein's apparent failure to carry out his commission as he had been paid to do. One is that, as an artist, Holbein painted what he saw with his inner eye, not what was literally there. Another, related theory suggests that Anne was deformed by pockmarks, which Holbein gallantly omitted from his portrait. And then there is Froude's theory that Cromwell had convinced Holbein that "an agreeable portrait was expected of him."

None of these theories stands up under scrutiny. Holbein was not a nineteenth-century romantic artist but a sixteenth-century craftsman who had been hired to perform a specific task that did not involve his inner sense of beauty. Nor did it involve gallantry. Though Marillac later mentioned that Anne's face showed signs of smallpox, the scars can't have been severe, since no one else mentioned them. In any case, though Holbein might have kindly overlooked a tiny scar or mole, he wouldn't have hidden large pockmarks—not if he wanted to keep his lucrative job at court. Nor would he have been stupid enough to believe Cromwell, or anyone else, who told him that Henry desired a prettified portrait. Unlike his painting of Jane Seymour, this was not a portrait of a reigning queen to whom the king was already committed. It was meant only to give Henry information in order to decide whether or not to marry her in the first place. The king wanted a beautiful wife for his bed, not a beautiful picture for his wall.

Finally, the proof is in the outcome. Had the king truly believed that he had been deceived about his intended bride, he would have punished those responsible. Holbein was a foreigner living in England; Henry could easily have had him sent back to Germany. He could even have thrown him into the Tower for treason. He did neither: he kept Holbein on at court and continued commissioning portraits from him. It's asking a lot to believe the man who executed Thomas More and Ann Boleyn, and drove Catherine of Aragon and Cardinal Wolsey to their deaths, would cheerfully reward a mere painter who had misled him on such a crucial issue.

And what of the others—Wotton, Southampton, Mont? Wotton, who had attested to the accuracy of Holbein's portrait, remained one of Henry's ambassadors. He was eventually named to the council of regents Henry created in his will to rule England during Prince Edward's minority. Southampton became lord privy seal. Mont also remained in Henry's service for years. All of them had seen Anne before she came to England; all of them, knowing how concerned Henry was about her looks, told him she was beautiful.

There was nothing deceitful in Holbein's portrait. It was indeed "lively," and its sitter at least attractive enough for honest men to find beautiful, for Henry himself to desire on the basis of the portrait. Then what accounts for Henry's vehement reaction when he first met Anne? In all likelihood, two factors were at work, and they fed into each other, creating a combination of disappointment and humiliation that sifted through Henry's narcissistic mind and forced Anne to become "ugly."

One is that, from an English patrician viewpoint, Anne did have serious drawbacks, as Wotton had told Henry. She lacked the graces deemed essential to an English lady. Remembering how dazzling Ann Boleyn had been, with her manners and accomplishments learned at the French court, we cannot be surprised that Henry would be disappointed with a German noblewoman—any German noblewoman. The housewifely skills that Anne of Cleves had been taught did not substitute for the elegance any English nobleman looked for in a wife or mistress. England itself seemed primitive by the courtly standards of France, which Henry was always trying to emulate, but the little courts of the German states were as far removed from England's as England's was from France's and Burgundy's. Perhaps Henry had actually thought of Malines when he envisioned Cleves, but despite its proximity, the exquisite court of Margaret of Austria was worlds away from the petty German principalities. To Henry, caught up in his fantasy of his fairy-princess bride, the real Anne might have seemed, on their first meeting, like a lumpy shepherdess. Dressed in her German garb and unprepared for visitors, she probably appeared awkward as well—especially when she tried to communicate in a strange language with her unexpected and bizarre visitor.

The other factor that must have influenced Henry's impression of Anne was her impression of him. Again, his sudden appearance made all the difference. Uncultivated she might have been, but Anne was neither stupid nor insensitive. Had she known she was meeting her new husband, she would have shown the proper reaction of modest delight, whatever her real feelings were. But the sudden invasion of her privacy by a vulgar, overbearing "messenger" who turned out to be the king left her no time for dissimulation. She can only have been dismayed by her first sight of this gross old man trying to act like an enthusiastic young swain. In the seconds it took to regain her composure, her horror must have been evident. In such a moment, Henry would have seen himself not as he wished to be, the magnificently handsome man of his youth, but as he was now. However much they might both try to erase the moment, it would always remain in the deepest recesses of Henry's mind. A humbler man might use such an experience as an occasion to take a sobering look at himself. But Henry could never look honestly at anything that threatened his great self-love. If he saw any hint of revulsion from Anne, all he could do was deflect it back on her. So the "Flanders mare" was born, to become an image more powerful in history than that of the pretty lady peering soberly out from Holbein's painting.

While Henry sulked in Greenwich, Anne continued on her progress as though nothing had happened. The king's bolt from Rochester was as ungracious as his descent on the bishop's palace had been ludicrous, but Anne was probably grateful for the time to regain her composure before seeing her betrothed again. Her trepidations about her marriage must have trebled. She had expected a tyrant, a wife killer, but she had not been prepared for an oaf. Royal marriages, she knew, were based not on attraction but on policy, and however she felt about him, she must marry this huge, ridiculous Englishman. But what could she do if he continued to avoid her? Her upbringing had taught Anne that she must acquiesce to the sexual demands of a spouse, but it had not trained her in the seductive arts of gaining that spouse's interest. Slowly Anne made her way toward London, smiling graciously from her litter at her cheering new subjects, moving closer and closer to her dreary, ominous fate.

For his part, Henry spent the time before Anne's arrival frantically trying to break the engagement. He summoned a council, whose members dutifully objected that Anne's precontract with the Duke of Lorraine was an impediment to the marriage. The ambassadors of Cleves were asked to produce documents to prove that the betrothal had been dissolved. They didn't have such proof with them, they told the council, but they could easily get it from the chancery in Cleves. The ambassadors were so clearly telling the truth that the weeks gained waiting for the papers to arrive would only delay the inevitable, as well as risk insult to the lady and her brother. Henry did not want to "make a ruffle in the world" and drive the Duke of Cleves into the camp of France and Spain. "Is there no remedy," he cried, "but that I must needs against my will put my neck into the yoke?"

Meanwhile, Anne was about to arrive in Greenwich, outside London. She and Henry had to go through the formality of their first official meeting.

It was a grandiose business, a smaller version of Henry's meeting with Francis I at the Field of Cloth of Gold in 1520. Henry was going through with it for the sake of his subjects, who would be ecstatic at getting a new queen, and for the foreign diplomats, who must be presented with an awesome spectacle of the union of two mighty anti-papal states. However unhappy the king might be with his bride (or, though it is doubtful that the thought occurred to him, however unhappy she might be with him), they had to put on a show of joyful extravagance.

Marillac, the ever-cynical French ambassador, and Hall, the ever-exuberant English chronicler, both give full descriptions of the event. "On the third day of January, being Saturday, on the fair plain of Blackheath, at the foot of Shooter's Hill," Hall writes, "was pitched a rich tent of cloth of gold, and divers other tents and pavilions, in which were made fires and perfumes for Her Grace and her ladies." All the greenery from the tents to the park gate at Greenwich had been cut down to allow space for the spectators, who presumably lined up by the hundreds. Decked out in velvet coats, English and foreign merchants were at the farthest ends of the clearing; next came the 160 aldermen of London and the members of the king's council. Closer still, next to the tents, stood knights and "fifty gentleman pensioners"; behind these stood the serving men, "well appareled that whosoever viewed them well might say that they, for tall and comely personages, and clean of limb and body, were able to give the greatest prince in Christendom a mortal breakfast." There were also gentlemen from the suites of the lord chancellor, the lord privy seal, the lord high admiral, and other high-ranking noblemen, all magnificently dressed and sporting gold chains.

Anne appeared at noon, accompanied by around a hundred of her own people as well as the noblemen who had met her at Calais and Dover. These marched solemnly toward Greenwich, where they were greeted first by the men Henry had appointed to her council—the Earl of Rutland, Sir Thomas Denny, and one Dr. Kaye, her almoner. The last presented her with her new servants and proceeded to deliver a stirring oration in Latin, which she did not understand. He was followed by sixty-five noble ladies, including Margaret Tudor's daughter Margaret Douglas and Mary Tudor's daughter Frances Brandon. Anne got out of her carriage and welcomed them all graciously: after much handkissing she was finally able, with her ladies, to enter their tents for warmth and a few moments of quasi-privacy before the king's arrival.

In equally splendid state, Henry came to greet his bride. They set out through the park, the trumpeter leading the way, followed by the officers of the king's council, the gentlemen of the privy chamber, the barons, the lord mayor of London, the bishops, the earls, and various foreign luminaries. All wore velvet or satin; most wore heavy chains of gold. Finally, behind all these but, as Hall is careful to tell us, "at a good distance" from them, came Henry himself, in a coat of purple velvet embroidered with gold and lace, lined with cloth of gold, and decorated with buttons of diamonds, rubies, and pearls. "His bonnet was so rich of jewels" that no one could estimate their value. Surrounding him were ten footmen, also bedecked in gold. Hall assures us that Henry himself, "his goodly personage and royal gesture," outshone his stunning jewels. Following Henry were his master of the horse, his pages of honor in "rich tinsel and crimson velvet," and finally the captain of the guard and his men.

At the edge of the park all the others moved to the sidelines, leaving the king in the middle of their rows. Anne, told that Henry had arrived, emerged from her tent wearing a gown of cloth of gold, a jeweled cap, and a partlet or ruff so full of costly jewels on the front of her dress that it "glistened all the field." She mounted a similarly bedecked horse, and with her bejeweled footmen surrounding her, rode to meet Henry. When the glittering couple saw each other they dismounted and formally embraced.

Perhaps if this gorgeous and artificial meeting had truly been their first, their marriage might have had a chance. Blinded by the brightness of their jewels and the adulation of the enthralled audience, they might have seen each other as Hall saw them: "so goodly a prince and so noble a king . . . so fair a lady of so goodly a stature and so womanly a countenance." Henry, once self-deceived, might have been able to continue his raptures long enough for Anne to bear him another son, and Anne might have discovered her husband's character in degrees safe enough to allow her to maintain her composure. But the damage had been done: the farce, however well carried off, was still a farce.

As the ritual of the formal meeting continued, the two groups joined together behind the king and his new lady, and the company rode on to Greenwich. Staged as the spectacle was, there was one homely, charming detail that gives us some insight into Anne's character. Among her entourage, "in a chariot all covered with black," were her three washer-women. She was a duke's sister on her way to becoming a queen, but her upbringing, although it had failed to teach her Latin and lute-playing, had taught her to value the people who worked for her.

Through more pageantry the royal procession finally arrived at Greenwich, where Henry, after one last loving embrace, dumped Anne in her new chambers and fled to his own. There he continued to berate Cromwell, who was now pathetically eager to admit that the new queen was "nothing fair," though he anxiously insisted that she had a "queenly manner." Henry agreed, but it was not a queenly manner he was interest-ed in. He demanded that Cromwell once more summon the Privy Coun-cil to find some pretext by which he could get out of the marriage. He no longer needed Leviticus to supply him with a motive. He wanted out, pure and simple.

The council once again asked the envoys from Cleves whether Anne hadn't been contracted to someone else. Wearily, the envoys repeated their assertions that Anne was free to marry Henry. Again, Henry told Cromwell that it was only his fear of the alliance between France and Spain that led him to go through with the marriage. Then he made one more desperate effort to extricate himself from it. Anne, he said, must be forced to swear that she was free from all precontracts.

It must have been tempting for Anne to take this chance to escape her unpalatable fate. But if she did, she would make a fool of her broth-er, to whose court she would be returned. Recognition of a precontract would render her useless to the duke, who would not be able to marry her off to any other monarch—or anyone else, for that matter. She would live her life under the thumb of the brother she had betrayed. There was, for now at least, no escape for her. She swore formally that she had never been contracted to marry anyone but King Henry. Informed of this, Henry repeated his anger at having to "put my neck into the yoke," and sulkily set the wedding date for the following Tuesday, which coinciden-tally was Epiphany, the feast of kings.

On Tuesday morning he was still sulking. Gorgeously arrayed in his diamond-bedecked wedding garb of crimson satin and cloth of gold, he awaited his bride and muttered to Cromwell that "if it were not to satisfy the world and my realm, I would not do that I must do this day for none earthly thing."

Doubtless his bride was having similar feelings—and for much better reason. She had had far less choice in this matter than Henry had. She had not been given the chance to send a portrait painter to see her mate. Henry might moan that princes suffered more than poor men because poor men could choose their wives while princes "take as is brought to them by others," but princesses far more than princes had to take spouses foisted on them. Not surprisingly, Anne was late to her own wedding. When she finally appeared she was as magnificently arrayed as her betrothed, in the obligatory cloth of gold gown on which were embroidered flowers made of pearls, and a coronet of gold studded with jewels and, interestingly enough, with sprigs of rosemary—an herb, Strickland remarks, "used by maidens both at weddings and funerals."

Archbishop Cranmer celebrated the marriage, following which the unhappy pair participated with pasted-on smiles in a round of jousts, masques, banquets, and "diverse disports" until the wedding day finally ended and her husband escorted her to her chambers.

When the inevitable moment came and the two were alone in bed, they did not consummate their marriage. Anne had prepared herself to submit to Henry's embraces, if only to give him the sons that would guarantee her safety. Henry fondled her enough to confirm his conviction that she was ugly, then gave up, but not before persuading himself that the quality of her belly and breasts proved that she was not a virgin—"which when I felt them strake me so to the heart that I had neither will nor courage to prove the rest." Whether it "strake Anne to the heart" to be briefly pawed and then rejected on her wedding night Henry did not report.

Henry announced his loathing for his bride and his failure to consummate his marriage to Cromwell the next morning, supplying the minister with the edifying information that Anne had "loose breasts." It was an ominous report. Henry had destroyed Wolsey merely for failing to free him from an unwanted marriage; Cromwell had thrown him into one. His only hope was that Henry would change his mind and find Anne virginally lovely after all.

One day soon after her marriage, several of her new ladies-in-waiting—Lady Edgecombe, Lady Rutland, and Lady Rochford—were chatting with the new queen in apparent innocence. The presence of George Boleyn's widow is worth noting. The lurid details of Ann Boleyn's trial and execution had been gossiped about in all the courts of Europe, and Anne probably knew the story of Lady Rochford's slanderous testimony against her husband and his sister. This was a dangerous woman.

The ladies expressed their hope that the queen was pregnant. Anne said emphatically that she was not. "How is it possible for your Grace to know that, and lie every night with the king?" asked Lady Edgecombe sweetly, if a bit ingenuously.

Anne might have been tempted to offer the lady a lecture on the menstrual cycle, but she settled for a firm, polite reiteration. "I know it well, I am not."

Persistently—we can almost see the gleam of malice in her eye—Lady Rochford said, "By our Lady, madam, I think your Grace is a maid still."

Wide-eyed, Anne replied, "How can I be a maid, and sleep every night with the king? When he comes to bed he kisses me and taketh me by the hand and biddeth me 'Goodnight, sweetheart,' and in the morning kisses me and biddeth me 'Farewell, darling.' Is this not enough?"

Lady Rutland continued. "Madam," she insisted, "there must be more, or it will be long ere we have a Duke of York, which all this realm most desireth."

But Anne answered only that she was "contented I know no more." She could not have been as naive as her startling, comical conversation with her ladies suggested. She was at least in her mid-twenties, and if the court in which she grew up was austere in its values, it was an austerity of simplicity, not of prudishness. Nor was this the Victorian era, when ignorance of sex was considered part of chastity. In sixteenth-century Europe, women were supposed to be chaste, but people had the wisdom to realize that a young woman going into a royal court had better know what goes on between a man and a maid if she were to preserve that great jewel of chastity. Anne was making certain that her English waiting women knew her marriage was unconsummated. She saw through their crude ploy, for she could not be unaware that Henry wanted to end their marriage, and she had no more interest than he in maintaining this farcical union.

Anne's feeling of alienation intensified shortly after her marriage, when Henry sent most of her Flemish ladies-in-waiting back to Cleves and replaced them with Englishwomen. He was not cruel enough—or brave enough—to send away the governess of the queen's ladies, her old confidante Mother Lowe, who remained to look after Anne and supervise the selection of her English ladies. It was Mother Lowe that noblewomen wishing their daughters to enter the queen's service approached, bribing her with the gifts that were so cherished a part of sixteenth-century patronage: wine, herring, exotic pets, and costly baubles of all kinds. These petitions must have amused Anne, who knew, as mothers far from court did not, that a daughter taken in by Anne of Cleves would not long be a lady-in-waiting to a queen.

As Henry's distaste for his marriage continued, the political situation that inspired it changed. The Franco-Spanish alliance began to founder. Though it would be months before the ties were formally severed, Henry realized that he had little to fear from either Charles or Francis. In fact, his continued alliance with the Protestant states, far from protecting him against the Catholic powers, created some motivation for them to maintain their shaky tie.

Henry himself disliked the Schmalkaldic League. He had never liked heretics; his religious instincts had always been conservative, and he would have gladly remained Defender of the Faith if only the Faith had defended his right to annul his marriage to Catherine of Aragon and marry elsewhere. Robert Barnes, one of the strongest Protestants at Henry's court, spoke for many true believers, both Catholic and Protestant, when he cried out, "My king does not care about religion." As Martin Luther said, "Junker Heinz will be God and does what he lust." The German alliance was seeming less and less useful to Junker Heinz.

When one of Anne's ladies-in-waiting attracted Henry's eye, his distaste for his marriage grew. As always with Henry, policy and passion became conveniently interwoven. Kathryn Howard was a niece of the Duke of Norfolk, who had helped another niece to the throne and then with equal alacrity helped destroy her. He instructed Kathryn to make herself attractive to the old king—a tactic perhaps lacking in originality, but with a solid history of success. Soon Henry was showering Kathryn with gifts, while the court snickered and waited expectantly for his conscience to attack again. Meanwhile, everybody knew his marriage to Anne was unconsummated—hadn't Anne herself said as much to Lady Rochford and her cronies?

All this inevitably led to the idea of annulment. It appealed as much to Anne as to Henry, though it was crucial that she allow everyone, including her husband, to think it was his idea alone. Her brother might be angry, but she was in a far better position than she had been before the marriage, when to escape it she would have had to publicly admit to a precontract. If Henry managed to annul the marriage, she could not be blamed. He had, the Duke of Cleves well knew, a habit of dropping wives he had wearied of. If Henry repudiated her now, she could expect pity, not censure, when she went back to her homeland.

But did she want to go home? Apart from her marriage, Anne had come to like her life in her new country. She wore damask and satin and diamond brooches; she played cards regularly with her ladies, and she had enough money that she could afford to lose a little of it gambling. She had a pet parrot. Music, which her own country deemed unseemly, was a new joy to her. True, she still couldn't play an instrument herself, but she had her own musicians to play whenever she wished them to, and from time to time she hired little Prince Edward's minstrels as well. The music that in her own country had been considered "an occasion of lightness" was here an occasion of joy. She had even learned to dance.

Anne wanted to maintain her comfortable life in England—without Henry. The king had ended two other marriages, and both wives had suffered horribly. She need not fear Catherine of Aragon's fate, for unlike Catherine she would not fight to hold on to her husband. She did have reason to fear Ann Boleyn's fate, however, if she gave Henry cause for anger. She must, when the time came, appear injured but obedient. As relations between France and the empire continued to deteriorate; as ugly rumors of Cromwell's fall from grace skittered through the court; as the Howard girl began wearing increasingly fine clothes and rich jewels, while the other maids watched her with sidelong glances and whispered among themselves, Anne waited and thought about her future.

Whatever the queen's thoughts were during those strange six months of her reign—while she sewed and danced, cooed over the toddler Edward, played with little Elizabeth, visited with the sad, haunted Mary, and amused herself with her musicians and her parrot—she confided them to no one, except perhaps for her beloved Mother Lowe, whose position in the queen's establishment remained firm.

Henry was spending less and less time with Anne. When they were together she continued her delicate balancing act of being meek but not alluring. According to Strickland, she once lost her temper with him. He brought up his scruples about their marriage, and she retorted that "if she had not been compelled to marry him she might have fulfilled her engagement to another, to whom she had promised her hand." The comment was assuredly calculated, helping Henry to the information he needed to end the marriage.

Anne's fear of Henry grew daily. The brutality he displayed toward others during those months frightened her into wanting to have as little as possible to do with him. As usual when he wasn't getting his way, Henry had begun indulging in deadly temper tantrums. On March 3, two stalwarts of the conservative faction, Henry Pole and Edward Courtenay, were executed for treason, and Pole's elderly mother, Margaret, Countess of Salisbury, was arrested and imprisoned in the Tower.

Not only conservatives suffered. Robert Barnes was arrested during Easter week and condemned to burn as a heretic. Most terrifying of all, Cromwell was arrested on trumped-up charges of treason in early June.

The arrest shocked the country, for in mid-April Henry had raised Cromwell to the peerage, creating him Earl of Essex. But the new earl had always had powerful enemies among the aristocracy, among whom Norfolk and Stephen Gardiner, Bishop of Winchester, figured prominently. They plotted to overthrow the powerful upstart, just as others had plotted to overthrow the powerful upstart Wolsey years earlier. Cromwell's orchestration of the marriage with Anne, combined with his own mildly reformist bent, gave his enemies the means to construct heresy charges against him. The charges of treason were added for good measure.

Shortly after Cromwell's arrest Henry sent Anne off to Richmond, allegedly because there were rumors of plague in London and he was worried about her health. This was, of course, absurd. Henry would have liked nothing better than for this inconvenient wife to die of the plague, and if there had been any danger of it, as Marillac dryly noted, Henry would hardly have remained in London himself, "for he is the most timid person in the world in such cases."

As a place of unofficial exile, Richmond wasn't bad; certainly it was superior to any of the castles Catherine of Aragon had been banished to. It had been Henry VII's favorite palace, dear to the heart of his persevering mother, Margaret Beaufort. Anne loved the place, and were it not for her anxiety, would probably have been content to remain there, away from her unpleasant spouse, indefinitely. But she was sick with worry. Would Henry be satisfied simply to divorce her, or would he discover some heinous crime, bolstered by cleverly constructed evidence, for which she would be executed?

Fortunately for Anne, Henry had no wish to harm her, provided he could remove her from his life and move on to his next marriage. The same Parliament that had so recently declared Cromwell a traitor now humbly requested permission to speak to the king on a matter that, it appeared, was greatly troubling the members. They were doubtful about the validity of their sovereign's marriage, and they begged him to submit the question to his clergy, now sitting in convocation. Not surprisingly, the king consented, thoughtfully adding that they would have to acquire the queen's approval as well.

In a scenario eerily reminiscent of Henry's first effort to obtain an annulment, the Duke of Suffolk and the Bishop of Winchester led a deputation to the exiled queen to persuade her to assent to the annulment. But this queen was only too glad to acquiesce. Her relief must have been intense. So fearful had she been of meeting Ann Boleyn's fate that, on first seeing the commissioners, she fainted. When she came to and realized that she was not about to be taken to the Tower, she quickly agreed that the question should go to convocation, and she made clear that she would abide by its decision.

Luckily Anne didn't have to give evidence in person, nor was she forced to listen to the king's distasteful testimony. Lady Rochford and the other ladies reported their conversations with Anne, indicating that the poor creature didn't even know what a man and his wife did in bed. Henry himself offered a written deposition asserting that he had been tricked into the marriage by reports of Anne's beauty, but was so repelled by her that he was unable to consummate the marriage, and added that "my physicians can testify according to the truth."

Which they did. The king's chief physician, John Chambers, repeated conversations Henry had had with him about his dilemma, which included the reassurance that "he thought himself able to do the act with other, but not with her." Dr. Butts added the pleasing information that Henry had had nocturnal emissions during the time he was married to Anne, which seemed to prove the absence of sexual intercourse.

There was one surprise. Though to Cromwell Henry had declared her to be "no maid" the morning after his wedding night, her virginity was now miraculously restored. Henry assured the jury that he had not taken her maidenhead from her, which was proved by the fact that she was still a virgin.

To Henry's minions among the council and the clergy, his inability to consummate his marriage was reason enough for an annulment—but to be on the safe side, they threw in the precontract with the Duke of Lorraine, which didn't exactly invalidate the marriage, they decided, but complicated the issue enough to make it questionable. With these murky bits of material, convocation constructed an annulment, and on July 9 the marriage between Henry of England and Anne of Cleves was formally dissolved.

⁂ Thomas Cromwell had been allowed to live only long enough to testify at the annulment hearings. He was executed on June 28. His few friends mourned him—including Archbishop Cranmer and Thomas Wyatt. Wyatt wrote of his dead patron,

> The pillar perished is whereto I leant,
> The strongest stay of mine unquiet mind.
> The like of it no man again can find. . . .

Henry would not find his like again either. The king had always underestimated Cromwell's importance. Two years earlier he had told the French ambassador that Cromwell "was a good household manager, but not fit to intermeddle in the affairs of kings." He was too dense to realize that Cromwell had to a large extent shaped the affairs of the king—at least his political affairs—and that he had been brilliant at it. With no Wolsey or Cromwell to run the country while he indulged his narcissism, Henry's policies after 1540 were, in Lacey Baldwin Smith's words, "either mistaken or inept."

Cromwell's execution was followed quickly by six others. On July 30 Robert Barnes and two other Protestants were burned at the stake. In a grand display of impartiality, Henry picked the same day to execute three Catholics, including Catherine of Aragon's old friend and supporter Thomas Abell. "It was wonderful to see adherents of the two opposing parties dying at the same time," Marillac wrote, adding that in the "perversion of justice of which both parties complained . . . they had never been called to judgment, nor knew why they were condemned."

But Anne of Cleves was safe. If she felt any grief at the loss of her husband and bedmate, she managed to comfort herself with the consolation prizes. Henry, though withdrawing from his position as husband, wanted to keep her in the family, and offered himself as her "loving brother." As Henry's sister, she would take precedence at court over all ladies except the king's current queen and his daughters. Henry provided his new sibling with a generous yearly income and a number of manors and estates, including Richmond and, ironically, Hever Castle, Ann Boleyn's childhood home. These would be taken back if Anne left England, so presumably Henry wanted to prevent her from ever returning to Cleves—perhaps, as Strickland suggests, out of fear that if she went home she would entreat her brother to avenge the injury to her honor and provoke a German war with England.

But Anne had little interest in returning home. She had formed a friendship with Princess Mary and, if the not always accurate seventeenth-century biographer Gregorio Leti is to be believed, she asked Henry to permit her to visit with Elizabeth from time to time. Henry agreed, so long as the girl addressed her as Lady Anne rather than Queen Anne. Elizabeth, who had herself been demoted from princess to lady in the wake of her mother's execution, would not have found the condition onerous, and Anne bore the loss of her title as cheerfully as she had borne the loss of her husband.

Henry found it hard to believe that Anne could let go of him with so little bitterness. He badgered her to write her brother to tell him that she was content with the annulment and with her new home. He repeatedly warned the members of the Privy Council that unless Anne committed herself in writing, all would "remain uncertain upon a woman's promise," which was untrustworthy; she could assure the reliability of her word only by "changing her woman's nature, which is impossible." Inconsistency, decided this master of caprice, was built into the female character.

Anne tolerated this nonsense with good humor, since she had every intention of staying in England. She promised her new brother that she would write anything he wanted to her old one. She agreed that Henry could read all her letters to and from her family—a wise decision, since she must have known he would do so anyway—and wrote to the duke in Cleves that she was happy with the arrangement, that all had been done with her consent, and that she was now Henry's cherished sister. She ended with a heartfelt "God willing, I purpose to lead my life in this realm." The duke grumbled, but once assured that Anne was well treated, he accepted the inevitable. With her dubious marital status she could be of little political use to him now, and if her new brother was willing to maintain her in a luxury he himself could ill afford, he would not quarrel over it.

Her letters written, her marriage annulled, the lady Anne quickly settled into her new life. Henry had withdrawn many of her ladies-in-waiting, but she had little reason to be fond of the Englishwomen who had baited her about her marriage bed. She still had the few Flemish ladies Henry had permitted to remain with her, as well as the formidable Mother Lowe, and Henry provided her with a smaller but reasonable-sized household staff.

Now that she had no need to attract—or avoid attracting—Henry, Anne blossomed. The French ambassador could scarcely believe his eyes, for instead of moping, as a newly abandoned wife should, she was preening herself like a peacock. "She is as joyous as ever," he told Francis, "and wears new dresses every day, each more wonderful than the last. She passes all her time in sports and recreations."

In their eagerness to please Henry, the clergy had made it clear that the annulment left Anne as well as the king free to remarry. She did not do so. After a harrowing six months with Henry, she had won a freedom few women of her era could dream of. She was taking advantage of it.

Chapter 8

THE ROSE WITH A THORN

KATHRYN HOWARD

There is no known likeness of Henry's fifth wife, but for many years this Holbein portrait was believed to show Kathryn. It would be nice to see the face of this much-maligned woman who dared to usurp the kingly prerogative of adultery.

Beheaded

athryn Howard was a cousin of Ann Boleyn and niece of the powerful Duke of Norfolk. She was the insignificant daughter of an insignificant Howard brother—a girl who might reasonably expect a good marriage to a man of equally noble blood, but who would never have imagined that she could become queen of England.

Like Jane Seymour's before her, Kathryn's relations were delighted when she was chosen as lady-in-waiting to the new queen. The duke was glad to find a use for the girl. If the king found her attractive, she might make him a pleasing mistress while he did his duty with his German wife. Though nominally religious, the duke had never objected to playing pander if it increased his leverage with Henry. He had encouraged the king's attentions to his other niece when she herself wanted nothing to do with Catherine of Aragon's husband. He had even offered Cromwell, whom he despised, the wife of one of his servants, obligingly throwing a backup into the deal—"a young woman with pretty proper tetins." About Kathryn herself, Norfolk knew, and cared, almost nothing.

Born around 1520, Kathryn was one of ten children of Norfolk's younger brother Edmund. She was farmed out to Horshaw, the household of her step-grandmother, the dowager duchess of Norfolk, where she lived in almost a boarding school environment with a group of other young daughters of the nobility. This was in no way remarkable. Few children of the sixteenth-century English nobility were raised by their own parents; it was considered better for all involved if the child was sent to be trained in the manners of his or her rank in the household of wealthy relatives or friends. Sometimes this worked out well for the child—as in the case of Ann Boleyn's sojourn at the courts of Margaret of Austria and of Queen Claude of France, and young Catherine Willoughby's life in the household of the French Queen and the Duke of Suffolk.

Kathryn's misfortune was that her step-grandmother's house offered neither the sophistication of the European courts nor the warmth of the

French Queen's home. She lived dormitory style with the other girls, learning the skills essential to girls of her class—reading and writing, ornamental needlework, and superficial training in music—but not much else. It was not a bad upbringing, only a very banal one, and the girls in the dormitories did what girls in dormitories usually do: they obsessed about their budding sexuality and the young men who responded to it. Flirtations of various degrees abounded, and the older girls soon figured out how to prevent their bedroom door from being locked at night, so their swains might sneak in with wine and strawberries. If, as one resident later admitted, there was "puffing and blowing" in one girl's bed, the others in this "maidens' chamber" would either tactfully ignore it or follow suit, according to their inclinations. The duchess apparently didn't care greatly about the extracurricular activities of her young charges, as long as they weren't caught. By the time Kathryn met her first suitor, she had a fairly good idea of what went on between the sexes. As she later said, she learned early how "a woman might meddle with a man and yet conceive no child."

Kathryn was fourteen when the duchess decided it was time for the girls to learn music. Their neighbor, George Manox, had a musical son who needed employment, and soon young Henry Manox had moved into Horsham to teach its nubile inhabitants to play the lute and virginals. His father may have hoped he would find a wife among the ladies of noble family, and Henry himself quickly became infatuated with Kathryn.

Kathryn found in Manox's attraction to her an opportunity to test her own sexuality. While she would not go as far as intercourse, she was willing to allow intimate caresses, provided that her frustrated suitor "desire no more." Manox clearly desired a great deal more, but he accepted her terms for the time being, and he later admitted that he "felt more than was convenient" of her body. He expected that his amorous skills and her own yearnings would eventually prompt her to go further, and he may well have been right. But before that could happen, the duchess discovered them in mid-caress. Her ladyship was furious. She forbade them to see each other again and seems to have dismissed Manox from his post. Predictably, this simply increased the aura of adventure for the pair and, with an obliging maid to act as go-between, they were able to arrange assignations. It was not a great romantic passion: Kathryn frankly told Manox that marriage between them was impossible since her family was so far above his.

At about this time a crucial change occurred in Kathryn's living situation. The duchess owned an estate in Lambeth, near London, which she had not used for many years. Now she decided that it was time to move her entourage to that more stimulating location. The move gave Kathryn and the country girls who lived with her a tantalizing glimpse of life across the river, where the king of England held his court. From time to time she saw the young courtiers who attended Norfolk when he visited the old duchess. Even her aging, thickset uncle must have seemed glamorous to Kathryn and her companions, who longed to be among those magical creatures who lived and worked at court, paying homage to the new queen, Jane Seymour. At Lambeth, staring across the water, they could imagine themselves ladies-in-waiting to Jane. Kathryn could daydream about being queen, as her cousin Ann had been—except that in her idle fantasies there would be no miscarriage, no axe, only jewels and cloth of gold and the deference of a worshipful court.

Meanwhile she was able to entertain herself in the here and now with her pretty musician. Manox too had moved near London, and was now in the employ of one Lord Bayment. His master presumably had no pretty young ladies in his household, for Manox and Kathryn resumed their semisecret liaison.

Once again they were discovered, this time by a maid who reported them to the duchess's chamberwoman, Mary Lascelles, adding that people were saying the two were secretly betrothed. Mary was furious. She confronted Manox, warning him that if he dared to marry a Howard, "some of her blood would kill thee."

But Manox laughed. His intentions, he assured her, were not honorable enough to include marriage. All he wanted from Kathryn was a sexual relationship, "and from the liberties the young lady has allowed me, I doubt not of being able to effect my purpose." Kathryn had promised him her maidenhead, he bragged, even though she feared the pain of being deflowered.

Crude as Manox's admission was, it had the virtue of honesty. He should not be judged too harshly, since Kathryn wanted no more from him than he wanted from her. She had already made it clear that she had no intention of marrying so far beneath her, and she seems to have wanted to experience her sexual initiation with an attractive and sophisticated lover. But word of Manox's blunt description of their relationship inevitably got back to a miffed Kathryn. They quarreled and, though she soon forgave him, her romantic interest in him faded.

The end was hastened by the appearance of a new and more exciting suitor. Francis Dereham, unlike Manox, was a gentleman, though far from a Howard. He was a "gentleman pensioner" of Norfolk's, and he soon discovered the household of the duke's stepmother. It wasn't long before he joined the ranks of the young men who sneaked into the dormitory to feast and make merry with the maidens. At first his chief companion in these pleasant pajama parties was Joan Bulmer, but he quickly turned to Kathryn. And she eagerly responded. The sexual awakening that had begun with Henry Manox's caresses now found its full expression behind the bedcurtains at Lambeth. For several months she enjoyed a passionate, intense affair with Dereham.

She had not reckoned on Manox's jealousy. He had learned of the nighttime escapades and was furious that Dereham was getting the full benefit of Kathryn's body, so he wrote a letter to the duchess advising her to visit the girl's chamber half an hour after she'd gone to bed: there, he said, "you shall see that which shall displease you." The duchess was indeed displeased, but not as alarmed as Manox had hoped, and after a bit of wrist-slapping, she again ignored the goings-on. The various pairs of lovers in the dormitory continued their romps unimpeded.

Kathryn was more smitten with Dereham than she had been with Manox, but she was still not interested in marriage. Unlike Manox, however, Dereham was. Whether he was deeply in love with her, or whether he merely wanted to marry above his station, he repeatedly begged Kathryn to marry him.

Though she was willing to pretend they were married while they courted, Kathryn was adamant that they were not truly betrothed—that as a Howard, she could only marry into the upper echelons of the nobility. She had feelings for Dereham, and she enjoyed their sexual relationship, but to her that was all it was. One could wish for Kathryn, in retrospect, that she had wed him sometime in those months between 1537 and 1539. Such a marriage would have given her a better husband than she ended up with—and a longer life. Yet it is important to remember that Kathryn herself never regretted limiting the nature of her relationship to Francis Dereham. She did not want to be his wife when they were lovers; she did not want to be considered his wife afterward. In the Tower, when she might have saved her life by admitting that she had been contracted to Dereham, she adamantly denied it.

The affair might have died naturally within a year or so, but circumstances intervened. In the autumn of 1539 the king was betrothed to Anne of Cleves, and once again ladies-in-waiting were needed at court. Competition was fierce, but the Duke of Norfolk's years of faithful service and even more faithful toadying had paid off. Kathryn Howard, along with another of his nieces, was chosen for the queen's suite.

Dereham was shattered by her departure, but Kathryn was too excited to waste much emotion on a lover whose attentions were already growing tedious. Their recollections of their parting differed. Dereham maintained that she wept to leave him, while she insisted that when he said he'd die of grief, she had told him he could "do as he list." They might both have been telling the truth. She was softhearted enough to cry at his pain, but she was anxious to move on to the next phase of her life. In December 1539, Kathryn Howard was at court, ready to serve her new queen. Neither of them knew at the time just how great a service the pretty girl would do her unhappy new mistress.

Henry was apparently attracted to Kathryn even before Anne arrived, for someone later told the dowager duchess that "the King's Highness did cast a fantasy to Catherine Howard the first time that ever his Grace saw her." This might explain some of his revulsion toward Anne of Cleves. Norfolk and his equally conservative crony, Stephen Gardiner, Bishop of Winchester, knew of Henry's distaste for his new bride as soon as he first voiced it, and Norfolk, who seemed to take a pimp's view of the women of his household, was thrilled. (The role of pander wasn't alien to Stephen Gardiner, either: for centuries the bishopric of Winchester had had legal control of the Westminster stews.) It is virtually certain that Norfolk commanded his niece to encourage the king's attention—probably, remembering Ann Boleyn and Jane Seymour, adding a warning that she must hold back the ultimate favor. It would not have occurred to him that his niece might have already chosen to grant her favors elsewhere. In his world, women acted on men's orders, not their own desires.

The motives of Norfolk and Gardiner were at once political and religious, for Anne represented the Protestant alliance and Kathryn, as a Howard, represented the conservative forces that supported traditional doctrine in an English church under the headship of the king. In fact, both women were conventionally but unenthusiastically pious, sharing a basic belief in God and a willingness to worship him in whatever way they were told.

It is doubtful whether the plotters told Kathryn the extent of their plans—and indeed, the plans were probably open-ended in the beginning. If the king could overcome his distaste for Anne of Cleves sufficiently to inseminate her, she might yet produce a son, rendering useless any dreams of a fifth marriage. In that case, the compliant Kathryn could become his mistress. If not, she would be saved for a more honorable use.

It is unfortunate that we have no accounts of the early relationship between Kathryn and Anne, but judging from their later behavior it was probably an amiable, even a warm one. We have no hints of the kind of rancor Ann Boleyn displayed toward Jane Seymour—no lockets ripped from the waiting woman's neck, no furious scenes with Henry. If Kathryn knew her task was to wrest Henry from his wife, she did it with no hostility toward the woman she was displacing. Perhaps she simply lacked conscience; or she may have sensed that Anne was no happier with her marriage than Henry was.

By April everyone knew Henry wanted to dump Anne and marry Kathryn. His attraction to the young woman had far exceeded the hopes of the duke and the bishop. He was wholly infatuated. She was his "jewel," he told members of the court, his "rose without a thorn." In her arms he recaptured his lost youth, the vision of himself as a chivalrous knight that Anne of Cleves had shattered that evening in Rochester.

He did not bother to conceal his feelings. Kathryn appeared in public in sumptuous gowns and jewelry given her by her besotted suitor, and she and Henry would dine together at Winchester House, where the honorable Bishop Gardiner obsequiously entertained them. It appears that the courtship was conducted in a spirit of chastity. As he had with Jane Seymour, the king contained his passions until he could be safely wed so that no doubt could be cast on the legitimacy of the son Kathryn would give him.

In July Parliament informed the king that there were reservations about the validity of his fourth marriage. Henry agreed to dissolve the marriage, Anne agreed to do as he asked, and Kathryn presumably agreed to become his wife. It is only this last fact about which there is any doubt, since no one saw fit to record Kathryn's views. Probably nobody had seen fit to find out about them in the first place. Henry had never doubted that any woman would be thrilled to be his wife; Norfolk had never doubted that his agreeable little niece would obey him for the good of the Howards.

Kathryn did obey him. She may have been blinded by the majesty of the regal trappings and simply failed to see the old, pus-oozing flesh beneath the king's robes. Or she may have seen exactly what Henry was, and decided that the glory of the Howards and the tangible rewards of being the young wife of an infatuated old king were worth the price.

If so, she realized that she might not have to pay it indefinitely. Everyone knew that Henry's sister Mary, forced to marry the aging and repulsive French king, had kept her old lord merry through three months of festivities until the king died and his young wife married her dashing duke. The thought of Mary would have been an encouraging one during the evenings of Kathryn's own wedding celebrations. But the months went by and Henry remained healthy, with no indication that he would soon follow Louis XII's generous example. If Kathryn was indeed this calculating, she can perhaps be forgiven in light of the callous nature of her new husband, who chose his wedding day to have Thomas Cromwell executed.

Henry was delighted with his bride. He chose a motto for her—"No other wish save his"—but as it turned out, Kathryn had a few wishes of her own.

Whatever she felt about the king, there is no doubt she enjoyed being queen. She was petted and pampered by her husband and deferred to by everyone else. There was plenty of entertainment. Anne of Cleves, in her persona as Henry's sister, cheerfully accepted her old lady-in-waiting as her new sister-in-law. The king had called on Anne at Richmond, and at the New Year she reciprocated with a visit of several days to Henry and Kathryn at Hampton Court. She brought them gifts—for Henry two horses with velvet trappings, for Kathryn a ring and two lap dogs—and knelt before the queen. It was a wonderful gesture, at once honoring Kathryn and showing that she held no grudge against the king for divorcing her, or the queen for replacing her. The three dined together; then Henry, his sore legs bothering him, went to bed, and the two queens danced with each other.

It is interesting to speculate about Anne's motives for befriending Kathryn. She might have pitied the girl who had inherited the precarious role she herself had so gladly escaped. She might have genuinely liked her: for all the contempt historians have displayed toward Kathryn, the pictures they paint show a generous, engaging, fun-loving woman, and such people tend to create enjoyment for others as well. Anne might simply have been going out of her way to assure Henry that she bore him no ill will. Almost as soon as they were separated and Henry had remarried, rumors had surfaced that he was unhappy with Kathryn and wanted Anne back. It was wise to show both the king and the world that she was delighted with Kathryn's succeeding her as consort and with her own status as "sister." There was no reason not to be. The grateful Henry treated her far better than her own brother would have, and as mock wife turned mock sister, she was faring better at Henry's hands than either his real sisters or his real wives had. It was a delight to be at court again, enjoying its splendors on her own terms without suffering any of the anxieties and uncertainties that had plagued her first few months there. Possibly too her friendship for Kathryn had something of guilt in it. She had acquiesced in, perhaps even furthered, Henry's desire to marry Kathryn, and she might well have felt some urge to play shepherdess to the pretty little lamb thrown mercilessly to the royal wolf.

There was another reason Anne wanted to be at court. She was fond of all the king's children, and had become good friends with the princess Mary. It required all of Anne's tact to remain friends with both Mary and Kathryn, for the relationship of the two was not good. Mary could be friendly with a woman like Anne, close to her in age and, like her, neglected and rejected. But Kathryn was younger than Mary, girlish in a way Mary had never been allowed to be—and, above all, she was Ann Boleyn's cousin.

Mary's life had become somewhat better since Jane Seymour had helped reconcile father and daughter. But Henry never again trusted the girl who had defied him, and she never forgave herself for giving in to him. When she signed Cromwell's humiliating confession, she became forever what she later dubbed herself—"the most unhappy lady in Christendom." Still, she tried to resign herself to her fate. Jane Seymour's friendship helped, and since Jane had married Henry after Catherine of Aragon's death, Mary could accept her as Henry's true wife. In Henry's mind, he was a bachelor when he married Jane; in Mary's he was a widower. When Edward was born, Mary rejoiced, sincerely, with the king and queen. It would have been sweeter had the son been Catherine's, but he was the king's true-born son, and the legitimate heir to the throne.

With Jane's death Mary lost her friend and ally, but she found another in the warm, sensible Anne of Cleves. Then Henry divorced the down-to-earth German noblewoman to marry Ann Boleyn's flirtatious cousin. However different this divorce was from his first, it could only bring back echoes of the terrible past. It was impossible for Mary to feel any warmth toward the queen whose very existence was a reminder of all that Mary had suffered.

We don't know exactly what Mary did to offend Kathryn, but it must have been fairly nasty to sting the good-natured queen into retaliation. All we know is that in some way Mary failed to treat Kathryn "with the same respect as her two predecessors." Probably she snubbed Kathryn openly, as she had snubbed Ann Boleyn years earlier, and implied that she was not truly queen since Anne of Cleves still lived. Kathryn retaliated by persuading Henry to dismiss two of Mary's favorite maids, one of whom was said to have died of grief as a result of the separation. Mary was "exceedingly distressed and sad." Later the queen and princess were less antagonistic, and even exchanged New Year's presents, but their relationship never seems to have progressed beyond civility.

Such pettiness was atypical of Kathryn, who was by nature an impetuously generous woman—too generous, in some cases. Francis Dereham appeared on her doorstep shortly after her marriage, soulfully reminding her of their times together and asking for a job in the royal household. She hesitated, but finally took him on as her private secretary, sternly warning him not to mention their former relationship to anyone. Her uneasiness did not prevent her from adding to her entourage other old and dangerous friends, four of her former companions from the duchess's household. None was noted for discretion.

There were other favors as well. She successfully interceded for the life of a spinning-woman named Helen Page, who had committed some capital crime. When Thomas Wyatt was once again imprisoned in the Tower, this time for his close association with Thomas Cromwell, she begged Henry to release him. Henry agreed, but only on the condition—wholly unrelated to his offense—that Wyatt return to his estranged and adulterous wife. It was apparently only to Henry that God gave the right to dispose of unwanted spouses.

While Kathryn was trying to make other people's lives easier, she was also taking care of herself. She was kind to the old king, who doted on her. She may even have had some affection for him. But at this point in his life he could hardly have been an appealing lover for a sexually experienced young woman. Someone else might be—someone like Tom Culpeper, one of the gentlemen of Henry's privy chamber.

Kathryn and Culpeper were distantly related, and they had known each other for some time, possibly since childhood. Before Henry made his interest in Kathryn public there had been rumors that she and Culpeper were planning to marry. He was one of Henry's most trusted servants, and it is even possible that in the days when Henry was trying to be discreet about his passion for the pretty little lady-in-waiting he used Culpeper as a go-between or chaperon. If so, the young woman would have had ample opportunity to contrast Culpeper's trim, youthful virility with the king's bloated mass.

The rumors about Culpeper naturally fell by the wayside when Henry and Kathryn were married, and the relationship between queen and courtier appeared properly distant on the surface. But only on the surface. Culpeper was a gorgeous, swaggering, unprincipled young man of the sort that many women find attractive. Their interest in each other continued unabated in the months following Kathryn's wedding. She knew that she would risk her life if she acted on her desire for Culpeper. She was willing to take that risk.

🕭 Here the temptation arises to make Kathryn's affair into a great romance. Risking death for love seems noble, the stuff of great tragedy: it takes on a mythic grandeur. We are willing to forgive women who betray their husbands for an overwhelming love. Guinevere, Isolde, Anna Karenina: we adore these mythic heroines and shed tears for their gallant, inevitable deaths. Knowing Kathryn Howard's sweetness and generosity, we want to include her in their company, rescuing her from the degradation of a merely sexual affair. Deprived of that image, we want to join her detractors who accuse her of wantonness, promiscuity, delinquency. Sophisticated though we like to think ourselves, we are still stuck in the ancient dichotomy of madonna and whore. Shaking free of those figures, however, we can see a very different Kathryn Howard, more human, more truly tragic than the various personae historians have allowed her.

The romantic image is the easiest to dispense with. Nothing in the reliable contemporary records suggests a great love, and much suggests otherwise. The romantic image began with the often inaccurate Spanish Chronicle, and the credibility of the tale can be gauged by the fact that it has Thomas Cromwell confronting the terrified queen about Culpeper. Cromwell found her, says the chronicler, "nearly dead"—which was reasonable enough, since he himself had been fully dead for some time.

The character of Culpeper himself also challenges the picture of a noble passion. Charming and seductive he may have been, but he was noble only in rank. He was in fact a rapist and a killer. In 1540, he pulled the wife of a park-keeper into the bushes, ordered his attendants to hold her down, and raped her. When some villagers attempted to rescue her, he killed one of them. Arrested, he was soon released on Henry's orders. Having gotten away with raping a park-keeper's wife, Culpeper was now free to engage in a mutually agreeable affair with a king's.

If Kathryn knew of Culpeper's unsavory activities, she didn't let the knowledge stand in her way. She was attracted to him, and she liked sex.

She had married as her family had told her to, aware that her marriage was based not on love or sexual desire, but on social rank. The mentality that allowed her to take a lover before her marriage while planning one day to wed someone else of more appropriate rank—exempting herself from the insistence on bridal virginity—carried into her life as Henry's queen. She had obeyed her family, marrying well enough to satisfy the most exacting Howard standards. She was doing her duty, and she was entitled to her pleasures.

A lot of pity has been wasted on Henry VIII over Kathryn's infidelity—much more than has been accorded Kathryn herself. The chroniclers of her own time treated her with contempt, which is at least understandable in an age when chastity and honor were synonymous when applied to a woman. Less understandable is the determination of twentieth-century writers to follow suit. Even her sympathetic biographer Lacey Baldwin Smith, in *A Tudor Tragedy* (1961), repeatedly refers to Kathryn as "wanton" and "promiscuous"; she was "a common whore" and "a juvenile delinquent." As late as 1991, Alison Weir described her as "certainly promiscuous."

Her defenders have done her an equal disservice. The Spanish Chronicle created a great romance. The nineteenth-century feminist historian Agnes Strickland, trapped in Victorian moral values, denied the affair, as though only as a victim of slander could Kathryn be defended.

Both defenders and detractors miss the point. Kathryn Howard was not a paradigm of chastity, but neither was she promiscuous: any "common whore" who lived as Kathryn Howard had would soon have starved to death. Neither whore nor martyr to love, she was something far harder for our mythologies to deal with—a woman who enjoyed both sex itself and the admiration she got from the men with whom she had her few sexual adventures. Looking at her life not through the eyes of her contemporaries, for whom the ownership of women by their husbands was a given, but from the perspective of a presumably more enlightened age, we should be able to recognize a kind of courage in her reckless affair with Culpeper. Kathryn Howard was a woman who listened to her body's yearnings, and in spite of all she had been taught, understood that she had a right to answer those longings. She was willing to risk whatever it took to be true to herself.

Her liaisons may have lacked the transcendent glamour of risking all for true love, but do they constitute promiscuity? Judged by the standards of her own age she was a "wanton," as was any woman caught engaging in nonmarital sex. Judged by the standards of ours, she can only be seen accurately as a woman with a healthy sexual appetite, which she indulged with a fair degree of restraint. No man would be judged sexually excessive, then or now, on the basis of two consummated affairs and some heavy petting. That her image remains so tarnished says more about our failure to accept female sexuality than about Kathryn Howard's morality.

We can perhaps with more justification call her foolish. The cousin of a woman executed on false charges of adultery, Kathryn knew she lived in a milieu where secrets were at best terribly difficult to keep. She warned Culpeper that when he went to confession he must not "shrive him of any such things as should pass between her and him, for surely the king . . . should have knowledge of it." Spies were everywhere, even in the holy confines of the confessional. Was a pleasant little fling with a pretty courtier worth risking her life for?

Perhaps it was. She was twenty and the king was fifty. That was considered old age, but many people lived into their seventies and eighties. She might be fifty when the king died—she might be as bloated and ugly as Henry was now. It cannot have been pleasant, looking into that vista of years that would be spent catering to the whims of the tyrannical old man, satisfying his sexual needs while her own went unmet. Perhaps the thought of Tom Culpeper—of a series of Tom Culpepers—made the vision a little more bearable: hidden, intense pleasures to make up for the dreariness of being Henry's wife, pleasures such as Henry himself had indulged in during his first two marriages. It may not have been so foolish to choose a course that made her life at least tolerable.

There was always the danger that she would conceive a child. But, as Kathryn had once declared, she knew how to avoid unwanted pregnancy. Whatever methods she had used with Dereham she could certainly transfer to Culpeper. Possibly she didn't bother. It had been drilled into her from childhood that hers was an old and noble family, one whose blood matched or bettered that of anyone in the land. The Tudors held the throne more by conquest than by blood, and were still regarded with some contempt by the old aristocracy. Kathryn may have decided that if she became pregnant it didn't really matter who the father was: legitimate Tudor or bastard Howard, her son would be worthy of the throne of England. Given Henry's desire to strengthen his dynasty with more sons, and his obvious difficulty in begetting live children, she may even have hoped to become pregnant by Culpeper. As long as she was still sharing the king's bed, no one need be the wiser.

So Kathryn began her affair. When, we can't be certain, but by the spring of 1541, less than a year into her marriage, she was giving him costly gifts—one was a jeweled cap, accompanied by a warning that he should hide it under his cloak and make certain no one saw it. In a letter written around the same time she spoke of how she longed for him, and said that it "makes my heart die that I cannot be always in your company."

In this letter she also referred to the woman who made their affair possible. "Come when my Lady Rochford is here, for then I shall be best at leisure to be at your commandment." Jane Lady Rochford was one of the most bizarre figures at Henry VIII's court. She had been Ann Boleyn's sister-in-law, and had testified against her husband. She had remained at court in the reigns of Ann's successors, but aside from her slightly prurient interest in the bedtime activities of Anne of Cleves, we hear little of her again until she took on the role of go-between for Kathryn and her lover.

Why she did so remains a mystery. The pandering of Kathryn's uncle and the Bishop of Winchester, distasteful as they are, at least make sense—with their pawn in the king's bed, they were assured of continuing to influence him. Lady Rochford had nothing to gain, and her life to lose. Whatever her motive, she did her job magnificently. In all the palaces and castles of the court, she ferreted out back stairs and hidden rooms where the two could meet, and carried messages between them. At her trial she claimed she had only done as the queen ordered. If so, she did it with astounding thoroughness. She was clearly an active and avid participant in the affair.

Kathryn and Tom must have managed their liaison with at least a modicum of discretion, since none of the Howard clan's ever-vigilant enemies at court seem to have noticed anything untoward. Then in the summer of 1541 Henry decided to make a progress to the northern provinces, where a brief insurrection had recently been quelled. Besides displaying his majestic power to his subjects, he would try to arrange a meeting with his nephew King James of Scotland in the border county of York.

It was to be the progress to end all progresses. Five hundred horses, two hundred tents, and a thousand armed soldiers would accompany the king and queen. So would the lords and ladies of the court, and the more important of both the king's and the queen's household servants. The members of the Privy Council would also come, for much of each day was to be spent attending to matters of government, in meetings that did not involve either the queen or the personal servants, who would have free time to entertain themselves as they would.

Before setting out, Henry sent word through the counties that any of his subjects who "found himself grieved for lack of justice" would have personal access to His Majesty. Then he executed the Countess of Salisbury, who had been held for the past two years on charges of treason. She did not die easily: the executioner hacked several times at her neck before she was dead. Perhaps, as an account written a century later claims, this was because she refused to cooperate, crying that she was not a traitor and should not die as such. She fought with the executioner, telling him that if he wanted her head "he must get it as he could." Horrifying though this gruesome picture is, it's also peculiarly refreshing. It is the one instance we know of, throughout the history of Henry's bloodbaths, in which someone defied the custom that innocent people must accept execution without complaint, since they were surely guilty of some grievous sin or other in the sight of God. Henry's councilors, interrogating the countess, had found her so intimidating that they said she was "rather a strong and constant man than a woman." But no man was strong and constant enough to die protesting as she did.

With the countess and a few other dubiously defined criminals out of the way, Henry proceeded north. He and his entourage stayed at royal palaces and the estates of various noblemen along the way. At each home, great hunting parties had to be arranged, as well as jousts, masques, and the other entertainments of royal life. It was the Duke of Suffolk's job to organize this at every stop. Throughout the progress the duke was constantly busy providing for the king's amusement.

Tom Culpeper and Lady Rochford spent their time providing for the queen's amusement—part of the time in the duke's own lush manor house, Grimsthorpe, where Henry had one of his longer stays. It's a pity, in a way, that Kathryn spent so much time there with her "sweet little fool," for she might have been better off getting acquainted with her hostess. Catherine Willoughby, the Duchess of Suffolk, was one of the most remarkable women of her era. On the surface, the two women had much in common. Both were the daughters of great noble families; both had been sent away from home as children. They were about the same age, and each had married a man nearly three times her age. Their husbands were in many ways similar. Like Henry, Charles Brandon had been much-married. Like Henry, he was a robust, hearty figure, fond of hunting, soldiering, and carousing. But he was neither as shrewd nor as cruel as Henry; he was a simple man, and if in his youth he was callous toward the women who loved him, he was a good husband to the king's sister and later to his young duchess. Catherine Willoughby was far luckier in her husband than Kathryn Howard was.

She was luckier, too, in her upbringing. Daughter of the intrepid Maria de Salinas, she had been a playmate of the princess Mary in the early, happy days of her childhood. Catherine had probably been tutored with the princess; Vives had strongly urged Catherine of Aragon to install Mary in a schoolroom with other girls, and the daughters of the senior ladies-in-waiting were obvious choices. At the very least Catherine was educated along the lines Vives presented to the enthusiastic queen. When her father died in 1526, the six-year-old girl had been sent to live with the Duke of Suffolk and his wife, Mary, still known affectionately as the French Queen. She was fortunate, for when the storm of Henry's conscience broke, she was at a safe distance.

When the French Queen died shortly after Ann Boleyn's coronation, the duke married his ward. She was fifteen; he was forty-seven. From the perspective of our age such a marriage seems a shocking abuse of a child, but in that era it was commonplace. As her guardian, the duke already had control of Catherine's fortune; as her husband, he consolidated that control. From her standpoint also the match offered advantages. A woman had little say over whom she married, and at least Catherine's husband was someone she knew and for whom she presumably had some affection. It seems to have been a happy marriage; the references that appear in contemporary accounts depict a comfortable, compatible couple. They had two sons, and Catherine, like many other noblewomen of her time, ran the household and in her husband's frequent absences also ran their estates.

At court during Ann Boleyn's reign, she listened to the sermons of the fiercely Protestant Hugh Latimer, Bishop of Worcester, and was impressed. They began a friendship that would last throughout their lives, and she called him her "father Latimer." The humanism that Vives had implanted in the child's mind grew into the Protestantism that fascinated the young woman and would define the mature matron.

Catherine Willoughby had also acquired a reputation for a biting wit—a wit, grumbled one victim of her sharp tongue, that "waited upon too froward a will." Another victim was Stephen Gardiner. Though the Bishop of Winchester was the duchess's godfather, he and Catherine despised each other. Perhaps their mutual antipathy had to do with religious differences, but it was probably exacerbated by Gardiner's uneasiness around strong women. Catherine Willoughby was not one to hide her contempt. Once at a dinner party given by the duke, Brandon announced that each lady must choose as her escort to the dining table the man she liked best, modestly excluding himself. Taking Gardiner's arm, Catherine sweetly declared that, since she was not permitted to choose the man she loved best, she would choose the one she loved worst. On another occasion she dressed a pet spaniel in bishop's vestments and named it Gardiner.

Gardiner, who along with the Duke of Norfolk controlled much of the young queen's life, probably warned her to avoid intimacy with the formidable young duchess. There is no record of the two women having spent any time together during the queen's stay. Entertainments kept the queen and the king's favorite in the privy chamber busy, but there were also the frequent meetings of the Privy Council, and Grimsthorpe, as both the duchess's biographers have noted, had two back staircases ideal for secret assignations. Aided by the energetic Lady Rochford, the lovers trysted while the duke attended the king in council and the duchess frantically saw to the needs of the dozens of courtiers and their servants who had taken over the house, to the great honor and greater exhaustion of its owners. Neither the duke nor the duchess had time to notice what else was going on under their roof.

Others did. Kathryn had enemies at court, not because of anything she did but because of what she was—the tool of the conservative faction. Since Cromwell's fall the Protestants had been searching for anything that would dislodge her from Henry's affection.

Among their number was one John Lascelles, who had been in Cromwell's service and was bitter both about his master's death and the conservative religious influence of Gardiner and Norfolk. Lascelles had a sister, Mary—the same Mary Lascelles who had reprimanded Henry Manox for his unchaste behavior with young Kathryn Howard. Mary had left the old duchess's service and married a Mr. Hall of Lambeth. John Lascelles approached his sister with the suggestion that she use her acquaintance with Kathryn to get a position at court, as so many others had. There, she would be able to act as his spy.

Mary sniffed; she would not demean herself by working for so loose a woman. To her brother's surprise, she went into a long account of the escapades of the future queen in the maidens' chamber.

Excited, John hurried back to London to report what he had heard to Archbishop Cranmer. The king believed he had married a fresh young virgin: he would not be happy to learn he'd bought used goods. Cranmer agreed, and carefully composed a letter to Henry, outlining Mary Hall's story.

When Henry returned from his progress, he was greeted with two pieces of bad news. One was that his sister Margaret had died in Scotland. The other was that his wife had been unchaste before they were married. He bore the loss of his sister stoically, but he wept over the loss of his illusions.

At first, however, he simply refused to believe Cranmer's letter. Someone was maliciously spreading lies to discredit the queen. Henry ordered Southampton and Wriothesley to investigate the story so that the culprits who dared to defame his wife could be brought to justice.

But Wriothesley quickly and efficiently determined the truth of Mary Hall's tale. He had Manox and Dereham arrested, and both, undoubtedly under torture, confessed their relationships with Kathryn. Southampton, interviewing Mary Hall, confirmed in glowing detail all that she had told her brother. The two men hurried back to the king. He and his council heard the story in its entirety.

Henry was thunderstruck. First he ranted and raved, calling for a sword so that he could slay the woman who had so abused his trust. Then he dissolved into tears, bemoaning his misfortune in "meeting with such ill-conditioned wives."

Drying his tears and blowing his nose, Henry ordered Cranmer and Norfolk to interrogate Kathryn. At first she frantically denied everything. Her inquisitors left, locking her in her chambers. They returned the next day.

By then, Kathryn had gotten hold of herself and realized that lies were useless. Her confession was hardly admirable. Desperate to escape the consequences of her actions, she admitted to her affair with Dereham but claimed he had forced himself on her. She soon dropped that lie as well, and wrote out her confession to Henry, acknowledging that, after Manox had "by many persuasions procured me to his vicious purpose," she had permitted him to "touch the secret parts of my body," and that Dereham had "used me in such sort as a man doth his wife many and sundry times."

She knew Henry well enough to know that the only way to save herself was to grovel. She was "the most vile wretch in the world," she said, and "unworthy to be called either your wife or subject." Henry by contrast was a man of "infinite goodness, pity, compassion, and mercy" who would, she hoped, spare her in light of her youth, ignorance, frailty and the "humble confession of my faults." But in spite of her interrogators' repeated insistence that she had been contracted to Dereham, she continually denied it. Dereham, they told her, was vehement in his claim that he had only lain with the woman who had promised to marry him. He lied, she said. They persisted. Henry wanted an excuse to annul the marriage, and a precontract with Dereham would make that possible. But Kathryn was a Howard, and Howards, though they might dally with the likes of Francis Dereham, did not marry them.

Kathryn's past had caught up with her, and it was dangerous enough. But worse was to come. Inevitably, as the members of the Privy Council continued their investigation into her premarital adventures, they learned of her current one. Soon they were questioning her about Tom Culpeper.

Kathryn admitted to the expensive gifts and the secret meetings, but she denied that she had had a sexual relationship with Culpeper. As she had blamed Dereham for her affair with him, she now blamed Culpeper for browbeating her into making assignations with him. For good measure, she added that Lady Rochford had also bullied her into meeting with the handsome courtier.

Culpeper, arrested and interrogated, also denied having had sex with the queen, although "he intended and meant to do ill with the queen, and that in like wise the queen so minded to do with him." He insisted that it was Kathryn who demanded their secret meetings, to which he had acquiesced with the greatest reluctance.

Lady Rochford rounded out the unsavory trio of confessions by blaming both of them and excusing herself as the unwilling servant forced to obey their orders. While conceding that she had not actually witnessed sexual acts between them, she was sure such acts had occurred, "considering all things that she hath heard and seen between them."

It is unfortunate to have to agree with that inveterate liar and troublemaker, but Lady Rochford's assessment makes sense. Culpeper and the queen were two sexually experienced people with a strong attraction to each other, and they knew they were courting death with their secret meetings. To take that risk without enjoying the pleasures it made possible seems imbecilic, and it's hard to imagine that Culpeper, who had forced himself on the park-keeper's wife, would put his life in jeopardy for a bit of innocent flirtation and pleasant conversation.

The King's privy councilors took no chances. Culpeper, they said, had confessed that he wished to bed the queen. According to the treason laws in Henry's England, the very fact of verbalizing a wish to harm the king was tantamount to doing it.

By an even more twisted logic, they declared that Dereham's entrance into the queen's service proved he wanted to seduce her, and thus he too was guilty of treason. All it really proved was that he wanted to use an old acquaintance's good fortune to boost his own. There was no indication whatever that his affair with Kathryn had resumed, or that either of them wished it to.

To make certain the case held, the council questioned all of Kathryn's waiting women, who testified to having heard various expressions of intimacy and affection between the queen and Culpeper. If none of the stories proved that the two had actually had sex, they did prove that Kathryn had looked longingly at a man other than Henry.

For this, she was doomed. It was not, as many historians claim, necessary for Henry to kill Kathryn. He could have chosen to believe Dereham and annulled the marriage based on her precontract. He could have belatedly remembered that she was a cousin of Ann and Mary Boleyn. Since one was his wife and the other his mistress, either relationship could make his current marriage incestuous. He had had, after all, a good bit of experience annulling marriages.

But Kathryn had wounded the royal ego, and it was because of this that he decided to kill her. If further proof is needed beyond Henry's own history, we need only to look at Francis Dereham's fate. There was no reason to believe Dereham wanted anything more from his ex-lover than a cushy job at court. But he, an insignificant gentleman, had been Kathryn's bedmate before Henry had, and he had lived at court, knowing that the king had not married a virgin. He could tell other men secrets about the body that Henry had embraced, about the acts that aroused Kathryn, about the ways she moved in sexual excitement. He could say, ah yes, I know what she does to please the king; it was I who taught her those caresses. His very existence made Henry fallible, less than majestic. Thus Dereham would suffer not the quick stroke of the axe, but the slow torture of drawing and quartering. Henry would not exact that punishment of the nobleborn Culpeper, who had truly betrayed him.

Both men were executed on December 10, at Tyburn, in front of the sort of crowd that always came to watch such events. It is grimly pleasant to imagine that one of the spectators was the park-keeper's wife, smiling a little as the man who had raped her and been excused by the king was beheaded for cuckolding that same king.

There remained now only Henry's last two victims. Lady Rochford had gone into "a kind of frenzy," in which she remained till her death. Her sanity seems always to have been questionable, and perhaps terror of her upcoming execution proved the last straw.

Kathryn, after her initial hysteria, seemed to have accepted the inevitability of her death. Before being taken to the Tower, she asked her jailers to beg the king to give some of her clothes to her waiting maids, since she had nothing else to give them. On the night before her death she requested that a block be brought to her so that she could practice how to place her head on it properly.

She was executed at 9 o'clock on the morning of February 13, so weak that she had to be helped up the scaffold. She managed a few customary words of self-recrimination. Then she laid her head down on the block. Swiftly, the executioner struck it off. Lady Rochford was executed immediately afterward.

Henry wallowed in self-pity. The lecherous Francis I wrote to him, commiserating over Kathryn's "lewd and naughty demeanor," but reminding him that "the lightness of women cannot bind the honor of men." The Spanish ambassador took a more cynical view of the king's grief. Henry, he wrote, was like the woman who lamented the death of her tenth husband more than the first nine because "she had never buried one of them without being sure of the next, but after the tenth husband she had no other one in view."

Henry deserved Chapuys's cynicism, and he deserves history's as well. This is not to deny compassion to the figure of an aging man desperately seeking to regain his youth. Nor is it to defend Henry's victim as an exceptional human being. Kathryn was simply a decent though somewhat ordinary young woman who enjoyed life. We don't know what kind of person she would have become over time. It's quite possible that had Kathryn Howard lived she would have grown into old age very much as Henry did, buying the attentions of some pretty young courtier, using his youth to negate her old age, convincing herself through his purchased affection that she remained the pretty, giddy young girl she had once been.

This is only supposition. We do not know what kind of old woman Kathryn would have been, because Henry did not permit her to become an old woman. He killed her for daring to exist outside his vision of her, to act on her own desires instead of his—to be the woman she was, on her own terms.

It is worth remembering this as we look at the sad old man taking time from his self-pitying sniffles to wipe away a tear, grab a pen, and sign his young wife's death warrant. For her there would be no self-deceiving old age. Henry made certain of that.

Chapter 9

THE CLERK

KATHERINE PARR

Henry's last wife was twice a widow when they married. She was smarter than Henry, and nearly lost her head for it.

Survived

athryn Howard was executed in February 1542, and Henry found himself once more without a wife, or a likely prospect of one. It had been hard enough to find a woman willing to marry him after Jane Seymour's death. Now, with another divorce and another execution under his ever-widening belt, Henry was even less of a matrimonial prize.

At first it seemed as though he had accepted that it was time to secure the succession by finding suitable spouses for his children rather than by producing more heirs himself. Nonetheless, he was keeping an eye on the ladies of his court. It wasn't too long before he settled on one.

And he picked her himself. Although there were plenty of pretty young things with ambitious relatives at court, the fate of Kathryn Howard made ambition dangerous. The act condemning Kathryn to death included an ominous provision that if any woman not "a pure and clean maid" married Henry without informing him about her lurid past, she would be guilty of high treason—as would anyone else who knew of her sins and failed to inform the king.

This changed the possible use courtiers might make of their marriageable relatives. Virginity was a difficult thing to prove, and Henry had established himself as a poor judge of such matters. He had believed Kathryn a virgin, though she was not. He had believed Ann Boleyn a virgin when he first bedded her, but later declared that she'd had had a hundred lovers before and during their marriage. He had concluded from his first night with Anne of Cleves that she was no maiden, only to swear later that she had been and indeed remained one after their marriage. As for any future wife, once she lost her maidenhead to Henry her past virginity would be unprovable, and anyone with a grudge or an ambition could declare newly discovered knowledge of her lack of chastity. The obvious solution was for him to marry a respectable widow—a woman who combined chastity with a legitimately vanished maidenhead.

Yet the widow he settled on seems at first glance a strange choice.

True, Katherine Parr had a drop or two of royal blood through that sower of ubiquitous seed, John of Gaunt. But she was thirty-one at the time of their marriage in 1543—fairly old for a king who wished to have more sons, and more significant, she had had no children in either of her first two marriages. Henry's grandfather, Edward IV, had raised eyebrows when he married the widowed Elizabeth Woodville, but he had blithely and astutely responded that her several sons and daughters proved her a fertile wife who would produce heirs to the throne.

Katherine, by contrast, was to all appearances barren. Why would the king who had turned the country upside down to get himself a son marry such a woman? Possibly he had simply given up hoping for more children, as some historians suggest. Perhaps he himself was impotent now, and wanted his impotence masked by the assumption of his wife's infertility. His health was increasingly bad. The ulcers he had had on both legs since the mid-1530s had worsened over the years. His great weight exacerbated the problem, and he had to be carried upstairs in a huge machine designed for that purpose. He had serious bouts of fever at various points in the early 1540s, each of which left him weakened and more vulnerable to the next. With all this, he needed a nursemaid more than a bedmate, and his attentions turned to Katherine Parr.

Henry had known Katherine since she was a child. Her father was one of his courtiers, and her mother was a lady-in-waiting to Catherine of Aragon. Thomas Parr died of a sudden illness in 1517, and his wife, Maud, continued to stay on in the queen's household. It is likely that Katherine studied for a while with the princess Mary, who was about four years her junior, under the curriculum suggested to Catherine of Aragon by Juan Luis Vives. Certainly in her later years Katherine demonstrated a great commitment to the humanism Vives espoused—though in a far different form than the firmly Catholic scholar had envisioned.

Maud Parr was a strong-minded woman, and she was determined to make the best possible careers for her three children. Katherine was given the most lucrative position a woman could hope for—marriage to a rich older man. She was fourteen when she married Lord Borough, a widower in his sixties.

In 1528 Lord Borough died, leaving Katherine a wealthy widow of sixteen. Her mother died the following year. Katherine had evidently found marriage agreeable, for, although she could have followed Maud Parr's example and led the comfortable life of a rich widow, she chose to remarry. Sometime in the early 1530s she married a widower in his mid-forties, John Neville, Lord Latimer. Latimer had been married twice before and had two children, so Katherine, not yet twenty, found herself a stepmother to a pair of children half her age.

Soon after Katherine's marriage her sister, Anne, married William Herbert. It may have been a love match; it most certainly was a match of comrades who shared religious and political affinities. Both were at court, and both were apparently influenced by the evangelism of the new queen, Ann Boleyn, since they showed distinct reformist leanings in the years ahead.

If Katherine's own interest in religious reform began at this time, she kept it well hidden. She had to, for her husband's sympathies were conservative. Latimer joined the northern rebels during the Pilgrimage of Grace, though he may have taken part under duress. He pulled back after the first set of uprisings, and was pardoned by the king—possibly at the request of the Herberts, for whom Henry seemed to have some fondness.

He evidently had some fondness for Katherine as well. In 1540, at her request and in opposition to the still-powerful Cromwell, Henry released from the Tower her relative George Throckmorton, accused of denying the royal supremacy. The attractive Lady Latimer seemed to have some influence on the king.

At that time her charm posed no threat to her. Katherine was safely married and, more important, Henry was safely infatuated. With Kathryn Howard's execution in 1542, the situation changed. Lord Latimer had fallen ill and was dying. Katherine suddenly began to receive expensive gifts from Henry. The implications of these gifts should not have been lost on her: she had been around the court for years, and she knew the king's patterns. Probably she hoped his interest would fade away as soon as one of the factions found a pretty young relative to dangle in front of the old king. There was little she could do to discourage Henry except to politely ignore the meaning of his gifts and try to avoid his company.

There was one man at court whose company she had no desire at all to avoid. Thomas Seymour, Queen Jane's brother, was handsome, charming, sexy—and considerably less intelligent than he thought himself to be. He too was taken with the gentle widow, and probably even more taken with her inheritance. He began paying court to her as soon as Lord Latimer died. She fell in love with him, and stayed in love for the rest of her life. "My mind was fully bent to marry you before any man I know," she wrote him four years later.

As Katherine's passion for Tom Seymour blossomed, so did the other great passion of her life. With her Catholic husband dead, Katherine Parr was free to explore the religious ideas that Henry had so reluctantly fostered. Tom Seymour inspired physical passion; the New Learning inspired intellectual passion. She became friends with such noted reformers as Hugh Latimer (no relation to her late husband), Miles Coverdale, and John Parkhurst. It was probably at this time that her old acquaintance with the Protestant Catherine Willoughby, Duchess of Suffolk, grew into close friendship. She must have been extraordinarily happy for a few brief weeks: in love with Tom Seymour, in love with the New Learning, and free, so she thought, to commit herself to both. But she was not free. The king had decided to marry her.

Another candidate for queen was being pushed on Henry. Once again, the comic courtship of Henry VIII and Anne of Cleves popped up—to the intense discomfort of both parties.

Henry and Anne had been miserable as man and wife, but they enjoyed each other as brother and sister. Anne seems to have absented herself from court almost entirely after Kathryn Howard's execution. The death of the pretty, flighty girl with whom she had danced during that happy Christmas season after her annulment must have angered and depressed her. For the most part, though, her own life kept her busy and content. She retained a certain celebrity, despite her own reticence. Rumors abounded that, after the divorce, she had given birth at various times to children sired by Henry. Henry feared she had taken a lover and had indeed had a child; he investigated and discovered that the story had arisen from Anne's brief confinement with a minor illness. The rumor was traced to one Frances Lilgrave, a tapestry weaver, who was promptly committed to the Tower for her slander.

Anne was satisfied with her anomalous position: others were not. One might have thought that Kathryn Howard's execution would have shown Anne's family that she had been lucky to escape her marriage to Henry unscathed. Instead they saw it as an opportunity for Anne to regain her former position. The ambassadors of the Duke of Cleves were soon besieging Henry with requests to take her back.

It must have been an uneasy time for Anne. She could hardly take it on herself to repudiate the duke's request without making her own distaste for Henry plain. She could only maintain a discreet silence and hope that Henry's physical aversion to her was unabated.

Incredibly, some of Anne's own ladies echoed the duke's sentiments, seeing Kathryn's execution as "God working his work to make the Lady Anna of Cleves queen again." One of them, Elizabeth Basset, had a more cynical reaction, which was undoubtedly closer to Anne's own. "What a man is the King!" Mistress Bassett exclaimed in disgust. "How many wives will he have?"

Henry's decision to marry Katherine Parr ended both hopes and fears that he might remarry his Flanders mare. Anne, pitying the new queen, reportedly sighed, "A fine burden Madame Katherine has taken upon herself!" Again she faded into the background, emerging only for an occasional visit with her friend the princess Mary.

The reluctant Katherine Parr took the foreground. She was in some ways a fitting last wife for the marriage-prone king, for her character combined qualities of all his other wives. Probably Henry was most aware of her similarities to his favorite wife, Jane Seymour. Each was a quiet, apparently prim woman, and each followed on the heels of a sexy queen with whom Henry had become painfully disillusioned. There was something of Jane's placid obedience in Katherine, something comfortable and unexciting that would soothe a wounded old man who had been forced to abandon his last fantasy of perpetual virile youth. The ostentatious subservience to male authority that led Jane to take as her motto "Bound to obey and serve" would cause Katherine to write, in evident sincerity, that women must "learn of St. Paul to be obedient to their husbands and to keep silence in the congregation and to learn of their husbands at home."

But there were other echoes as well in the deceptively smooth character of Katherine Parr. Most historians compare her with Catherine of Aragon, for the two shared a serious, scholarly attachment to humanistic learning. This parallel between the first and last wives makes a nice frame, with Henry ending his marital career as he had begun it, in the lap of a gently intellectual, pious wife.

Shift the prism again, and another Katherine emerges—the borderline Protestant, the intense evangelical whose religious convictions harkened back to those of Ann Boleyn. Like Ann, she would bravely bring to court controversial Protestant bishops, including Ann's friend Hugh Latimer. She was a great admirer of another of Ann's old friends, Marguerite of Navarre, whose life and writings showed such a curious blend of worldliness and piety. Later, during her fourth and last marriage, Katherine would prove herself similar to Ann in yet another way, for she had a temper equal to Ann's, and a vocabulary uncompromising enough to match even that proud virago's.

There was something too of Anne of Cleves in her makeup: both were firmly domestic, in tune with the small, practical things that make a household pleasant, that could lend stability to even the shifting, nomadic court life, regardless of which castles the members of the royal family were scattered among. Like Anne, Katherine was able to compromise easily, willing to suffer what the world would see as humiliation if it provided security and safety to herself and those she cared for. Also like Anne, she would manage to be close to all three of Henry's children, despite their differences with her and with each other.

And though no one could guess it at the time, there was a powerful undercurrent of sensuality in her nature, suppressed through three arranged marriages, that would flare forth when she was finally able to marry the man she adored. The extent of that adoration would have surprised any of her predecessors except for Catherine of Aragon, but the streak of wild, giddy sexuality that wove through it would have been familiar to Kathryn Howard.

If Henry admired Katherine's resemblance to Jane Seymour, he was less pleased with her evident attraction to Jane's brother. In the early days of his infatuation with Ann Boleyn he had used his royal power to end Ann's relationship with Henry Percy. Now he sent Tom Seymour off on an embassy to the regent of the Netherlands. Katherine's brief chance at happiness was gone, and there was nothing she could do about it. Henry wanted her, and Henry would have her.

What made the experience bearable for Katherine was its religious significance. Henry might be a tyrant personally, but he was the man who had freed England from the yoke of Rome. As his queen, she could help keep him from turning back. She saw this as a vocation, as God pulling her in the direction of his choice. As she later explained, she resisted this pull at first, but "God withstood my will therein most vehemently for a time, and, through his grace and goodness, made that possible which seemed to me most impossible; that is, made me renounce utterly my own will and to follow his will most willingly."

After a deep and painful struggle with her conscience, Katherine resigned herself to a dangerous and unappealing husband. They were married on July 12 at Hampton Court, in a lush ceremony. She was surrounded, at least, by women she loved and respected. In addition to the two princesses, her attendants included her sister Anne and her dear friend Catherine Willoughby. Their presence was a good omen, for these and a handful of other women would help to make her reign tolerable, reinforcing the strong religious faith that was now the guiding force in her life.

If she hoped to ease Henry into greater sympathy for the Protestant cause, she was unsuccessful, at any rate in the early days of their marriage. Writing to a friend, a Protestant merchant reported that Henry had "within these two days burnt three godly men. For in July he married the widow of a nobleman named Latimer, and he is always wont to celebrate his nuptial by some wickedness of this kind."

Though Katherine could not save heretics from the stake, she could quietly spread a delicate reformism in her own court circles, choosing as her chaplains men like John Parkhurst and Miles Coverdale and as her ladies-in-waiting Anne Stanhope, Joan Denny, and Catherine Willoughby.

The women formed a group at once similar to the pious noble-women of Margaret Beaufort's time and significantly different from them. As John King argues, they "fused Bible reading with popular theological study," and deliberately set out to spread Protestant humanism not only among the women of the nobility but also among those women of the lower classes. Katherine patronized Protestant writers, and encouraged making the gospel available to everyone.

She did not, however, confine herself to patronage. This was an age when few women wrote anything beyond private letters; Thomas More had praised his daughter Margaret because she wrote for no audience other than her father and husband. Sometimes women like Margaret Beaufort wrote translations of others' works for publication. But across the sea, in France, the king's sister Marguerite of Navarre was boldly writing her own works, both religious and secular, for the edification of at least a large circle of the nobility.

Katherine Parr decided to follow suit. Basing her work on Thomas à Kempis's *Imitation of Christ,* she composed a small book of *Prayers and Meditations*—unpretentious, traditionally pious little prayers, harmless enough to win the king's approval, which were published during her reign and remained popular years after their author's death. Unexceptional in themselves, they are significant for two reasons. One is the simple fact that a woman—a queen—had written them. The other is that they paved the way for the stronger work that would appear after Henry's death.

If God had called Katherine to help solidify the Henrician Reformation in England, he had also called her for a more personal task. It is one of the great charms of Katherine Parr that she seemed always to combine the abstract and the concrete—religion with charity, love of God with love of his creatures. She saw what Henry had done to his children—even the boy Edward was more an extension of the king's ego than a beloved son. The new queen set out to supply what was missing in their lives and to create a personal, loving relationship with each of them. It wasn't easy in a time when royal children rarely lived with each other or their parents. Elizabeth, now nine, attended the king's wedding and then did not see her stepmother for a full year.

Mary, however, came to live at court when Katherine married Henry. The friendship that had almost surely begun in girlhood, while Maud Parr waited on Catherine of Aragon, flourished. If Mary objected to a position at court inferior to that of the woman whose mother had once served hers, she gave no sign of it. Soon Katherine was talking with her new step-daughter about a project she had in mind that would interest them both. Erasmus had written a Latin paraphrase of the New Testament. Perhaps Mary—whose Latin, she delicately said, was much better than her own—might translate the paraphrase of the Gospel of Saint John into English?

Mary enthusiastically began the work, though ill health prevented her finishing it. The queen eventually commissioned others to complete it, under the editorship of Nicholas Udall. The book was finished in 1545, though not published until three years later, and in his dedication Udall glowingly described the court of the new queen.

> Neither is it now any strange thing to hear gentlewomen, instead of most vain communication about the moon shining in the water, to use grave and subtle talk in Greek or Latin with their husbands in godly matters. It is now no news in England to see young damsels in noble houses and in the courts of princes, instead of cards and other instruments of vain trifling, to have continually in their hands either Psalms, homilies, or other devout meditations.

This was in part the inevitable fawning hyperbole of the writer toward his patron, and it had been no news for quite some time that various noble-women, including Mary, Katherine, and the Duchess of Suffolk, enjoyed both godly talk and card-playing. But certainly Katherine brought to the court a new intensity of intellectual and religious seriousness.

At the same time she maintained a sense of fun. She dressed elegant-ly and ostentatiously. The crosses she wore around her neck hung beside diamond pendants and other rich jewels. Even her shoes were trimmed with gold. She loved to dance, refusing to forgo her favorite pastime even when, as one Spanish ambassador reported, she was feeling ill.

Katherine's influence at court and her own intellectual growth were given a chance to flourish by the fortuitous occurrence of a new Anglo-imperial war against France in the summer of 1544, a year after her mar-riage. Henry appointed Katherine regent, as he had done so long ago with Catherine of Aragon, and went off to play soldier. She did her job conscientiously, like the first Catherine, overseeing the war with Scotland that inevitably accompanied any war with France, although most of the military decisions were made by her friend and co-religionist Edward Seymour.

Katherine's letters to Henry are surprisingly affectionate. "Although the distance of time and account of days is neither long nor many of your majesty's absence," she wrote in one, "yet the want of your presence, so much desired and beloved by me, maketh me that I cannot quietly pleasure in any thing until I hear from your majesty." It's hard to believe she really cared for the man whose tyranny she knew so well, but the letters have a ring of authenticity. Her feelings were not romantic; Tom Seymour remained her great passion. But Henry was her king, and the Moses who had, however self-centeredly, rescued England from the clutches of the papacy. God had given her the job of being Henry's wife, and she did it with grace and spirit.

Henry won his latest skirmish, and Katherine composed a victory prayer, which emphasized not the joy of conquest but the hope of peace: "We most humbly beseech thee, O Lord God of Hosts, so to turn the hearts of our enemies to the desire of peace, that no Christian blood be spilt. Or else grant, O Lord, that with small effusion of blood and to the little hurt and damage of innocents, we may to Thy Glory obtain victory." Victory, to Katherine, was secondary to saving lives.

The months of her regency increased both Katherine's influence at court and her inclination toward Protestantism. She grew close to Archbishop Cranmer, whose conciliatory manner, so similar to her own, masked a deeply held Protestant faith. She spent more time than ever with her ladies, who, relieved of the hovering bulk of the tyrant, were able to spend their time discussing the ideas that most intrigued them—the evangelical beliefs that so often bordered on what Henry called heresy.

She also took advantage of the king's absence to help solidify the royal family. Elizabeth had committed some offense for which she had been banished from court for a year, and she now wrote to Katherine, begging her intercession, because she dared not risk Henry's wrath by writing to him herself. Elizabeth was soon back at court under the loving care of her stepmother. She showed her gratitude in her New Year's gift in 1545, her own translation of Marguerite of Navarre's *Mirror of the Sinful Soul*, inscribed with the words "To our noble and virtuous Queen Katherine, Elizabeth her humble daughter wishes perpetual felicity and everlasting joy." (Did the girl think of her real mother as she wrote this—the queen who had been at Marguerite's court, and who had so admired Marguerite, all those years ago?)

It may have been during these months that Katherine found the emotional leisure to begin writing her openly Protestant *Lamentation of a Sinner*. Henry would never see this work. In spite of its extreme flattery of the king himself—it was here that she compared him to Moses—it was full of ideas that Henry vehemently rejected. She attacked the ceremonial practices of the Church of Rome, to which Henry himself remained utterly attached, and she stated outright that good works come from faith but that faith alone is necessary for salvation.

A triumphant Henry returned in October, and Katherine greeted him with dutiful expressions of joy. How deeply she felt that joy is debatable; Henry was far more lovable in his absence. Though he was cheerful when he returned home puffed with victory, his health problems and the increasing religious dissension among his people soon plunged him into irascibility. Conservatives clung to the beliefs they had grown up with, and those with more Reformist tendencies stubbornly continued to push at the door Henry's break with the pope had opened.

"Heretics"—to the extent that anyone could be sure of what heresy meant in Henry's fluid theology—abounded. They were encouraged by members of his own court, like Catherine Willoughby, and by people outside court like the popular "gospelers," among whom was a fiery young woman from Lincolnshire, Anne Askew.

Askew is one of the most intriguing figures of the era. Katherine Parr and her ladies knew of her, as did everyone else in London, and no one with any Protestant sympathies could fail to be drawn to her. She was an awesome woman, this stark, witty, charismatic Protestant who had dared to appropriate two rights that belonged to Henry alone. She had decided for herself what constituted religious truth, and she had abandoned her spouse, resuming her family name and moving to London to spread the gospel.

Born in 1520, Anne was the daughter of a minor knight, Sir William Askew. He had allowed his daughters to be educated well enough to read and write English. Their learning was supplemented informally when their older brothers, Francis and Edward, were at Cambridge. On visits home the young scholars talked about the Protestant ideas floating around the university town—ideas that intrigued the girl, bored with the flat, conservative world of Lincolnshire.

Whatever affection she might have retained for the conservative religion of her childhood Anne lost in 1536, during the uprisings in Lincolnshire. Sir William, a loyal Henrician, opposed the rebels. In retaliation, they attacked his house while he was away, leaving the terrified women to watch helplessly as they seized Francis and another son, Thomas. The rebellion was defeated and the brothers returned unharmed, but Anne's loathing of the old religion was solidified.

Her father sympathized with her feelings, but he didn't let that stand in the way of practical decisions—such as the choice of a husband for Anne. Thomas Kyme, a cloddish neighbor who was traditional in his religion, made up in wealth what he lacked in intellect. He was originally betrothed to Anne's sister Martha, who died suddenly before the marriage. Thomas's father was quite willing to settle for another Askew girl.

Anne escaped from the dreariness of life with Thomas Kyme as best she could. We may assume that she spent as much time as possible with her sister Jane, whose husband, George Saint Paul, was a Protestant and a friend of the Duke of Suffolk and of his outspoken young wife. There are no records of a meeting between Anne Askew and Catherine Willoughby, but with so close a connection, the two intense Protestant women must have met on several occasions.

Anne had other outlets as well in the early days of her marriage. In 1538, in one of his swings toward progressivism, Henry had decreed that every parish must have a large English Bible in its church so that the parishioners "may most commodiously resort to the same and read it." This allowed literate parishioners with Protestant or evangelical leanings to conduct informal public Bible readings in the churches. The priests could only watch in dismay as their former privilege was exercised by all sorts of laymen—and even laywomen.

The reading of scripture went beyond the churches. Wealthy householders read the Bible to their families and servants—and, of course, with the readings came explanations, interpretations, conversations. Anne Askew took full advantage of the opportunity. She read in the churches, and she read to her household—to Thomas Kyme's household, turning a conservative country manor into a Protestant breeding ground. The birth of their two sons did not put a damper on Anne's biblical enthusiasms: if pregnancy confined her temporarily to the house, it gave her all the more time to read the Bible to the servants who attended her.

In 1543, Henry was in a more conservative mood, and he passed the Act for the Advancement of the True Religion, prohibiting men below the rank of gentleman, and all women, from reading the Bible. Thomas Kyme rejoiced. Anne was not daunted. She had a prodigious memory, and she had spent long hours in scriptural reading. If she could not read the precious book herself, she could recall large sections of it verbatim. The prohibition meant that she could, and must, use her gift to help others now deprived of access to God's word. Her gospeling continued.

Thomas Kyme, driven to the end of his limited wits, sought out the local priests for advice on how to handle his unruly wife. They advised Kyme to kick her out of his house, reasoning that the humiliation would force her to see the error of her ways and return to him. Far from chastened, Anne took her sons and moved in with her brother Francis, pursuing her gospeling with renewed vigor. For Saint Paul had written that a good Christian married to an unbeliever must remain with his or her spouse—unless the spouse decided otherwise. "If a faithful woman have an unbelieving husband which will not tarry with her she may leave him. For a brother or sister is not in subjugation unto such." Kyme and his priestly advisers, not knowing the Bible as well as she did, had inadvertently released Anne from her wifely duty. She would never return to him. As the Protestant martyrologist John Foxe, her contemporary, later wrote, "She could not think him worthy of her marriage which so spitefully hated God, the chief author of marriage."

The Lincoln courts rejected her petition for divorce, and Anne decided to go to London and get her divorce there. Like the king's new wife, Anne revered Henry for freeing his people from the evil of popery. She was certain that the king, who had himself disposed of several unworthy spouses, would allow a godly woman to be free of her unbelieving husband.

In London Anne resumed her family name and took rooms near the Inns of Court, where she must have been an odd sight among her fellow lodgers, nearly all male, and young students of law. She contacted an old neighbor who was now at court, one of Henry's three "sewers"—men who supervised the arrangement of the king's table, seated his guests, and tasted the royal meals for poison. He was, in fact, John Lascelles, the man whose obliging sister had supplied him with the details of Kathryn Howard's early love life.

Lascelles gladly took his young friend under his wing, introducing her to the seething world of London Protestantism. After the claustrophobic traditionalism of Lincolnshire, Anne was in her glory. All around her were Protestants whose devotion to their faith matched her own. Men who had once been legends to her became her regular associates—Hugh Latimer, bishop of Worcester; Nicholas Shaxton, bishop of Salisbury; the renegade priest Dr. Edward Crome. All were her friends, as they were the friends of the new queen, Katherine Parr.

The city was full of Bible study groups, whose members were a mixture of nobility and commoners, merchants and apprentices, shopkeepers, students—anyone, high or low, male or female, who revered scripture. The ban on Bible reading had intensified the hunger for it, and those who knew the Bible well became known as gospelers, a new breed of lay preacher, collecting an audience in every nook and cranny of London, from churchyards to taverns, expounding illegally but openly on God's word, as they now heard it not in beautiful, mysterious, inaccessible Latin, but in their own clear, vibrant English. Anne was familiar with such activities, though her audience had been small. Quickly, exuberantly, she became one of London's most famous and beloved gospelers, her beauty and high rank marking her as the Fair Gospeler. She had found her home, and soon all London had heard about the lovely young gentlewoman who talked equally with servants and masters, who had such thorough knowledge of God's word, who spoke with such intense conviction.

Unfortunately, not all London was pleased. Bishop Gardiner had been warned of her by the disgruntled priests in Lincoln even before her celebrity in London. The Bishop of Winchester's idea of a good woman was a quiet and submissive one—a woman like the king's third wife, whose only fault was dying in childbirth and leaving the king vulnerable to more aggressive women. Gardiner did not like the queen. He did not like his goddaughter, the sharp-tongued Duchess of Suffolk. And he did not like the Fair Gospeler. The new religion, he thought bitterly, bred such women. Angrily he wrote to one Protestant correspondent, "ye give women courage and liberty to talk to their pleasure so it be of God's word." The queen and the duchess were, as yet, too powerful to keep from their dabbling in religious reform, but this arrogant young gentlewoman was another matter. Undoubtedly Gardiner's spies had told him of Anne's link to Catherine Willoughby—and a link to Catherine Willoughby was a link to Katherine Parr. If the bishop could use this to discredit the queen, perhaps he could pick the king's seventh wife.

He chose his henchmen well. Chief among them was Thomas Wriothesley, the lord chancellor. Wriothesley was utterly without scruple, willing, as opportunism dictated, to persecute Catholic or Protestant, conservative or radical. George Blagge described him as one who "by false deceit, by craft and subtle ways" had allowed cruelty to creep "full high, borne up by sundry stays." Together the two men sent their spies out to catch Anne Askew, and to uncover her connections with Katherine Parr and her circle.

How strong those connections were we don't know. Certainly Anne had managed to get to court and at least had seen, from whatever distance, the king she idolized. With her connection to the duchess and to John Lascelles, she had some access to the outer circles of the court, and later she mentioned in a poem that she had once seen Henry on his royal throne.

In June 1545 she was arrested with two of her co-religionists on charges of heresy, but there were no witnesses and the charges were dropped.

Anne was in London, happily gospeling, on Christmas Eve, when Henry addressed Parliament. His speech was a masterpiece of hypocrisy, calling for Christian charity, brotherly love, and an end to religious quarrels. "What love and charity is amongst you, when one calleth the other papist and anabaptist, and he calleth him again papist, hypocrite, and pharisee? Are these the signs of fraternal love between you?"

Coming from a man whose commitment to fraternal love had led him to execute numerous papists and heretics, as well as assorted wives, friends, courtiers, and ministers, the speech must have lacked credibility to its hearers. But Henry took no responsibility for the climate of religious dissension, blaming instead the clerics "who preach against one another, teach one contrary to another." He continued carrying on for a while about love and charity, then got to the point. Anyone who knew of a clergyman who taught "perverse doctrine" was to report him to the king's council, and the laity were not to "dispute and make Scripture a railing and taunting stock against priests and preachers." Henry returned to his unctuous exhortations that his hearers should love one another, but the message was not lost on them: spy on heretics, and report them to the council. In a spirit of Christian love, they were to root out heresy—and if Christian love needed reinforcement, there was always the rack.

Early in 1546 Anne's petition for divorce came up in Chancery. But though she had been certain she would win her appeal in London, she didn't. Her plea was dismissed, and she was ordered to return to her husband.

She could not bring herself to obey. On March 10, 1546, Anne was arrested again on heresy charges. This time she was tried before the "quest," a kind of grand jury whose job was to determine whether the accused was likely to be heretical, and if so to turn her over to a higher court for further examination.

The court was jammed with Anne's supporters, and her prosecutors had a hard time of it. To begin with, although they included the bishop's chancellor, Dr. John Standish, it was clear that none of them had anything like Anne's grasp of the Bible. Standish began by accusing her of violating Saint Paul's prohibition against women speaking the word of God. Oh, no, she answered—Paul had said that women mustn't teach in the congregation. Had Standish ever seen her in the pulpit? No, he admitted, he'd never seen any woman preaching in the pulpit. Well, then, she scolded, he "ought to find no fault in poor women," unless they had broken the law.

Anne continued to play the "poor woman" theme, with ironic relish. When they reprimanded her for refusing to answer their questions directly, she said she was "but a woman" and thus ignorant of procedure. When they could get no response to their questions about her belief in transubstantiation, they asked why she had so few words. Replied the Fair Gospeler, "Solomon said that a woman of few words is a gift of God." Dr. Standish, hoping to trap her into making heretical statements, asked her to explicate one of Paul's texts. The modest maiden demurred. "I answered that it was against St. Paul's learning that I, being a woman, should interpret the Scriptures, especially where so many wise men were."

The wise men were perplexed and frustrated. They could hardly fault Anne for her womanly modesty, but they knew they were being mocked. They threw her back in jail, waiting to resume the hearings until two weeks later, when Edmund Bonner, the Bishop of London and a savvy hunter of heretics, could interrogate her. Bonner fared no better than his colleagues had. To all his questions, she simply replied that she believed what the scriptures said, refusing to elaborate. Finally the exasperated bishop released her, and she returned to her brother's house in Lincoln.

Anne apparently resigned herself to living in Lincoln. However much she might miss London, at least her brother shared her beliefs, and she might read scripture in peace. Her career as the Fair Gospeler was over, but she could savor her memories of it in this drab but Protestant haven.

She had not reckoned on Stephen Gardiner's vindictive heresy hunting. Anne's friends and co-religionists were being rounded up—Latimer, Shaxton, Crome, and Henry's cheerful courtier Sir George Blagge (whose girth had earned him the affectionate royal nickname of "my pig") were all arrested on suspicion of heresy.

By returning not to Thomas Kyme but to her brother's house, Anne had given Gardiner a useful weapon against her. She was summoned to London and ordered to return to her husband. Once again she was questioned about her religious beliefs, this time by members of the king's council. One of them was Katherine Parr's brother, William, whom Anne berated, along with other Protestant sympathizers, for arguing "contrary to their knowledge." She made her contempt of Gardiner even clearer. He had promoted the royal supremacy, gotten rich on monastic lands, and yet maintained a nearly papist theology. She sneered at him and asked "how long he would halt on both sides."

Anne no longer attempted to evade admitting her own beliefs. She treated transubstantiation as a joke. Of course Jesus had said he was the bread of the Eucharist. He had also said he was the door to salvation—did that mean he was present in any door a priest chose to bless? She was courting martyrdom, and on June 18, she was condemned to die at the stake.

She was moved to the Tower of London to await execution. There something extremely unusual happened. Anne was visited by two council members, Richard Rich and Gardiner's sleazy henchman Wriothesley, who asked questions about her "sect." Did it include any of the queen's ladies? The Duchess of Suffolk, perhaps, or the Ladies Sussex, or Hertford, or Denny? Anne shrugged. She knew nothing about those ladies and their beliefs. But the king, they said, had been told otherwise. The king, she retorted bitterly, had been lied to about many things. When she continued to deny knowledge of the queen's women, she was put to the rack.

The lieutenant of the Tower, Anthony Knevet, was appalled. Torture was a tool for eliciting confessions, and this woman had already been condemned to die. Moreover, it was not to be used on a gentlewoman. When the first turns of the rack elicited only grim silence, he refused to continue. Rich and Wriothesley rolled up their sleeves and began turning the rack themselves. Knevet fled to the court, forced his way into Henry's presence, and there, flinging himself to his knees, told the king what was going on. He begged to know if it was His Majesty's will that he torture the woman. Publicly confronted, Henry had no choice but to affect ignorance and horror. He thanked Knevet and ordered the racking stopped.

Word of it had already leaked out to an enraged populace. The merchant Otwell Johnson wrote that Anne "hath been racked since her condemnation (so men say), which is a strange thing to my understanding. The Lord be merciful to us all."

The torture left Anne so weakened that she could not walk, but it had not broken her determination. While she awaited execution, she wrote about her arrests, interrogation, and torture, and gave the account to her maid. After her death, the maid—about whom we know nothing except her loyalty and courage—managed to get the manuscript to some Protestant German merchants, who took it to the exiled Protestant zealot Bishop Bale. He published the work and then passed it on to his friend John Foxe, who included it within a larger account of Anne's life and execution.

Anne was unable to walk to the stake, so she was carried on a chair. She was executed along with three men, among them her old friend and mentor John Lascelles. As the faggots were piled high about them, Wriothesley made his way through the throng to offer the four a pardon if they recanted. Anne spoke for them all, crying out loud that she "came not hither to deny my Lord and Master!" The torch was lit and the four died quickly, thanks to gunpowder a friend had thrown into the flames. A fortuitous thunderstorm, breaking out suddenly, added to the legend that grew to surround the death of the Fair Gospeler: the thunder, the eighteenth-century ecclesiastical historian John Strype tells us, "seemed to the people to be the voice of God, or the voice of an angel."

꘎꘎ Anne Askew died without betraying the queen or any of her ladies. Whatever Katherine Parr's relationship to the Fair Gospeler, she could hardly have been pleased to see the young woman die so horrible a death for beliefs with which she herself sympathized. She may even have shown her anger in some way to Henry, and thus elicited *his* anger. He was beginning to show signs of disaffection. He disliked her increasingly Protestant beliefs. There were rumors that Henry planned to divorce her and marry someone else: inevitably, Anne of Cleves was suggested. Even more ludicrous were suggestions that Henry was eying Catherine Willoughby, whose religious convictions were far more radical and whose tongue was far sharper than the mild Katherine Parr's. Farfetched though they were, the rumors reflected something ominous: Henry was no longer enchanted with Katherine Parr.

Stephen Gardiner realized this. The Bishop of Winchester listened zealously to conversations between the king and queen; he watched carefully Henry's reactions to his wife. And he smiled: Katherine was playing into his hands. On one occasion she had the temerity to disagree with Henry on some point of theology in Gardiner's presence. Henry said nothing until she had left the room, then turned to the bishop and snarled, "A good hearing it is when women become such clerks; and much comfort to come in mine old age, to be taught by my wife!"

It was the opening Gardiner had been looking for, and he seized it gleefully. First he offered Henry the cloying flattery that Katherine had failed to provide. Henry was a genius, a man "not only above princes of that and other ages but also above doctors professed in divinity." That being the case, it was "an unseemly thing for any of the King's subjects to argue with him so malapertly as the queen had just done." Words, he noted ominously, led to deeds, and Henry was in danger.

Henry nodded. But what could he do to protect himself? The bishop was ready with a suggestion. Why not issue a warrant for the queen's arrest? If she were taken to the Tower and interrogated, they could find out the extent of her heretical activities. The king who had so firmly forced his attentions on the widow Latimer now agreed with alacrity to her arrest.

The warrant was made up, but somehow, on its way to the bishop, it got into the hands of one of Katherine's ladies. Foxe described this as a happy coincidence. A few modern biographers suggest it was the work of Henry himself, playing one side against the other. More likely it was managed by one of Katherine's sympathizers close to the king—Blagge, her brother William, her brother-in-law William Herbert, or her friend Anthony Denny.

However the warrant got into her hands, Katherine saw it. She acted at once. First she made certain that it got back where it was found so that no one would suspect she had seen it. Then she went into hysterics. Her apartments were near the king's, and he heard her shrieks. Either concerned for her well-being or irritated at the noise, Henry sent his physician to her. Dr. Thomas Wendy was fond of the queen and, in a less open way, shared her beliefs. He sent word to Henry that Katherine was dangerously ill because of some mental distress.

Henry was concerned enough to visit her and to enquire about the cause of her unhappiness. She told him that she knew he was displeased with her, and the knowledge of that displeasure had thrown her into such sorrow that she had become ill.

This was the kind of answer Henry liked, and he assured her that he loved her as much as ever—that, in fact, he had been meaning to come to her and ask her opinion on some theological issues that had been troubling him.

Katherine took her cue. How could she, "a poor, silly woman, so much inferior in all respects of nature" to Henry, council him on religious matters?

Ah, but she had, Henry reminded her. Just the other day she had argued with him on that very subject.

But that wasn't a real disagreement, Katherine assured him. She had pretended to argue with him because she knew his leg was hurting him badly, and she wanted to get his mind off his pain. Prettily, she confessed to another motive as well. If she claimed to disagree with him, he would put forth his own arguments, and she "might receive to myself some profit thereby." Katherine's reconstruction of what had happened of course made excellent sense to Henry, who kissed her heartily and announced that they were "perfect friends" once more.

The next day Henry and Katherine were sitting together in the palace gardens when Wriothesley approached them, the ominous warrant in his hand. Henry saw the paper, and was alarmed. Suppose Katherine should learn what he had intended to do? Before the chancellor could open his mouth, Henry was shouting at him. "Beast!" he cried. "Fool! Knave!" Wriothesley beat a hasty retreat while Katherine turned toward her husband, her face full of womanly compassion. Whatever Wriothesley had done to displease Henry, she begged that he would forgive it for her sake, for surely it was well intentioned. "Poor soul," Henry replied, "thou little knoweth how evil he deserveth this grace at thy hands."

Katherine had won, but only for the time being. After that incident she kept her opinions to herself. It must have been galling. She had married the king because he had led England away from papacy, but she had not been able to help guide him in a more godly direction. He had begun their married life burning men whose beliefs were not all that different from her own; he had killed the Fair Gospeler. Now he had threatened Katherine Parr herself. As long as he lived, she would fear for her life.

Fortunately for her, Henry did not live long. He fell ill in September with what appeared to be a severe cold. He recovered, but in December was struck with a fever. Again he rallied, but remained weak. The Spanish ambassador wrote that he feared the next fever would kill the king.

As the year drew to a close Henry grew weaker. He closed himself in his bedroom, seeing only his physicians, his priests, and a few of his councilors. In the dark early morning of January 28, 1547, Henry died, clutching the hand of Archbishop Cranmer.

Public mourning was ostentatious and probably sincere. Henry had been well loved. Every parish held a solemn dirge and tolled its bells. He was buried, according to his instructions, with his favorite wife, Jane Seymour.

Henry's will had provided generously for Katherine, but he did not see fit to appoint her to the sixteen-man council that was to rule during the minority of the nine-year-old Edward VI. It would not have mattered if he had. Edward Seymour, quietly conspiring with two other councilors, William Paget and John Dudley, calmly assumed the unchallenged title of Protector of the Realm, rendering the regency council ineffectual. Until Edward reached manhood, Seymour decided, he himself would rule England: he would be, in all but title, the new king. He quickly persuaded the council to make him Duke of Somerset.

Edward Seymour was an ambitious man, and a humorless one, but he had a true concern for the needs of England's people. Occasionally he showed touches of genuine sensitivity. Before Henry's death was announced to the public, he made certain that a messenger was sent to inform Henry's dear sister, Anne of Cleves.

Katherine left court quietly, retiring to her manor house in Chelsea.

There, when the weather allowed, she roamed through the lovely gardens that bordered the Thames, safe in her widowhood.

Then her old friend Thomas Seymour came to see her. He was as enamored of her as ever, and the man who had stood between them was dead. Katherine wasted no time. The king had prevented their marriage three years before, and the regency council might prevent it now. The queen dowager could not marry without the approval of the new king, and that meant the approval of the new council. Like Henry's sister Mary so many years before, Katherine was determined that, on the death of the husband she did not want, she would grab the one she did before anything else interfered.

Tom Seymour may have been a shallow opportunist—he was described by the late-sixteenth-century writer John Hayward as "fierce in courage, courtly in fashion, in personage stately, in voice magnificent, but somewhat empty in manner"—but he brought out marvelous things in the once-docile Katherine. If she had to fight for the man she had wanted so long, she could, and would, fight. For some reason both Edward Seymour and his wife, Katherine's former lady-in-waiting Anne Stanhope, adamantly opposed the marriage, though neither had anything to lose by it. Somerset at first simply hedged on the question. He would visit Katherine soon and discuss it with her, he promised. But he never came. Katherine was furious. In the middle of a tender love letter she told Tom of his brother's broken promises—a habit, she said, that he had acquired from his wife, "For it is her custom to promise many comings to her friends, and to perform none." Apparently there had been some falling-out between the one-time friends.

The widow who in her youth had been the model of propriety now, in her thirty-fifth year, entered into a secret love affair. The tone of Katherine's letters plotting her assignations reveals a gleeful sense of adventure that admirers of the mild queen would have found shocking. But she was a sensible woman, and even her passion was conducted sensibly. Instructing Seymour on how and when to sneak into the manor unseen, she told him of her longing to be his "humble, true and loving wife," and laid out plans to get the king's permission for their marriage. If the protector remained obdurate, his brother was to "obtain the king's letters in your favor, and also the aid and furtherance of the most notable of the Council."

Katherine waited only as long as practically necessary, and not as long as propriety demanded. They were secretly married sometime in May, as evidenced by King Edward's diary and by a letter Seymour sent her while staying with her sister and brother-in-law, Lord and Lady Herbert. The

Herberts had twitted him about his nocturnal visits to Katherine, and then admitted that they knew the truth and were delighted. Later Seymour would be accused of marrying the queen so soon after Henry's death that "had she proved a mother so soon as she might have done, it would have been a doubt whether the child should have been accounted the late king's" or Seymour's. The charge, however, is ludicrous. The wedding was at least three months after Henry's death. Katherine was besotted, but no fool, and she would hardly put her country at risk of the civil war that might ensue if the boy king died and she had a son of possibly royal paternity.

The newlyweds hid the fact of the marriage from Katherine's royal stepchildren, hoping to gain their approval before giving them the news. It was most important to win over Edward, for without his consent the marriage could be nullified. Approaching his nephew through a servant, John Fowler, Seymour coyly tried to get the young king to suggest the marriage himself. Seymour was thinking seriously of finding himself a bride, Fowler said. Did Edward have any thoughts about who that bride should be? Edward's first two suggestions, his sister Mary and Anne of Cleves, were met with polite resistance. Finally the boy rose to the bait. What about his most recent mother, Katherine Parr? Seymour was charmed by the suggestion. So convinced was Edward that the idea had originated with him that when he learned Katherine had agreed to marry Seymour, he wrote a letter thanking her "for the gentle acceptation of our suit."

Edward's eldest sister reacted very differently. Seymour entreated Mary for her help in getting the regency council's approval, only to be met with a cold rebuke. She would not be "a meddler in this matter," and she thought it odd that he should ask it of her, "considering whose wife her grace was of late." She was shocked that Katherine could "forget the loss of him who is, as yet, very rife in mine own remembrance" and appealed to Elizabeth to back her up. Elizabeth's reply, however, was politic—classic Elizabeth. Of course, she agreed, their stepmother's hasty remarriage was shocking. But the thing was done, and it was best to remain silent and try to live with it.

In fact, Elizabeth was living with it quite happily. She had moved to Chelsea with Katherine, and must have known, or guessed, about Seymour's secret visits. She had loved and revered their father as much as Mary had, but she also loved Katherine, and she could see—too well, as it turned out—Tom Seymour's attractions. She would try to placate Mary by agreeing with her disapproval; she would not risk alienating Katherine by letting her know of it. What she really believed, who can say? She had learned young the value of guarding her true feelings.

Somerset and his wife accepted the marriage with little grace. The duchess refused to continue bearing the queen dowager's train, since Katherine, as the wife of Somerset's younger brother, was now of lower rank than she was. She insisted, absurdly, on being the first lady to enter any room—a privilege that precedent reserved for the queen, who was followed by the king's daughters and then his sisters. She was thus obligated to yield place not only to Katherine but to Mary, Elizabeth, and Anne of Cleves. Egged on by his wife, Somerset and the council refused to give Katherine the jewels Henry had left her in his will, claiming they had been not the king's personal property but the crown's. Somerset also took it on himself to lease one of her properties, Fausterne, to a friend of his, despite her express wish that the place be available for her own use.

The once mild Katherine wrote to her husband that she was glad she was nowhere near the protector, for if she had been she "would have bitten him." She blamed his wife for his nastiness, and she may have been right. Anne Stanhope was especially vindictive toward the woman she had once served. She is reported to have said that Henry VIII had married Katherine "in his doting days, when he had brought himself so low by his lust and cruelty that no lady that stood on her honor would venture on him." Sadly, two of the most intelligent and progressive women in England were now bitter enemies.

But Katherine was gloriously happy. Even the fury in her letters suggests a new exuberance. She was deeply, brazenly, sexily in love. She also had her religion, which she could now openly embrace. She was able to share this religious joy with others, and with one other in particular. Her worst enemy might be one of England's two duchesses, but her best friend was the other. The warmth of Catherine Willoughby's companionship remained constant.

She continued to focus her maternal concern for Henry's children on young Elizabeth and on Elizabeth's cousin, seven-year-old Jane Grey, the granddaughter of Henry's sister Mary. Jane's own parents, a greedy, vicious pair, were delighted when Seymour suggested that their daughter move into his new household. He apparently believed that he could bring about a marriage between the girl and her cousin, King Edward, and that in the wake of such a marriage he would replace his brother as the power behind the throne. The plots came to nothing, but Jane was given a few happy months in which she was coddled instead of beaten.

Elizabeth too blossomed in her new environment, but her flowering brought with it new perils. She was in the throes of adolescence, and strongly aware of Tom Seymour's attractiveness. Seymour in turn found the presence of the pretty and nubile young princess in his household exciting. He began to flirt with her. In the beginning it was harmless. In fact, Katherine, liberated from her years of matronly staidness, sometimes joined in their giddy frolics. Seymour would enter Elizabeth's bedroom before she arose, pulling open the curtains and bidding her good morning. Coyly, she would pull back into the bed. The game soon escalated, and he was kissing her, to the dismay of her governess, Kat Ashley. But Ashley could do little to stop it, especially on the mornings when Katherine herself came in with Tom, and they both began tickling Elizabeth in her bed. On another occasion the three were romping in the garden and Seymour cut the girl's gown to pieces as the laughing Katherine held her down.

Then one day Katherine walked in on her husband and the princess locked in each other's arms. She was hurt and angry at their betrayal. She was also sensibly aware, as they seemed not to be, that this was dangerous territory. Elizabeth was second in the succession to the throne. If her pre-marital shenanigans resulted in pregnancy, Tom Seymour might face execution, and everyone in the household, including Katherine herself, could end up in the Tower. Moreover, Elizabeth would lose all possibility of inheriting the throne or even of making a suitable match. Bidding Elizabeth a tender farewell, Katherine sent her to live with her old friends Sir Anthony and Joan Denny, where she was sure the girl would be kindly and respectfully treated, and still exposed to progressive religious influence.

For a time, Katherine seemed happy again. She was pregnant, and Tom was once more a devoted husband. When their daughter was born, even Somerset was moved to write, congratulating his brother for becoming "the father of so pretty a daughter."

But Katherine's apparently healthy delivery was followed by puerperal fever. In her delirium she berated her husband. "My lord, you have given me many shrewd taunts," she cried. Seymour, for once thinking of someone other than himself, lay on the bed and tried to soothe her, but she continued her remonstrances. Soon she drifted into sleep, and later seems to have forgotten her delirious fury. Her will, made soon afterward, left all her goods to Seymour, affectionately expressing the wish that they were a thousand times more valuable than they were.

The last woman Henry married died on September 5. But the legacy of his marriages remained—in the cheerful existence of the wife turned sister, Anne of Cleves; in the country's deep religious divisions; and in the reigns of the children three of his wives had given him, at such cost to themselves.

BOTH KING AND QUEEN

MARY I

Daughter of Henry and Catherine of Aragon, she survived all of Henry's marital escapades to become, briefly and unhappily, queen of England.

The Tudor dynasty began with one woman's fierce ambition for her son. It ended with another woman's fierce ambition for herself. Between the two came Henry VIII with his tribe of wives.

Each of those wives had influenced the quiet, intense girl who lay in her own sickbed, mourning the death of her last stepmother, Katherine Parr. Elizabeth Tudor, sick with one of the bouts of stress-induced illness that haunted her adolescence, had loved this woman. More than any other, Katherine had provided the maternal love that had been so conspicuously lacking in Elizabeth's life. Elizabeth was angry with herself for flirting with Tom Seymour, and so angry with him that she refused to send him a letter of condolence. Her communications with him henceforth consisted of business letters related to property, though he appears to have had some half-baked fantasy of marrying her.

In Edward's reign, the Protestantism that Katherine Parr had embraced and Elizabeth had somewhat reluctantly embodied was flourishing. Released from Henry's equivocations, the English church was now fully reformist. The nine-year-old king was controlled by his uncle, the power-hungry Edward Seymour, Duke of Somerset, and Somerset's ally, the even more power-hungry John Dudley, soon to be Earl of Northumberland. The boy had been much influenced in his religion by Katherine Parr, but he had not inherited her instinct for gentle tolerance. His own religion was a harsh, judgmental Protestantism that his uncle and later Northumberland carefully fostered.

Elizabeth, like Edward, was Protestant—the circumstances of her birth made that inevitable. She had already begun the habit of image creation that would stand her in such stead during her own long reign. She knew that gossip still linked her, dangerously, to Thomas Seymour. Free from Seymour's magnetism, she realized that his ambitions could only lead him, and anyone associated with him, into trouble. The image she now chose to convey was that of somber, pious maidenhood. If her romps with

Seymour suggested a somewhat different personality, her garb and her public behavior portrayed her in the light best calculated to please her brother and the English people. Edward styled her his "sweet sister Temperance," approving of her quiet manners and her simple, unornamented dress.

On the surface it seemed that Elizabeth was the more fortunate of the two sisters, for Mary's Catholicism, as passionate as Edward's Protestantism, put her at odds with her brother and the regency council. The protector permitted Mary to hear the Catholic mass in her own household, but only secretly, and she chafed under restrictions she found odious and sinful.

But Elizabeth had her own problems. The reign of a child-king was inevitably tense, lending itself to the abuse of power by an unscrupulous regent. The time of Richard III, who had usurped his young nephew's throne, was not all that remote. Edward and those who followed him in the line of succession were always in some danger. Seymour's escapades posed another threat to Elizabeth's safety. But along with the Protestantism that, for the moment, was an asset, Elizabeth had an important advantage over her sister. She had never been happy. Mary's inability to compromise with misery came from an early knowledge of joy. Always, through all the agony of the years after Ann Boleyn, Mary remembered how things had been before her mother had been cast off, before the break with Rome, when she had been the golden princess basking in her father's and England's love. All the rest of her life would be a passionate, futile attempt to bring those times back.

Elizabeth had never been a golden princess. She was the unwanted daughter, the seed of her mother's destruction, and there had never been a time when she had not known fear, rejection, contempt. Her bitter birthright was the knowledge that to survive she must learn to dissemble, to hide her true feelings, to watch and study the actions of others. That bleak heritage gave her an ability to manipulate her surroundings that Mary would never possess. The abrupt end of her interlude in Katherine Parr's household, when she had begun to allow her sexual feelings to hold sway over her, reinforced the distrust she learned in childhood.

Elizabeth needed all her resources now. Seymour had become involved in the deadliest and stupidest game of his none too intelligent career. Not contented with his appointment as lord high admiral soon after Henry's death, he begrudged his brother's preeminence on the council without recognizing the superior political acumen that made it possible. In the middle of the night on January 18, 1549, he and a handful of confederates crept into the king's bedchamber, planning to kidnap the boy and proclaim Thomas Seymour the new lord protector. Edward's little spaniel barked at the intruders. Panicking, Seymour grabbed his sword and killed the dog. An officer of the guard heard the commotion and rushed to the king's room to find Edward staring at the body of his pet and the bloody sword in his uncle's hand. Seymour was arrested for treason and sent to the Tower.

Unfortunately for Elizabeth, word of Seymour's earlier shenanigans had spread. Northumberland, who was on the regency council and was doing a fair job of shamming friendship for Somerset, saw a chance to discredit the protector and at the same time clip the wings of the shrewd girl who could pose a threat to his own plans to rule England. Several members of Elizabeth's household were arrested, and she herself was summoned to court to answer charges that she was pregnant by Seymour. She was indignant at the charges, continually denying any wrongdoing, and indifferent, apparently, to the fate of the man she had once been so infatuated with. On hearing of his execution, she is reported to have responded coldly, "This day died a man of much wit and little judgement." Scholars have debated the authenticity of the quotation—one suggesting that she knew Seymour too well to accuse him of having much wit—but none have disputed her cold attitude. If she grieved, she grieved in private.

The princess's concern now, as always, was survival. She must somehow get through the years of the protectorate until her brother was old enough to rule in his own right. Then she could trust that his affection would keep her safe.

Her safety was further threatened by a series of terrifying events. Northumberland's plot to discredit his erstwhile friend Somerset moved on to another stage. In late 1549 he headed an attempt to overthrow the Protector. Somerset was arrested, accused of treason, and stripped of his powers. His place as Protector was taken by John Dudley, Earl of Northumberland. For two years, Somerset was shuttled back and forth between his estate and the Tower, but he never regained his power. He was executed in January 1552.

Northumberland did not enjoy his triumph long. In April 1552, four months after Somerset's execution, King Edward fell ill. He rallied within a month, and all appeared well. But Northumberland realized the recovery was deceptive. The unspecified illness was apparently the early stages of a deteriorating condition. If the boy died, his sister Mary would become queen. Northumberland had treated Mary far worse than Somerset had, and in any case he could hardly expect to have any influence in the reign of a middle-aged Catholic monarch. As the months passed, the Protector wove a plot to keep Mary from the throne. He was helped enormously by Henry VIII's will.

Even from his grave, Henry was causing problems for the women in his life. His will had reinstated his daughters in the line of succession, but failed to stipulate their legitimacy. They were still, officially, bastards, and as such had no legal claim to the throne.

Before pointing that detail out to the ailing young king, Northumberland needed to gain control of the girl who was next in the line of succession—Henry's great-niece, Lady Jane Grey, who was now fifteen years old. He approached her parents and suggested a marriage between their daughter and his son. He would take care of the succession if they would share control of the throne with him when Jane became queen. On May 21, 1553, Jane Grey married Guildford Dudley. She had not wanted the marriage, but her parents beat her into submission.

Northumberland now turned to Edward, persuading the sickly but still zealous boy that the Catholic Mary would destroy the work of the Reformation if she were allowed to become queen. What argument he used to eliminate Edward's "sweet sister Temperance" from the succession we don't know. Whatever it was, it worked. Edward wrote out a new will, proclaiming Jane his heir. Then on July 6, in the lovely palace of Greenwich, the king died.

Jane Grey, miserably unhappy in her new marriage, was dragged out of bed on the morning of July 10 and told, to her astonishment, that her cousin was dead and that she was now queen. If Northumberland and her parents expected a joyful response to their startling announcement, they were badly mistaken. Jane had no desire for political power, and she respected the line of succession established in Henry's will, with sovereignty falling next to Mary. "The lady Mary is the rightful heir," she said, aghast. "The crown is not my right." Her angry parents were unable to fall back on their old methods of procuring obedience, for they could hardly use physical violence against a girl they had just declared their queen. They could, however, use emotional pressure, persuading her, as Northumberland had persuaded Edward, that her rule was essential for the continuance of the Protestant religion. Again, we hear nothing of any reference to Elizabeth, the logical Protestant alternative to a Catholic monarch. Jane was in no position to argue, and was probably too shaken by all the sudden events in her life to think clearly.

We do not know what Elizabeth's response to these events was. If she wanted to be queen herself, she wisely kept silent about it. She had sensed that she was in danger even before she was told of her brother's death. As the king lay dying, Northumberland sent orders to both sisters to come attend their ailing brother. Sisterly affection might have urged her to set out at once, but caution took over. If her brother had already died, or died when she arrived, she would be wholly in the power of his unscrupulous guardian. She sent word that she was herself ill, and would come as soon as she was able.

Mary, more trusting, received the same summons and unquestioningly set out to Greenwich. She was approached on the way by a mysterious messenger, who warned her to turn back. She did, and promptly mobilized an army to defend her claim to the throne. Within nine days, she and her forces had marched, unresisted, into London. The unwilling usurper was thrown into the Tower, and Catherine of Aragon's daughter was queen of England.

This left Ann Boleyn's daughter in a very sticky position. She was now next in the line of succession, half sister to a fanatically Catholic queen who deeply distrusted her.

At first all seemed harmonious between the sisters. Elizabeth was summoned to London to pay homage to the new queen, and she did so with every appearance of joy. In Mary's coronation procession, she rode in the same carriage as their honorary aunt, Anne of Cleves.

The sisters were both aware that the cheers of the people along the route of the procession were as much for Elizabeth as for Mary herself. The Spanish ambassador, Simon Renard, noted with alarm the love the English people had for the young princess. Mary trusted Renard, as she had once trusted Eustache Chapuys, not realizing that the gallantry of the old ambassador had been replaced by the self-serving cynicism of the new. His agenda was Spain's, and he viewed Mary, with her sentimental attachment to her mother's homeland, only as a useful and somewhat contemptible tool.

Renard saw Mary's vulnerability, and used it mercilessly. She was thirty-seven. Her looks were gone, worn away by time, ill health, and the bitterness of her life. Yet she was unworldly and inexperienced. It was an unfortunate combination. She was as naive as a girl, but without a girl's freshness; as weathered as an older woman, without an older woman's experience. She could not conceal her feelings, as an older woman might; she was not even aware of them. But her vulnerability seemed pathetic rather than alluring.

Renard realized, as Mary herself did not, that she was a woman with stifled sexual passion that, approached carefully in the language of religion, could be manipulated. He wanted her to marry Philip, Charles V's son and heir to the Spanish throne. He spoke to her of Philip's great virtue and piety, and had a portrait of the handsome prince sent over from Spain. Staring at the picture, listening to the soft, suave voice of the ambassador, Mary fell in love with the prince who would rescue her from her loneliness and help her restore the world to the way it had been before the witch queen had come and destroyed it.

The queen's innocence amused and astounded Renard. Once he found her weeping in front of the portrait. She could not marry Philip, she cried; she had found out something terrible about him. Aghast, Renard asked what it was. He had a mistress! she cried.

The ambassador stared. Philip was twenty-seven years old, a widower, a man. Did she really expect . . . ? Obviously she did. Hastily Renard assured her that Philip was chaste, the victim of vicious lies by calculating heretics. Reassured, she returned to her plans for the marriage.

There were, said Renard, only two obstacles. One was the continued life of Jane Grey who, willingly or not, remained a potential focus for an attempt to overthrow the queen. Mary refused to have her cousin executed.

The other problem was Elizabeth. She was a Protestant, a heretic. This Mary was willing to address. She was certain that, given the chance, her people would abandon heretical error and return to the true faith, the faith of her mother, the faith of England when it was a happy, uncomplicated land. If Elizabeth was a good person, she too would return to the true faith.

Mary spoke to her sister. Would Elizabeth attend mass with Mary? Elizabeth hedged. She could not attend mass without believing in Mary's faith. Would Mary help her to learn the truth? Mary agreed; Elizabeth went to mass, read the devotional literature her sister gave her, and pretended to be converted.

Mary remained, reasonably enough, skeptical, but they lived in seeming concord until the following January, when an insurrection erupted, aimed at deposing Mary and placing Elizabeth on the throne. Its leader was Sir Thomas Wyatt the Younger, whose father had once written poetry about Elizabeth's mother. Another major plotter was the hare-brained Henry Grey, Duke of Suffolk, who somehow believed he could get his daughter Jane back on the throne. When the insurrection was quickly suppressed, its ringleaders were executed.

Elizabeth could understand and approve her sister's treatment of the contemptible Henry Grey. His daughter was another matter. Mary knew that Jane was an innocent pawn in her elders' games. But the queen's advisers insisted that the girl had to die to ensure the country's security, and Renard firmly declared that Philip would not come to England as long as Jane Grey lived. Infatuation and desperate loneliness won out over compassion and wisdom. Jane was executed on February 12, 1554.

Elizabeth grieved for her young cousin, but even more, she feared for herself. Before his execution, Wyatt had denied under torture that Elizabeth knew anything of the plot. Elizabeth's own denial was coupled with expressions of fury and contempt for the unfortunate Wyatt. Mary did not believe either of them; Elizabeth was arrested. In a bitter cold rain, a barge carried her through Traitor's Gate and into the Tower. She was terrified, the more so because she had not been allowed to speak to her sister. Gardiner had interrogated her, and Gardiner, she was convinced, wanted her dead. Elizabeth was certain that Mary's own affection would save her, if she could only talk with her. She wrote Mary a letter begging for an audience, reminding her that "I heard my Lord of Somerset say that if his brother had been suffered to speak with him, he had never suffered."

Mary remained unmoved. Elizabeth remained in the Tower thinking about the other women who had left there only for their executions—Jane a few weeks earlier; Kathryn Howard; Margaret Pole, the Countess of Salisbury. Above all, there was Ann Boleyn. Brooding in the dank rooms of the Tower, the princess despaired, for a time, of her sister's mercy, and she thought glumly of her mother. She hoped only that Mary would imitate their father's one concession to the woman he had worshiped and then destroyed; she resolved that, when the time came, she would beg Mary to send for a French swordsman to behead her.

But however much Mary hated her sister, she knew Elizabeth's execution could lead to civil war. The people loved Elizabeth, and even Gardiner regretfully conceded that killing the girl would be dangerous. Bringing her to court, where her youth and popularity would inevitably stir trouble, would also be a mistake. Instead she was sent to the palace of Woodstock, in Oxfordshire, and given into the keeping of the dour Sir Henry Bedingfield. Under Mary's orders, she was lodged in four rooms in the gatehouse—not in the royal apartments, where a princess would be expected to stay. She was permitted to walk in the orchards, always under the careful surveillance of ladies handpicked by the queen. When one of these ladies appeared to form a strong attachment to the princess, she was dismissed.

Daily Elizabeth learned of the deaths of heretics at her once-gentle sister's hands. Hugh Latimer and Nicholas Ridley were burned at the stake in October 1555. Archbishop Cranmer, Ann Boleyn's old friend, followed in March 1556. Other victims were less exalted. Working with grim loyalty for the Catholic queen, the Protestant-leaning William Cecil noted that in 1556 eighty people were burned, "whereof many were maidens"; the next year forty-four men and twenty women were burned. If Mary decided her sister was a heretic and not merely a traitor, Elizabeth would have more to fear than a clumsy axman. She was a prisoner: she could not, as Catherine Willoughby had, stealthily flee the country before the queen could attack.

Then suddenly Elizabeth found herself back at court, at the behest of a strange ally. Philip of Spain had come to England, dutifully married the woman he privately referred to as his "beloved aunt," and learned quickly of the popularity of his new sister-in-law. Mary was, as they both believed, pregnant. If she conceived a healthy son, Philip's job would be done, and he could slowly drag England into Spain's control. But the queen was aging and unhealthy: there was a strong chance she would miscarry and die. That left two possible heirs to the throne: the Protestant Elizabeth, and the Catholic but French Mary Queen of Scots, the granddaughter of Margaret Tudor. To a Spanish prince, a French monarch was far worse than a heretical one. He insisted that Mary release her sister and reconcile with her. Elizabeth stayed at court for several months, and when she returned to Hatfield, it was not as a prisoner but as an honored princess—and, though Mary would not admit it, as the heir to the throne.

Mary's pregnancy had been an illusion—a hysterical pregnancy, or dropsy, or possibly uterine cancer. Philip suddenly discovered that he was needed in Spain. He left in August, vowing to come back soon.

He returned a few months later, in February 1557—but not to stay. Spain was once more at war with France, and the emperor wanted England's help. Mary was less fond of war than her father had been, but she was hopelessly in love with Philip, and she agreed. Her council objected, but she overruled it.

She could not, however, overrule her sister. Philip was determined to marry Elizabeth to his cousin Philibert of Savoy, a puppet of the emperor. The idea appealed to Mary, who had been trying to marry the girl off to some foreign nobleman or other for months. It did not appeal to Elizabeth. She did not want to marry *anyone,* she kept insisting. Mary, like everyone else, attributed her reluctance to coyness, perversity, or maidenly modesty, but she gave in to the girl's adamant refusals.

Having achieved his more crucial goal of gaining an ally against France, Philip left for Spain once more. Maybe Mary believed his assurance that he would return: she had proved herself as expert at self-deception as her father had been. She again believed herself pregnant, and certainly Philip would come back when his son was born. Elizabeth set about embroidering tiny garments for the child who would replace her as heir to the throne.

In the middle of all this, Elizabeth suffered another loss. Anne of Cleves, now living in Katherine Parr's old manor house at Chelsea, fell ill and died in the spring of 1557. Anne had arranged her dying with the placid common sense with which she had arranged her life. She left a will that provided for the well-being of all her many servants and dependents. She also left a number of interesting bequests. To Mary she bequeathed "our best jewel," along with a request that the queen take care of her servants "in this time of their extreme need." She left Elizabeth her second-best jewel, and the request that Elizabeth take into her service Anne's "poor maid" Dorothy Curzon.

Like the first, Mary's second pregnancy turned out to be a fabrication of her desperate mind and her ailing body. As she faced her failure to conceive, the wretched queen also faced her failure to retain her people's love. The war with France was a fiasco that cost the British their last stronghold on French soil, the port city of Calais. Mary now realized that, with no further use for a sickly and unpopular wife, Philip would never be back. She was ill, and she had nothing left to live for. In the early morning hours of November 17, 1558, surrounded by sweet visions of singing children dressed in white, the "unhappiest lady in Christendom" died, ready to be reunited with the God she had been true to all her life.

Elizabeth was at Hatfield, standing in front of an oak tree in the park, when the old queen's council brought her the news. Kneeling before her, William Cecil, a canny and principled survivor of three Tudor reigns, told her she was now queen of England. She looked at him for a moment, then up at the gray November sky, and quoted from Psalm 118: "It is the Lord's doing," she exulted. "It is marvelous to our ears."

Her first act was to appoint Cecil as her chief secretary. More discerning than her sister or her father, Elizabeth chose her advisers astutely. For fifty years she would seek Cecil's advice, consider it, then accept or reject it as her own reason decreed. He was never, like Wolsey or Cromwell, the true ruler of England, nor was he ever in danger of dying, as those ministers did, when he was no longer of use. But then, he was always of use, as Elizabeth knew he would be that first day at Hatfield.

The new queen decided at the beginning of her reign—had probably decided long before—that she would never marry. She announced that to Parliament early on, when a deputation urged her to choose a husband and settle the succession. "In the end," she said bluntly, "this shall be for me sufficient, that a marble stone shall declare that a queen, having reigned such a time, lived and died a virgin." The men—even Cecil, the wisest of them all—looked at each other and smiled. It was predictable and admirable for a virgin to speak so: had not Queen Mary once said she had no desire to marry?

But Elizabeth was never especially modest. She had strong passions, and had marriage been politically safe, she would probably have chosen a handsome, lusty nobleman for a husband, had a few sons and a lot of fun in the bargain, and ruled England with all the brilliant skill the "virgin queen" was to show.

Marriage, however, was not safe. Mary had destroyed herself through marriage. Ann Boleyn had briefly gained power by marrying Henry VIII, then lost both the power and her life. And her successors? The insipid Jane Seymour had died providing Henry with a son. Kathryn Howard had been the king's pretty toy, crushed and discarded when it became soiled. Wise, motherly Katherine Parr had survived two marriages, barely escaped execution in a third, and then died in childbirth after being betrayed by the one husband she really loved. Even the ghost of Henry's first wife haunted Elizabeth. The daughter of the most powerful ruler in Europe had been abandoned when her body could no longer offer pleasure or produce a son. Only one of Henry's wives had lived happily, the wife who was not a wife, Anne of Cleves. But she lived in obscurity.

Elizabeth had learned her lesson from all these women. For fifty years she reigned alone, her own consort, her own ruler. She courted various princes for political reasons, and she flirted with various courtiers both for personal gratification and to maintain her useful image as the ever-young and desirable maiden queen.

She had some ambivalence about her decision not to marry. It showed in her cruelty to those of her maids of honor who married without her consent, which was rarely given. It showed most poignantly when her bubble-brained rival Mary Queen of Scots gave birth to a son, and Elizabeth cried out in agony, "The queen of Scots is lighter of a fair son and I am but of barren stock!"

She was capable of love both passionate and permanent, and for most of her reign she maintained an intense romantic relationship with Robert Dudley, the Earl of Leicester. Many believed that she was his mistress, and probably their relationship did include sexual satisfaction, but it is safe to assume that it never involved actual intercourse. An illegitimate child would have cost Elizabeth the throne. And it was the throne she loved above all—that, and the people of England. To maintain her power, it was not enough to be queen. The savvy Scots ambassador, Sir James Melville, visiting her court a year into her reign, told her he knew she would never marry. "Your Majesty thinks that if you were married you would be but Queen of England, and now you are both King and Queen."

Elizabeth's great-grandmother Margaret Beaufort had spent her life making her son king of England. Ann Boleyn and Henry's other wives had tried to give him sons to be kings. But his daughter, the girl who was meant to be a boy, took the lessons that each of them had given her and molded a reign so powerful it defied all the assumptions of history. The legacy of those six queens was not the worn-out furs of Catherine of Aragon or the "best jewels" of Anne of Cleves. It was the forty-five-year reign of Henry's daughter Elizabeth—both king and queen of England.

ELIZABETH I

Daughter of Henry and Ann Boleyn, she paid dearly for failing
to be a son, but ruled England for fifty triumphant years.

BIBLIOGRAPHY

In writing this book, I used four groups of sources. To begin with there are the standard contemporary and near-contemporary sources—documents of Henry's reign, the Spanish and Venetian diplomatic calendars, Roper's *Life of Sir Thomas More*, Foxe's Book of Martyrs, etc. Similarly, I have used the standard later works, such as Mattingly's *Catherine of Aragon* and the various biographies of Henry VIII, without which no book on anyone of the period can be written.

In addition, I have used two other types of sources that were necessary to shape this particular work. The first is the studies of the lives of women of the era—some written earlier in this century, but most since the 1970s, when the discipline of women's studies carved out a place in scholarly research.

Second, I have used the works of writers who do not particularly deal with the sixteenth century but rather interpret, from a feminist perspective, the realities of women's lives, taking as their starting point the understanding that in male-dominated societies, male interpretations of reality in general and women in particular determine any look at women, past or present. Although I have only occasionally mentioned them in the text, they are the foundation of all my interpretations of these women's lives and experiences.

Because notes can distract the reader, and because this book focuses on reinterpretation of accepted facts rather than on disputing the facts themselves, I have avoided using notes.

Ashdon, Dulcie. *Ladies in Waiting.* New York: St. Martin's Press, 1976.

Atkinson, Clarissa W. *The Oldest Vocation: Christian Motherhood in the Middle Ages.* Ithaca, N.Y.: Cornell University Press, 1991.

Bainton, Roland. *The Reformation of the Sixteenth Century.* Boston: Beacon Press, 1952.

———. *Women of the Reformation in France and England.* Boston: Beacon Press, 1973.

Bale, John. *Select Works.* Ed. H. Christmas. London: Christmas Society, 1849.

Beilen, Elaine. *Redeeming Eve: Women Writers of the English Renaissance.* Princeton: Princeton University Press, 1987.

Belloc, Hilaire. *Cranmer.* London: Cassell, 1931.

Bengis, Ingrid. *Combat in the Erogenous Zone.* New York: Knopf, 1972.

Brewer, J. S. *The Reign of Henry VIII.* London: Murray, 1884.

Byrne, Muriel St. Clare, ed. *The Letters of Henry VIII*. London: Casrell and Co., 1968.

———. *The Lisle Letters*. Chicago: University of Chicago Press, 1981.

Calendar of Letters and State papers . . . between England and Spain. Vols. IV, V, VI. Ed. P. de Goyangos et al. London: Her Majesty's Stationery Office, 1862.

Calendar of State Papers, Milan. Vol. 1: 1385–1618. Ed. A. B. Hinds. London: Longman, 1912.

Calendar of State Papers, Venice. Vols. II, III, IV. Ed. Rawdon Brown, et al. London: Longman, 1894.

Cavendish, George. *The Life of Cardinal Wolsey*. Ed. S. W. Singer. London: Hardin and Lepard, 1825.

Chapman, Hester. *Anne Boleyn*. London: Cape, 1974.

———. *The Last Tudor King*. New York: Macmillan, 1958.

———. *The Thistle and the Rose*. New York: Coward McCann Geoghegan, 1969.

Chrimes, S. B. *Henry VII*. London: Methuen, 1972.

Clifford, Henry. *The Life of Jane Dormer*. London: Burns & Oates, 1887.

Clive, Mary. *This Sun of York*. New York: Knopf, 1974.

Crabites, Pierre. *Clement VII and Henry VIII*. London: Routledge & Sons, 1936.

de Ionge, Jane. *Margaret of Austria, Regent of the Netherlands*. New York: Norton, 1953.

Dickens, A. G. *The English Reformation*. New York: Schocken, 1964.

Dowling, Maria. "A Woman's Place? Learning and the Wives of Henry VIII." *History Today* 41 (June 1991).

du Boys, Albert. *Catherine d'Aragon et les Origines du Schisme Anglican*. Paris: V. Palme, 1880.

Dworkin, Andrea. *Woman Hating*. New York: Dutton, 1984.

Ehrenreich, Barbara, Elizabeth Hess, and Gloria Jacobs. *Re-Making Love: The Feminization of Sex*. New York: Anchor Press, 1986.

Ellis, Henry. *Original Letters*. London: Harding, Triphook & Lepard, 1846.

Elton, G. R. *Reform and Reformation: England 1509–1558*. Cambridge, Mass.: Arnold, 1977.

———. *The Tudor Constitution: Documents and Commentary*. Cambridge: Cambridge University Press, 1960.

Erickson, Carolly. *Mistress Anne*. New York: Summit, 1984.

———. *Bloody Mary*. New York: Doubleday, 1978.

Farley, Lynn. *Sexual Shakedown: The Sexual Harassment of Women on the Job*. New York: McGraw-Hill, 1978.

Ferguson, Charles W. *Naked to Mine Enemies: The Life of Cardinal Wolsey*. Boston: Little, Brown, 1958.

Figes, Eva. *Patriarchal Attitudes: The Case for Women in Revolt*. New York: Fawcett, 1970.

Firestone, Shulamith. *The Dialectic of Sex*. New York: Morrow, 1970.

Fisher, John. *Early English Works*. Ed. John E. B. Mayor. London: N.p., 1886.

Foxe, John. *Acts and Monuments.* Ed. S. R. Cattley. London: Seeley, Burnside, & Seeley, 1843–1849.

Fraser, Antonia. *Mary Queen of Scots.* London: Delacorte, 1969.

———. *The Wives of Henry VIII.* New York: Alfred A. Knopf, 1992.

Froude, J. A. *The Reign of Henry VIII.* London: Everyman's Library, 1909

Goff, Lady Cecilie. *A Woman of the Tudor Age.* London: J. Murray, 1930.

Green, Mary Ann Wood. *Lives of the Princesses of England.* London: N.p., 1849.

Greer, Germaine. *The Female Eunuch.* New York: McGraw-Hill, 1970.

Gunn, S. J. *Charles Brandon.* London: Blackwell, 1988.

Hackett, Francis. *Francis the First.* New York: Literary Guild, 1934.

———. *Henry the Eighth.* New York: Liveright, 1929.

Hall, Edward. *Chronicle Containing the History of England.* London: J. Johnson, 1809.

Harris, Barbara. "Marriage Sixteenth-Century Style: Elizabeth Stafford and the Third Duke of Norfolk," *Journal of Social History* 15 (Spring 1982).

———. "Power, Profit, and Passion: Mary Tudor, Charles Brandon, and the Arranged Marriage in Early Tudor England." *Feminist Studies* 15 (Spring 1989).

———: "Women and Politics in Early Tudor England." *The Historical Journal* 33 (June 1990).

Harvey, Nancy Lenz. *Elizabeth of York, Mother of Henry VIII.* New York: Macmillan, 1973.

———. *The Rose and the Thorn.* New York: Macmillan, 1975.

Ives, E. W. *Anne Boleyn.* Oxford: Blackwell, 1986.

Jenkins, Elizabeth. *Elizabeth the Great.* New York: Coward McCann, 1958.

Kelly-Gadol, Joan. "Did Women Have a Renaissance?" In *Becoming Visible: Women in European History,* Ed. Renate Bridenthal, Claudia Koonz, and Susan Stuard. Boston: Houghton Mifflin, 1987, 2d ed.

Kendall, Paul Murray. *Richard III.* New York: Norton, 1955.

King, John. "Patronage and Piety: The Influence of Catherine Parr." In Margaret P. Hannay, ed. *Silent but for the Word: Tudor Women as Patrons; Translators and Writers of Religious Works,* Kent, Ohio: Kent State University Press, 1985.

Krailsheimer, M. A., ed. *Three Sixteenth-Century Conteurs.* Oxford: Oxford University Press, 1966.

Lerner, Gerda. *The Creation of Feminist Consciousness.* Oxford: Oxford University Press, 1993.

Letters and Papers, Foreign and Domestic, of the Reign of Henry VIII. Ed. J. S. Brewer, James Gairdner, and R. Brodie. London: Her Majesty's Stationery Office, 1864.

Letters of Royal and Illustrious Ladies. Ed., M. A. E. Wood, London: H. Colburn, 1846.

Levin, Carole. "John Foxe and the Responsibilities of Queenship," *Medieval and Renaissance Women: Historical and Literary Perspectives* ed. Mary Beth Rose, Syracuse, University of Syracuse Press; 1986.

———. "Lady Jane Grey: Protestant Queen and Martyr." In *Silent but for the Word: Tudor Women as Patrons, Translators and Writers of Religious Works,* ed. Margaret P. Hannay, Kent, Ohio: Kent State University Press, 1985.

———. "Queens and Claimants: Political Insecurity in Sixteenth Century England." In *Gender, Ideology and Action,* ed. Janet Sharistanian, Westport, Conn., Greenwood, 1986.

———. "Women in *The Book of Martyrs* as Models of Behavior in Tudor England." *International Journal of Women's Studies,* 4 (March/April 1981).

———. "Women Scholars and Intellectuals of the English Renaissance." In *The Study of Women: History, Religion, Literature and the Arts,* ed. Helen Tierney, Westport, Conn., Greenwood, 1990.

Lindsey, Karen. "Sexual Harassment on the Job." *Ms.,* November 1977.

Luke, Mary, *Catherine the Queen.* New York: Coward McCann Geoghegan, 1967.

———. *A Crown for Elizabeth.* New York: Coward McCann Geoghegan, 1970.

Marius, Richard. *Thomas More.* New York: Knopf, 1985.

Mattingly, Garrett. *Catherine of Aragon.* Boston: Little, Brown, 1941.

———. "Eustache Chapuys: A Footnote in English History." Unpublished. Bowdoin Prize essay, 1922.

Mayer, Dorothy Moulton. *The Great Regent: Louise of Savoy 1476–1531.* London: Weidenfeld and Nicolson, 1966.

Millett, Kate. *Sexual Politics.* New York: Doubleday, 1970.

Molland, Judy. "Those Wicked Witches: Anita Hill on Trial." *Sojourner* 18 (October 1992).

Muller, James Arthur. *Stephen Gardiner and the Tudor Reaction.* New York: Macmillan, 1926.

Mumby, F. A. *The Youth of Henry VIII.* London: Constable, 1913.

Neale, J. E. *Queen Elizabeth I.* New York: Doubleday/Anchor, 1934.

Plowden, Allison. *Tudor Women: Queens and Commoners.* New York: Atheneum, 1979.

Prescott, H. F. M. *Mary Tudor.* New York: Macmillan, 1953.

Read, Evelyn. *My Lady Suffolk.* New York: Random House, 1962.

Reinhart, Hans. *Holbein.* Paris: Hyperion, 1938.

Reynolds, E. E. *Margaret Roper.* London: Burnes & Oates, 1960.

Richardson, Walter. *Mary Tudor, the White Queen.* London: Owen, 1970.

Ross, Charles. *Richard III.* Berkeley & Los Angeles: University of California Press, 1981.

Routh, E. M. G. *Lady Margaret: A Memorial of Lady Margaret Beaufort, Countess of Richmond and Mother of Henry VII.* Oxford: Oxford University Press, 1924.

Scarisbrick, J. J. *Henry VIII.* Berkeley & Los Angeles: University of California Press, 1968.

Seymour, William. *Ordeal by Ambition.* New York: St. Martin's Press, 1972.

Simon, Linda. *Of Virtue Rare: Margaret Beaufort, Matriarch of the House of Tudor.* Boston: Houghton Mifflin, 1982.

Smith, Lacey Baldwin. *Henry VIII: The Mask of Royalty.* Boston: Houghton Mifflin, 1971.

———. *A Tudor Tragedy: The Life and Times of Catherine Howard.* London: Clay, 1961.

Strickland, Agnes. *Lives of the Queens of England.* Vols. 3, 4, 5, 6. London: Henry Colburn, 1902.

———. *Lives of the Queens of Scotland.* Vol. 1. London: Henry Colburn, 1851.

———. *Lives of the Tudor and Stuart Princesses.* London: Henry Colburn, 1888.

Sylvester, Richard, and Davis P. Harding, eds. *Two Early Tudor Lives.* New Haven: Yale University Press, 1962.

Warnicke, Retha M. *The Rise and Fall of Anne Boleyn: Family Politics at the Court of Henry VIII.* Cambridge: Cambridge University Press, 1989.

Watson, Foster. *Vives and the Renaissance Education of Women.* New York: Arnold, 1912.

Webb, Maria. *The Fells of Swarthmore Hall and Their Friends, with an Account of their Ancestor Anne Askew the Martyr.* London: Alfred W. Bennett, 1895.

Weir, Alison. *The Six Wives of Henry VIII.* London: Pimlico, 1991.

Williams, Neville. *Henry VIII and His Court.* New York: Macmillan, 1971.

Wilson, Derek. *A Tudor Tapestry.* London: Heinemann, 1972.

Wriothesley, Charles. *A Chronicle of England During the Reigns of the Tudors.* London: Camden Society, 1885.

Wyatt, Sir Thomas. *Collected Poems.* Ed. Joost Daalder. London: Oxford University Press, 1975.

INDEX

Chapman, Hester, 118
Chapuys, Eustache, xvi, 47, 63, 82,
    84, 88, 95–97, 100, 104, 107,
    109–113, 117, 119, 127, 129,
    130, 132, 178, 209
Charles I, 39
Charles of Burgundy, 49, 51
Charles V, xvi, 33–35, 43–44, 55, 60,
    63, 66, 67, 68, 72, 76, 77, 88,
    95, 112, 138, 139, 152, 210
child-rearing practices, 4, 159–160,
    187
Christina, Duchess of Milan, 139
church doctrine, xxvii–xxix, 100–101,
    190, 195–196
Clement VII, Pope, xvi, 66–69,
    72–74, 76, 78, 80, 83–85, 91,
    98, 100, 103, 140
Cleves, Duke of, 143, 152, 156, 157,
    184
Cobham, Ann, 122
Compton, Sir William, xxv
Constantine, George, 139
court
    atmosphere of, xxvi
    entertainments, xxiii–xxiv, 18,
        28–29, 30, 51–52, 172
    life, 152–153
    politics, xxv
Courtenay, Edward, 153
Coverdale, Miles, 184, 187
Cranmer, Thomas, xvi, 82–84, 87, 88,
    91, 95, 125, 140, 150, 155, 174,
    189, 199, 211–212
Crome, Dr. Edward, 192, 195
Cromwell, Thomas, xvi, 70, 84, 87,
    88, 96, 98, 105, 119–128, 130,
    132, 137, 139, 140, 142, 144,
    149, 150, 153–156, 159,
    165–168, 174, 213
Culpeper, Thomas, xvi, 141,
    167–172, 176
Curzon, Dorothy, 213

Darcy, Lord, 95
Defender of the Faith, xxviii, 28, 83,
    87, 100, 152
Denny, Anthony, 198, 203
Denny, Joan, 187, 196, 203
Denny, Sir Thomas. See Rutland, Earl
    of
Derby, Earl of, 21

Dereham, Francis, 162–163, 167, 170,
    175–177
Dormer, Lady, 108
Dormer, Sir Robert, 108
Dormer, Will, 108
Dorset, Marquis of, 97
    See also Grey, Thomas
Douglas, Margaret, 148
Dudley, Guildford, 208
Dudley, John, Earl of Northumber-
    land, 52, 199, 205, 207–209
Dudley, Robert, 214
Dworkin, Andrea, xx, 119

Edgecomb, Lady, 150, 151
Edward III, xxvi, 3
Edward IV, xvi, xxvi, 3–7, 15, 60,
    182
Edward VI, xvi, 134–135, 145, 153,
    166, 187, 199–202, 205–208
Elizabeth I,
    arrest, 211
    becomes queen, 213
    birth, 99
    character, 206–207, 214, 215
    as Mary I's heir, 212
    popularity, 211
    relations with Mary I, 209–212
    sexuality, 214
    succession to throne, 208–209
    and Tom Seymour, 202–203,
        205–206
    also mentioned, xvi, 102–104, 120,
        128, 153, 156, 187, 189, 201,
        216
Elizabeth of York, xxiii, 8–10, 16, 20,
    39
Empress Matilda, 62
English Reformation, the, xxi,
    xxviii–xxix, 12, 100, 191–193,
    205
Erasmus, Desiderius, xxix, 28, 34, 43,
    138, 188
Evil May Day, 41–42
Exeter, Marchioness of, 95, 103

Fair Gospeler, the. See Askew, Anne
Felipez, Francisco, 67, 77, 97, 109,
    110
Ferdinand of Aragon, xvi, 13, 15,
    18–23, 29, 30, 31, 33, 35, 39,
    49, 62, 63

relations with Anne of Cleves, 149, 150

relations with Catherine of Aragon, 27–33, 39–45

relations with Jane Seymour, 131, 133, 134–135

relations with Katherine Parr, 185, 189, 197–199

religious convictions, xxvii–xxix, 27–28, 99–100, 152, 191

religious persecution, 103–104, 112, 140, 153, 156, 186, 194, 196

repudiation of Catherine of Aragon, 40, 56–57, 61, 64–69, 71–91

search for new wife, 135, 137–141, 181

succession to throne, 208

also mentioned, 2, 12, 16, 17, 21, 26, 34, 94, 101, 116, 136, 141, 158, 167, 169, 180, 201, 203–205, 215, 216

Herbert, Lady, 200

Herbert, William, 183, 198, 200

heresy, xxviii–xxix, 47, 88, 112, 189, 194

Herman, Richard, 101

Heron, Giles, 126

Hertford, Lady, 196

Holbein, Hans, 136–138, 140, 144, 145, 158

Holinshed, Raphael, 8

Holland, Bess, xxv, 85, 106

Holy Roman Emperor. *See* Charles V; Maximilian I

Howard, Edmund, 159

Howard, Elizabeth, 85

Howard, Kathryn,
  affair with Tom Culpeper, 167–172
  birth and childhood, 159–160
  character, 162, 165–167
  execution, 178, 181
  and Francis Dereham, 162–163
  and Henry Manox, 160–162
  as lady-in-waiting, 152, 162–164
  marriage to Henry VIII, 165
  motto, 165
  sexual activities exposed, 175–177
  sexuality, 160–162, 167–170
  also mentioned, xvii, xx, xxi, 153, 158, 173, 184, 186, 192, 211, 214

Howard, Thomas, Duke of Norfolk, xvii, xxv, 32, 41, 42, 85, 93, 98, 103, 106, 126–127, 134, 152, 154, 159, 161, 163, 174

Husee, John, 125, 133, 134

Hussey, Lord, 95, 106

Hutton, John, 140, 143

infidelity, xxv, 22, 32, 37, 40, 53, 71, 85, 107, 159, 169

Isabella of Castile, 13, 15, 16, 18–21, 22, 27, 49, 62, 63

Isolde, 168

Ives, E. W., xx, 50, 57, 100, 118, 126, 128

James III of Scotland, 36

James IV of Scotland, 20, 31, 36, 62

James V of Scotland, 62, 63, 139, 171

Joan of Arc, 103

John of Gaunt, 3, 13, 182

Johnson, Otwell, 196

Juana of Castile, 13, 21–23, 63

Juan of Aragon, 49

Julius II, Pope, 31, 66, 72, 76

Karenina, Anna, 168

Kaye, Dr., 147

Kelly-Gadol, Joan, xix

Kempis, Thomas à, 187

King, John, 187

King Hal. *See* Henry VIII

Kingston, Lady, 124

Kingston, Sir William, 123–124, 129

Knevet, Anthony, 196

Knight, William, 68

Kyme, Thomas, 191–192, 195

ladies-in-waiting, xx, 48, 103
  affairs, 40
  apparel, 133–134
  dowries, 21
  duties, xxii–xxiv, 129, 150–151, 198
  pastimes, 189
  relations with mistresses, 106–107
  as source of information, 55, 105, 122, 177
  types, xxii

Lancastrians, 4–5, 6, 7

Lascelles, John, 174, 192, 193, 196

Lascelles, Mary, 161, 174

Willoughby, Catherine, Duchess of
    Suffolk, xviii, xxiii, 97, 142, 159,
    172–174, 184, 186, 187, 188,
    190, 191, 193, 196, 197, 202,
    212
Winchester, Bishop of. *See* Gardiner,
    Stephen
Wolman, Richard, 66
Wolsey, Thomas, xviii, 29–30, 41
    42, 44, 45, 51, 52, 54, 57, 59,
    61, 65–68, 71–75, 77–81, 84,
    86, 90, 122, 145, 150, 154, 156,
    213
Woodville, Elizabeth, xviii, 5–9, 11,
    60, 182

Worcester, Lady, 122
Wotton, Nicholas, 140, 141, 143–145
Wriothesley, Charles, 127
Wriothesley, Thomas, xviii, 139, 175,
    193, 196, 198–199
Wyatt, George, 48, 55
Wyatt, Sir Thomas, xviii, 55, 59, 90,
    92, 125, 129, 155, 167
Wyatt, Sir Thomas the Younger, 210,
    211
Wycliffe, John, xxviii

Yorkists, 4, 5, 7

Zouche, Ann. *See* Gainsford, Ann